OUR UNDERACHIEVING COLLEGES

OUR UNDERACHIEVING COLLEGES

A Candid Look at How Much Students Learn and Why They Should Be Learning More

Derek Bok

With a new afterword by the author

Princeton University Press
Princeton and Oxford

Copyright © 2006 by Princeton University Press
Published by Princeton University Press, 41 William Street,
Princeton, New Jersey 08540
In the United Kingdom: Princeton University Press, 3 Market Place,
Woodstock, Oxfordshire OX20 1SY
All Rights Reserved

Eighth printing, and first paperback printing,
with a new afterword, 2008
Paperback ISBN: 978-0-691-13618-9

*The Library of Congress has cataloged the cloth edition
of this book as follows*

Bok, Derek Curtis.
Our underachieving colleges : a candid look at how much students
learn and why they should be learning more / Derek Bok.
p.   cm.
Includes index.
ISBN-13: 978-0-691-12596-1 (hardcover : alk. paper)
ISBN-10: 0-691-12596-1 (hardcover : alk. paper)
1. Education, Higher—Aims and objectives—United States.
2. Academic achievement—United States.   I. Title.
LB2322.2.B65   2006
378.73—dc22   2005023229

British Library Cataloging-in-Publication Data is available

This book has been composed in Electra and American Gothic by
Princeton Editorial Associates, Inc., Scottsdale, Arizona

Printed on acid-free paper. ∞

press.princeton.edu

Printed in the United States of America

9   10

CONTENTS

ACKNOWLEDGMENTS

In writing this book, I have benefited much from the work of three research assistants, Dolly Bross Geary, Kiernan Mathews, and Elena Zinchenko, who have found many valuable sources to enlighten my inquiries. Other colleagues—Darla Deardorff, Tiziana Dearing, Howard Gardner, Richard Hackman, Deborah Hughes-Hallett, Carol Geary Schneider, Nancy Sommers, Dennis Thompson, and Dean Whitla—have kindly read and commented helpfully on individual chapters. Five people—my longtime colleague Richard Light, Spencer Foundation president Michael McPherson, my former collaborator James Shulman, my daughter Hilary, and my wife Sissela—have read the entire manuscript and offered valuable comments. Finally, my assistant, Connie Higgins, has once again displayed exemplary patience and fortitude in preparing more drafts and redrafts than I care to remember. To all of them I am extremely grateful.

OUR UNDERACHIEVING COLLEGES

INTRODUCTION

During the 1980s, as major U.S. companies felt the hot breath of foreign competition and Japanese goods invaded our stores and showrooms, Americans began to ask what had gone wrong with the economy. Government officials, journalists, and analysts of every kind looked for anyone or anything that might be responsible for our seeming competitive weakness. Business executives were the first to bear the brunt of public scrutiny. Education's turn came soon after. In 1983, a national commission on the public schools wrote a widely publicized report, A Nation at Risk, which referred to "a rising tide of mediocrity" and warned of "unilateral educational disarmament."[1] A flood of commentary followed, urging all manner of reforms.

As public schools came under heavy assault, old university hands predicted that higher education would eventually suffer the same fate. They were soon proved right. Within a few years, Secretary of Education William Bennett and Lynne Cheney, head of the National Endowment for the Humanities, issued sharp critiques of the undergraduate curriculum along with concrete proposals for reform.[2] Public intellectuals, such as Dinesh D'Souza, and journalists, such as Charles Sykes, quickly weighed in with harsh attacks on a broad array of university policies.[3]

Professors too—almost all from the humanities—began publishing critical essays of their own. The titles of these books capture the prevailing tone: The Closing of the American Mind, The University in Ruins, The Moral Collapse of the University, Tenured Radicals, The War against the Intellect, Impostors in the Temple, Killing the Spirit.[4] Allan Bloom's The Closing of the American Mind made the New York Times Best-Seller List. Other books were not so fortunate, but almost all were published by well-known houses and respectfully discussed in the pages of leading reviews.

The authors do not come from the same point on the ideological spectrum, nor do they all emphasize the same concerns. Nevertheless, their writings have certain features in common. Almost all their criticism is directed at leading research universities rather than the full range of undergraduate institutions. Their books are mainly polemics, containing little that is positive about the work of universities or the professors who teach there. Among their complaints, moreover, certain common themes recur that seem to have resonated widely with their readers.*

Many of the authors deplore the lack of any overarching purpose in the undergraduate curriculum. As Allan Bloom declares, "There is no vision, nor is there a set of competing visions, of what an educated human being is."[5] In the words of Bill Readings, "The story of liberal education has lost its organizing center—has lost, that is, the idea of culture as both origin and goal, of the human sciences."[6] Without a compelling, unifying purpose, universities are charged with allowing their curricula to degenerate into a vast smorgasbord of elective courses. Knowledge itself has splintered into a kaleidoscope of separate academic specialties with far too little effort to integrate the fragments, let alone show students how they might connect. Hence the education offered undergraduates has become incoherent and incapable of addressing the larger questions "of what we are and what we ought to be," a point elaborated at length by Bruce Wilshire in his *Moral Collapse of the University*.[7]

A number of the detractors have pilloried universities for cheapening their students' education by allowing intellec-

---

*Since this book is concerned with the quality of undergraduate education, no effort has been made to discuss complaints involving such topics as college costs, admissions policies, or financial aid.

tual standards to deteriorate.[8] As they see it, discourse on campus is seriously inhibited by the orthodoxies of political correctness. Affirmative action has undermined the integrity of faculty hiring. The great canonical masterpieces of litera-ture have been downgraded to make room for lesser works whose principal virtue seems to be that they were authored by women, African Americans, or Third World writers. The very ideals of truth and objectivity, along with conventional judgments of quality, are thought to be endangered by at-tacks from deconstructionists, feminists, Marxists, and other literary theorists who deny that such goals are even possible.[9]

Another theme in several of the critical writings empha-sizes the growing tendency to turn colleges into training camps for careers. As former Assistant Secretary of Educa-tion Diane Ravitch has observed, "American higher educa-tion has remade itself into a vast job-training program in which the liberal arts are no longer central."[10] According to Eric Gould, "What we now mean by knowledge is informa-tion effective in action, information focused on results. . . . We tend to promote the need for a productive citizenry rather than a critical, socially responsive, reflective individ-ualism."[11] Those who share this view observe disapprovingly that the number of students majoring in vocational programs has risen sharply over the past several decades, while the per-centages majoring in traditional liberal arts subjects, espe-cially the humanities, have declined. With students flocking to courses in business administration, computer science, and the allied health professions, more and more colleges seem preoccupied with serving the occupational needs of under-graduates instead of preparing them to live a full life as widely informed, reflective human beings.

A final complaint accuses the faculty of neglecting their students. Authors such as Charles Sykes in *Profscam* have assailed tenured professors for caring only about their re-search and appointing new colleagues almost entirely for their scholarly reputations, with little heed to the quality of their teaching.[12] The few young faculty members who manage to inspire their students are regularly passed over for promotion. Meanwhile, according to the authors, professors content themselves with lecturing to large audiences, leaving the real teaching to inexperienced graduate students in small sections. Lost in the crowd, many undergraduates finish college without knowing a single faculty member well enough to ask for a letter of recommendation.

Many people were surprised that books about undergraduate education, such as *Profscam* and *The Closing of the American Mind,* could sell so many copies. Yet their success is not so difficult to explain. More than half of all young people in America go to college, and more than a quarter receive a bachelor's degree. Virtually every aspiring lawyer, doctor, minister, scientist, and schoolteacher must earn a college diploma, and almost all future corporate executives, legislators, and high public officials will do the same. If colleges miseducate their students, the nation will eventually suffer the consequences. If they can do a better job of helping their students communicate with greater precision and style, think more clearly, analyze more rigorously, become more ethically discerning, be more knowledgeable and active in civic affairs, society will be much the better for it. Small wonder, then, that critics care enough to write with such passion and that large numbers of people want to read what they have to say.

Since most of these books were published, developments overseas have given a new reason to care about undergraduate education. A revolution in technology has enabled any work that can be digitized to be performed virtually anywhere on the globe. Today highly skilled employees in Bangalore, Beijing, and other distant places on the planet can communicate with colleagues in American companies almost as easily as if they were working down the hall. Already, several hundred thousand U.S. tax returns are being prepared every year in India; CAT scans from American hospitals are being analyzed by doctors in Australia; scientists in China are doing research for Microsoft; Russian engineers are working on aircraft design for Boeing. No longer are bright Americans who went to the right schools protected from overseas competitors in forging careers in the world's most prosperous economy.[13] Ambitious young men and women all over the world are eager to take their place and are empowered by technology to do so. In this environment, the quality of education in American colleges has assumed greater importance than ever before. Reason the more for casting a critical eye at what goes on in undergraduate classrooms across the nation.

American universities, too, face the prospect of growing competition from abroad. Over the past half century they have come to take their preeminence for granted, while higher education in other advanced countries has suffered from low faculty salaries, overcrowded conditions, inadequate facilities, and excessive state control. Educators in the United States have grown accustomed to being able to attract the ablest students from around the world to enrich their faculties and raise the quality and quantity of highly skilled people working in American companies, hospitals, and other institutions. In recent years, however, there have been signs that countries in Europe and Asia are beginning to pay more attention to their universities, recognizing that first-rate research and advanced education are essential ingredients of success in today's global economy. As India and

China continue to develop, they can offer more challenging, better paid jobs to the hordes of young scientists and engineers graduating from their universities. In the future, it may no longer be as easy as it has been in decades past to have our pick of the world's talent.

In view of these developments, neither American students nor our universities, nor the nation itself, can afford to take for granted the quality of higher education and the teaching and learning it provides. To be sure, professors and academic leaders must keep a proper perspective. It is especially important to bear in mind all the purposes universities serve and to resist efforts to turn them into instruments preoccupied chiefly with helping the economy grow. But resisting commercialization cannot become an excuse for resisting change. Rather, universities need to recognize the risks of complacency and use the emerging worldwide challenge as an occasion for a candid reappraisal to discover whether there are ways to lift the performance of our institutions of higher learning to new and higher levels.

Unfortunately, the widely publicized critiques of the past 20 years are not a particularly helpful guide for deciding what needs to be done. Indeed, there is something very odd about their indictments. If they were anywhere close to correct, prospective students and their families would be up in arms. After all, going to college costs a lot of money, even in public universities. Those hoping to attend and those who pay the bills presumably expect a first-rate education in return. If colleges were truly in crisis, burdened by incoherent curricula and uncaring professors, students would hardly be applying in such large and growing numbers. Nor would parents be seeking out well-paid counselors to help with college applications or paying for special tutoring to teach their children how to get higher scores on college entrance exams.[14]

Critics may reply that students are not affirming under-graduate education in its current form but are merely anxious for an impressive credential now that a college degree has become so important to future success. But this response will hardly bear scrutiny. Survey after survey of students and recent graduates shows that they are remarkably pleased with their college years. Americans may dislike their government and distrust most institutions in the society, but 75 percent or more of college alumni report being either satisfied or very satisfied with their undergraduate experience.[15] Just after many of the hostile books appeared, a nationwide poll found that more than 80 percent of undergraduates expressed satisfaction with the teaching at their college.[16] In subsequent surveys, large majorities of students have reported being satisfied with their contacts with professors.[17] Two-thirds would choose the same institution if they had to make the choice again.[18] Among the most selective colleges that are repeatedly singled out by critics for special scorn—the Stanfords, Princetons, Harvards, and Yales—the percentages of contented graduates are even higher, and alumni support their alma maters with exceptional generosity.[19]

How can writers condemn our colleges so harshly if students, parents, and graduates value them so highly? On this point, the authors are silent. Whether they are simply unaware of student opinion or consider undergraduates incompetent to judge (this was clearly the view held by Allan Bloom), they fail to explain why those attending college do not complain more loudly. Are the critics right and the students wrong? Or is it the reverse? Or are both right or both wrong? These questions provided the initial impetus for writing this book.

Having examined the evidence on the effects of college, I find good reason for the satisfaction of most alumni with their education. Countless studies have found that college students, overall, achieve significant gains in critical thinking, general knowledge, moral reasoning, quantitative skills, and other competencies.[20] Most seniors agree that they have made substantial intellectual progress. The marketplace affirms these conclusions by giving large additional rewards to those who carry their education beyond high school to acquire a B.A. degree.

These positive results suggest that the critics were too harsh and too one-sided in their judgments. They do not prove that all is well with undergraduate education. Far from it. Despite the favorable opinions of undergraduates and alumni, a closer look at the record in the chapters that follow shows that colleges and universities, for all the benefits they bring, accomplish far less for their students than they should. Many seniors graduate without being able to write well enough to satisfy their employers. Many cannot reason clearly or perform competently in analyzing complex, nontechnical problems, even though faculties rank critical thinking as the primary goal of a college education. Few undergraduates receiving a degree are able to speak or read a foreign language. Most have never taken a course in quantitative reasoning or acquired the knowledge needed to be a reasonably informed citizen in a democracy. And those are only some of the problems.

These weaknesses are not the ones discussed in the widely publicized critiques of American universities. There is little in these polemical books that takes a serious look at how much students are learning or gives hard evidence of what is actually being accomplished in college classrooms. Fortunately, however, the more important weaknesses have not gone entirely unnoticed. Most of the problems have been recognized and many have been investigated in detail by specialists in educational research who try to discover how much students are learning and what methods help them learn best. But these researchers rarely spend much time describing the policy implications of their work. Moreover, their findings normally appear piecemeal, usually in specialized professional journals and little-known reports that few people (other than educational researchers themselves) ever read. Although some professors are aware of the problems and try new methods of teaching to overcome them, their concerns are rarely shared by the faculty as a whole. Even the faculty committees that periodically review their colleges' curricula give little sign of having studied the relevant research or recognized the weaknesses it exposes in their undergraduate programs. Throughout undergraduate education, a great wall separates the world of research from the world of practice—even though the practitioners involved are professors, trained in research, who would seem ideally prepared to take full advantage of whatever findings empirical investigators have to offer.

In writing this book, I have tried to breach this wall by making ample use of the published work on how students learn and what effect colleges have on their development.*

---

*This book does not concern itself only with the large research universities or the highly selective colleges that rank near the top of the annual rankings in *U.S. News and World Report*. Instead it treats undergraduate education in all kinds of four-year colleges. Some readers may wonder whether one can write a single book that encompasses vast public universities, small liberal arts colleges, church-related institutions, women's colleges, and urban universities. The differences among these institutions are obvious and will be noted where it is important to do so. Nevertheless, despite the contrasts in such matters as size, facilities, and student abilities, a remarkable feature of American undergraduate education is how little effect these differences seem to have on the development of students during college (once account is taken of variations in the talents and back-

Although there is much we still do not know about teaching and learning, we know enough to throw light on many of the most important problems affecting the quality of undergraduate education. What emerges is a clearer picture of how students develop in college together with an agenda for reform quite unlike the ones advanced by either the well-known critics of universities or the faculty committees that periodically review undergraduate programs.

The good news is that most of the serious deficiencies can be overcome, at least to a significant degree, given the will to do so. The bad news is that most of the problems are not being seriously addressed on campuses today, nor will they be until they are correctly identified and clearly understood by those responsible for the quality of teaching and learning in our colleges. That is the real reason why I have written this book.

---

ground of freshmen at the time they enter). As two noted researchers concluded after reviewing hundreds of studies, "on just about any outcome, and after taking account of the characteristics of the students enrolled, the dimensions along which American colleges are typically categorized, ranked, and studied, such as type of control, size, and selectivity, are simply not linked with important differences in student learning, change, or development"; Ernest T. Pascarella and Patrick T. Terenzini, *How College Affects Students,* Vol. 2: *A Third Decade of Research* (2005), p. 641. Community colleges do seem different enough from four-year colleges that they will not be treated in this book. With this exception, however, it does seem possible to write a single book about the effectiveness of American undergraduate education despite the diversity of the colleges that provide it.

1 | THE EVOLUTION OF AMERICAN COLLEGES

Undergraduate education today bears no resemblance to the instruction masters and tutors gave to the trickle of adolescents entering one of the nine colleges that existed prior to the American Revolution. Even a century later, less than 2 percent of young people were attending college. Serious research had barely gained a foothold on the nation's campuses, and entire fields of knowledge that are common today were still unknown. As late as 1940, fewer than 1 in 20 adults had a B.A. degree. It is only within the past 50 years that universities have come to boast the huge enrollments, the elaborately equipped research laboratories, and the legions of faculty members and other instructors that fill their campuses today.

Some understanding of the evolution of American colleges is needed as the background for a serious discussion of the contemporary college experience. Only through acquaintance with this history can one tell whether critics are correct in asserting that the quality of liberal education is in serious decline. Without some knowledge of the past, one cannot fully appreciate which aspects of the undergraduate program are amenable to change and which seem to stubbornly resist reform. Lacking historical perspective, one cannot even be sure whether "new" proposals are truly new or merely nostrums that have been trotted out before with disappointing results. At the very least, anyone wishing to criticize or reform undergraduate education should know its history well enough to understand what

11

important changes have occurred and what features of undergraduate education have remained essentially the same over time.[1]

THE EVOLUTION OF UNDERGRADUATE EDUCATION: A BRIEF SUMMARY

Until the Civil War, colleges in the United States were linked to religious bodies and resembled finishing schools more closely than institutions of advanced education. Student behavior was closely regulated both inside and outside the classroom, and teachers spent much of their time enforcing regulations and punishing transgressors. Rules of behavior were written in exquisite detail. Columbia's officials took two full pages merely to describe the proper forms of behavior during compulsory chapel. Yale turned "Sabbath Profanation, active disbelief in the authenticity of the Bible, and extravagant [personal] expenditures" into campus crimes.[2]

Most courses were prescribed in a curriculum that usually included mathematics, logic, English, and classics, with a heavy dose of Latin and Greek. In a typical class, students recited passages from an ancient text under the critical eye of the instructor. Although many colleges offered courses in the sciences, such as astronomy or botany, classes were taught more often by invoking Aristotle and other authorities than by describing experiments and the scientific method. By most accounts, the formal education was sterile. Many students felt that they learned much more outside the classroom in informal clubs and literary societies, where they engaged in debates, read modern literature, and discussed serious subjects.[3]

Despite their quaint ways, colleges before the Civil War were deliberately organized to pursue two important objectives: training the intellect and building character. The most influential defense of the prevailing model appeared in an 1828 report from Yale College, which held that the principal aim of college instruction was not to supply all of the important information that students might some day use but to instill mental discipline.[4] According to the report's authors, a classical education was ideally suited to this purpose.

Mental discipline was supposed to emerge from hours of demanding work translating ancient languages, disputing arcane questions in class, and solving mathematical problems. As one college president put it, "If you seek to bring your mental powers up to a high degree of efficiency, put them to work, and upon studies that will tax them to the uttermost. When one has been mastered, take a second, and a third, and so go on conquering and to conquer, victory succeeding victory in your march to mental conquests and triumphs."[5] Not until the end of the century did this inspiring message fall victim to Edward Thorndike's experiments suggesting that the skills acquired through painstaking translations of Cicero and Virgil would rarely help students to analyze and solve problems outside the realm of Latin texts.

Character would be forged by having undergraduates study classical texts, demanding strict compliance with the detailed rules of campus behavior, and requiring daily attendance at chapel. As a culminating experience, most colleges prior to the Civil War offered a mandatory course for seniors on issues of moral philosophy, often taught by the president himself. Ranging over ethical principles, history, politics, and such issues of the day as immigration, slavery, and freedom of the press, this capstone course served multiple objectives. It set forth precepts of ethical behavior, it prepared students for civic responsibility, and it brought together knowledge from several fields of learning. For many students, it was the high point of an otherwise dull and stultifying education.

By the middle of the nineteenth century, the traditional program was showing signs of strain. Experimental scientists and scholars of modern languages and literature were gradually gaining a foothold in the curriculum. Instructors chafed at having to spend so much time enforcing rules of behavior. Expressing their displeasure with the status quo, students began to vote with their feet. From 1850 to 1870, undergraduate enrollments in America actually declined as a proportion of the total population. As Francis Wayland, the president of Brown, succinctly put it, "We have produced an article for which the demand is diminishing."[6]

With the end of the Civil War, higher education began a period of unprecedented reform. Aided by federal land grants and by the philanthropy born of industrial fortunes, college presidents such as Charles W. Eliot, Andrew White, William Rainey Harper, and Benjamin Gilman built new institutions and radically transformed old ones. Inspired by the model of the great German universities, these leaders encouraged research, welcomed science, and introduced Ph.D. programs to build new cadres of scholar-teachers.

Undergraduate education soon felt the impact of these changes. The old classical curriculum gave way to offerings of a newer and more practical kind. Instruction in modern languages and literature continued to spread. Courses in physics, biology, and chemistry sprung up everywhere. Private universities introduced new programs in vocational subjects such as commerce and engineering. Public universities carried occupational training even further. According to Laurence Veysey, "such untraditional disciplines as pedagogy, domestic science, business administration, sanitary science, physical education, and various kinds of engineering were all becoming firmly established at a number of leading universities by the turn of the century."[7]

More radical still were the reforms at some of America's most prominent institutions. At Harvard, for example, President Charles W. Eliot not only rejected the old prescribed classical curriculum, he urged that *all* requirements be abolished, leaving students free to study whatever appealed to their interests. By the end of his 40-year term of office in 1909, only a course in English composition and the study of one foreign language were required of freshmen. Sophomores, juniors, and seniors were left completely free to study what they chose. At Cornell, another advocate of student choice, President Andrew White, explained the reasons for shifting to a freer curriculum: "The attempt to give mental discipline by studies which the mind does not desire is as unwise as to attempt to give physical nourishment by food which the body does not desire. . . . Vigorous, energetic study, prompted by enthusiasm or a high sense of the value of the subject, is the only kind of study not positively hurtful to mental power."[8]

Religious orthodoxy also lost its grip on many colleges. Nonsectarianism was increasingly considered conducive to sound university governance. Faith was no longer thought central to the development of moral character. Compulsory chapel began to give way on many campuses, making religious observance little more than another option within a broad array of extracurricular pursuits.

Not all college presidents agreed with the trend toward greater freedom of choice. Some clung tenaciously to the old classical model and mounted a spirited defense of the status quo. President James McCosh of Princeton was particularly outspoken in opposing Harvard's reforms, denouncing President Eliot in words reminiscent of William Bennett's ripest prose during his term as secretary of education:

Tell it not in Berlin and Oxford that the once most illustrious university in America no longer requires its graduates to know the most perfect language, the grandest literature, the most elevated thinking of all antiquity. Tell it not in Paris, tell it not in Cambridge in England, tell it not in Dublin, that Cambridge in America does not make mathematics obligatory on its students. Let not Edinburgh and Scotland and the Puritans in England know that a student may pass through the one Puritan college of America without having taken a single class of philosophy or a lesson in religion.[9]

President Eliot was unmoved. As time went on, he would watch the currents of reform begin to turn in his direction. In 1890, 80 percent of the curriculum was required in the average college. By 1901, curricula in more than one-third of American colleges were at least 70 percent elective.[10] By 1940, the share of mandatory courses in the typical college curriculum had declined to 40 percent.

In the end, however, Eliot's vision proved too extreme to survive intact even at Harvard. Although no one wanted to return to the old, classical curriculum, most educators felt that the doctrine of total elective choice went too far in the other direction. Such freedom clearly did not produce "the vigorous, energetic study" that enthusiasts like White had promised. By the time Eliot finally retired, 55 percent of Harvard students were graduating having taken virtually nothing but elementary courses. More than 70 percent did not pursue any single field of knowledge in real depth.[11] Many undergraduates studied as little as possible and relied on paid tutors—or "crammers"—to fill their heads with just enough information at semester's end to pass their exams.

Meanwhile, social clubs and fraternities flourished. Intercollegiate sports took hold, as football games attracted tens of thousands of raucous students and alumni. At colleges across the nation, undergraduates decorated their rooms with posters reading "Don't let your studies interfere with your education."[12] For many undergraduates, college was not a serious intellectual experience but an excuse for making social contacts and enjoying the good life. As one dean of students, LeBaron Briggs, candidly admitted, "Social ambition is the strongest power in many a student's life."[13]

In retrospect, it is likely that the casual attitude toward coursework reflected the spirit of the times more than the nature of the curriculum. Even in the more conservative atmosphere of Yale, the typical student was described as "a careless boy-man who is chiefly anxious to 'have a good time,' and who shirks his work and deceives his instructors in every possible way."[14] Whatever the underlying causes, critics of the elective system seized on such carefree undergraduate behavior as a justification for imposing greater structure on the curriculum. By the early twentieth century, both the extreme free-choice model embraced by universities such as Stanford and Cornell and the more rigid, traditional system still in place at Princeton seemed equally out of touch with the times.

Once Eliot retired, revisionist forces took over at Harvard. His successor, A. Lawrence Lowell, soon persuaded the faculty to require students to choose a major, or field of concentration, to stop them from taking a long series of introductory courses. The resulting curriculum, with its combination of breadth and depth of study, had already been adopted by most other colleges. Depth was achieved through concentrations that consisted of a number of courses within a single discipline. Breadth was typically ensured by requiring students to take two or three courses in each of several broad areas of knowledge, such as the humanities, social sciences, and sciences.

By the start of World War II, college curricula were divided between two models. Most public universities offered a wide assortment of vocational majors along with the standard liberal arts concentrations, while achieving breadth through some form of distribution requirement. Most leading private universities tended to resist occupational majors (save for engineering and business). A few, among them Stanford and Columbia, went beyond distribution requirements by requiring students to complete specially created survey courses on such broad topics as Western Civilization or the Great Books, in an effort to ensure that every student graduated with a basic grounding in the intellectual heritage of the West.

These patterns of breadth and depth were nourished by constant growth in the number of courses, made possible by the steady expansion of university faculties. Entirely new disciplines, with courses of their own, gave undergraduates a wider range of options from which to choose electives, fulfill their distribution requirements, or select a major.

In the aftermath of World War II, universities underwent further substantial change. Encouraged by the GI Bill and later by the demands of an increasingly sophisticated economy, larger and larger numbers of young people crowded into colleges. Existing universities expanded, and new ones were founded. From 1945 to 2000, the number of B.A. degrees awarded annually rose almost eightfold, from 157,349 to approximately 1.2 million.

The rapid growth in the undergraduate population meant that higher education was no longer reserved for the elite but now attracted a majority of American youth. Student bodies became more diverse, as blacks, Hispanics, Asians, and other ethnic minorities entered private and public colleges alike. As applicant pools grew larger, the best-known institutions became highly selective, teachers' colleges evolved into multipurpose universities, and community colleges sprouted like mushrooms. Many of the new students (and their parents) were more interested in preparing for jobs than in acquiring a broad liberal arts education. Responding to this demand, more and more colleges began to offer vocational programs. Before long, the number of students choosing vocational majors exceeded the numbers concentrating in traditional arts and sciences disciplines.

The rapid rise in the undergraduate population was matched by growth in other dimensions. The number of faculty members increased severalfold. Aided by generous federal support, especially in the sciences and social sciences, the volume of research expanded massively. Academic specialties proliferated, producing new majors, new academic journals, and ever greater intellectual fragmentation.

University faculties responded to these developments in various ways. Although the basic structure of the curriculum remained intact, with its provision for breadth and depth, the steady growth of new knowledge pushed aspects of science once reserved for graduate students back into intermediate and even introductory college texts. As researchers separated themselves into more and narrower specialties, colleges began developing interdisciplinary programs to focus on large societal issues, such as environmental problems or the impact of science and technology on society. Challenged by a more diverse student population, many faculties launched other multidisciplinary ventures in fields such as women's studies, Afro-American studies, and ethnic studies. In response to America's new international prominence, and aided by significant outside support, other faculty members created research centers and interdepartmental programs aimed at understanding major regions of the world, such as Western and Eastern Europe, Africa, and East Asia.

As student numbers continued to rise and individual universities grew larger, colleges launched a variety of experiments to provide more individualized instruction, at least for portions of their student bodies. Honors programs were established for qualified students. Research internships offered opportunities for undergraduates to work in laboratories alongside experienced investigators. Freshman seminars, group tutorials, and small senior colloquia afforded students at least a modicum of personal contact with faculty members.

Meanwhile, advances in technology brought changes in the way professors taught their classes. In the 1950s, the spread of paperback books and photocopiers expanded the depth and variety of course materials far beyond the single hardcover text that had been the staple of most earlier college courses. Several decades later, the Internet brought an even wider array of readings within easy reach of students. Some professors actually put entire courses on line so that students could not only obtain syllabi and homework assignments at their computers but also participate in discussions with their classmates or ask questions of the instructor. Never before had such extensive intellectual resources been so readily available to enhance the undergraduate educational experience.

RECENT CRITICISMS IN HISTORICAL PERSPECTIVE

All the new courses, interdisciplinary programs, and other curricular innovations could not forestall the wave of criticism briefly described in the Introduction. Disapproving voices from within the academy and beyond attacked universities for lacking a clear vision for undergraduate education, failing to counteract the growing fragmentation of knowledge, sacrificing the liberal arts in favor of vocationalism, and neglecting undergraduates to concentrate on research.

Most of the critical writings suggest that the quality of undergraduate education today has declined from some elusive pinnacle of prior greatness. For Allan Bloom, the moment of excellence seems to have occurred between World War II and the 1960s. For Charles Sykes, the best days came decades earlier. For Martin Anderson, the peak of educational achievement is never specified.

Sorting through fragments from the past, however, one is hard put to discover any true golden age. What Henry Adams said of Harvard in the mid-nineteenth century—"it taught little and taught that ill"—could have been said equally well of most other colleges of the period.[15] By the end of the century, old universities had been reformed and new ones added, but few who remember the indolent, socially ambitious students of that era would regard the education obtained in the leading colleges as a model worthy of emulation.

Colleges in the late 1930s likewise seem to have offered something less than a peak educational experience, even for the best students at the most prestigious institutions. In terms reminiscent of Henry Adams, McGeorge Bundy dismissed most of his studies at Yale as "a terrible waste of time."[16] Elliot Richardson was no kinder in describing his own Ivy League experience: "I did not think much of Harvard education in those days before the Second World War. In most cases, it wasn't worth going to class."[17]

The end of the war brought to American campuses a flood of GIs with a new seriousness of purpose that gladdened the hearts of many professors. Even so, by the 1950s studies appeared that described undergraduates in unflattering terms and concluded that "colleges rarely succeed in bringing about important changes in attitudes or values."[18] Contemporary critics who deplore the political correctness of today seem to forget the social pressures of the postwar years, which stunted the ambitions of so many college women, ignored any need to recruit minority students, and silenced radical voices for a generation. The conformities of that age may have seemed less visible than the campus orthodoxies of today, but that is only because they were much more closely aligned with the prevailing social attitudes of the time. According to one large-scale study of undergraduates in the early 1950s, "the main overall effect of higher education upon student values is to bring about general acceptance of a body of standards and attitudes characteristic of college-bred men and women. . . . There is more homogeneity and greater consistency of values among students at the end of their four years than when they begin."[19]

It is equally difficult to find any period during the past century and a half when educators were united around a common unifying vision of liberal education. After the Civil War, as previously noted, colleges took very different paths, with some advocating almost total freedom in the choice of courses, others clinging to a largely prescribed, traditional curriculum, and still others adding programs of a more practical, vocational sort. Humanists argued for the primacy of liberal learning and the cultivation of intellect, refinement, and judgment. University presidents such as Woodrow Wilson spoke of a commitment to public service. Research-minded faculty were preoccupied with attracting and preparing their successors. Far from choosing among these visions, leading educators such as Henry Tappan, Andrew

White, and Charles W. Eliot seemed to embrace them all. As Lincoln Steffens put it in describing the University of Wisconsin, the university stood ready "to teach anybody-anything-anywhere."[20] Observing this smorgasbord, Abraham Flexner, the leading authority on higher education at the time, remarked that "the [American] college is without clear-cut notions of what a liberal education is and how it is to be secured . . . and the pity of it is that this is not a local or special disability, but a paralysis affecting every college in America."[21]

The interwar period did not bring new clarity. In 1942, the Progressive Education Association concluded its eight-year study of undergraduate education with the mournful lament that "Liberal arts college faculties seldom state what they mean by liberal or general education. Perhaps they do not know."[22] One noted educator of the period, President Robert Maynard Hutchins of the University of Chicago, did propose a new model to counteract what he termed the "disunity, discord, and disorder" that had overtaken undergraduate education.[23] But his idea of a curriculum founded on a study of the great works of Western civilization never gained much of a following among other colleges in the United States.

After World War II, several major universities tried anew to build a model program of general education that would prepare young people to take their place as knowledgeable, thoughtful members of a free and democratic society. Again, however, no consensus emerged. The vast majority of colleges were content to go on imparting breadth of knowledge merely by requiring students to choose a designated number of courses in the catalogue from each of the three major divisions of learning: the humanities, sciences, and social sciences. By 1977, Frederick Rudolph concluded his history of curricular reform in America by observing that "the general education movement is hopelessly engaged in the respiration of a lifeless ideal."[24]

In short, anyone seeking a common purpose must go all the way back to a time before the Civil War, when colleges united around a classical curriculum aimed at mental discipline and character building. No one today would willingly return to that antebellum model of student recitations, ancient languages, and rigid disciplinary codes. Ever since the demise of the classical curriculum, faculties have clung to several different visions of education, with no one model proving itself superior in a clearly demonstrable way. As Laurence Veysey points out in his survey of curricular change since 1900, "when one stands back and looks at the entire pattern of the American curriculum from a distance, the changes (aside from course proliferation) seem usually to mark variations on themes begun long ago."[25]

There is nothing surprising about the variety of aims and philosophies represented in contemporary American colleges. Uniformity of purpose and curriculum has always been more characteristic of European universities than of their counterparts in the United States. The traditional hallmark of higher education in this country has been its variety, featuring large colleges and small, secular and religiously affiliated institutions, single-sex and coed student bodies, and a rich mix of educational opportunities and programs. Now that student populations here and in Europe have expanded to include young people with widely differing interests and needs, many foreign educators look upon the diversity of our colleges as a strength rather than a weakness.

While the aims of a liberal education may be no more confused or contested today than they were a hundred years ago, specialization has undoubtedly increased. But specialization itself is not a new phenomenon. Even at the beginning of the twentieth century, William James complained of the narrowness of "the Ph.D. octopus."[26] When educators called for a convention in 1904 to reaffirm the unity of knowledge "in this time of scattered, specializing work," the effort failed completely.[27] By the 1920s, Rexford Tugwell could declare that "no one any more can hope to understand the whole of science as was very definitely hoped by the scientists a century or two ago; and so modern scientists gradually have abandoned the hope of a great intensive integration in favor of frankly specialized work in particular fields."[28]

Ensuing decades of academic research have fragmented knowledge even further, and colleges have admittedly paid a price. Many academic books and articles published today seem uncomfortably narrow, bound too closely by the confines and conventions of their discipline to do full justice to the problems they address. At the same time, it is hardly fair to ignore the progress that specialization has produced or to argue as though different branches of knowledge could be combined in some finely integrated whole if only blinkered professors would try a little harder. No one yet has demonstrated convincingly that the drawbacks of fragmentation have outweighed the contributions to knowledge made possible by specialization. Nor has any general theory or universal method emerged to knit the separate disciplines together. The unity of knowledge remains an elusive ideal. Although college presidents prior to the Civil War may have drawn on knowledge from many different sources to teach their seniors about the major issues of the day, few knowledgeable observers would bring these opinionated patriarchs back into the classroom if they were alive today.

As for the rise of vocational education, it is true that the proportion of B.A. recipients graduating with occupational majors has grown since the 1970s. Yet the proportion today is not significantly higher than it was in the 1940s and 1950s.[29] Moreover, vocational courses are hardly new; they have been a fixture in American higher education at least since the Morrill Act of 1862 declared that the leading object of the new land grant universities would be, "without excluding other scientific or classical studies, to teach such branches of learning as are related to agriculture and the mechanic arts."[30] As Frederick Rudolph reported in his classic study of the curriculum, undergraduate education in the United States has always had a practical, vocational aspect.[31] In the words of Christopher Jencks and David Riesman, "the question has always been *how* an institution mixed the academic with the vocational, not *whether* it did so."[32]

The recent growth in the number of students pursuing vocational degrees seems to have come about primarily for two reasons, both external to the university. One is the tendency of American employers to demand higher levels of knowledge and skill from those whom they employ. Thus increasing numbers of young people believe that they must look to college for the competence they need to secure a good job. Many of them are students who would previously have gone directly into the workforce to learn the necessary skills on the job.

The other reason for the growth of vocational majors is the marked increase in the number of students who look upon making money and succeeding in one's career as primary motivations for going to college. Since 1970, the percentage of freshmen who rate "being very well off financially" as an "essential" or "very important" goal has risen from 36.2 to 73.6 percent, while the percentage who attach similar importance to "acquiring a meaningful philosophy of life" has fallen from 79 to 39.6 percent.[33] It is hardly a surprise that these trends have been accompanied by a growing number of students seeking to prepare themselves for a career.*

Against this backdrop, can one really blame universities for offering more vocational programs? Surely colleges have *some* responsibility to respond to the desires of their students. In a system in which colleges must compete vigorously for enough applicants to fill their classrooms, they could hardly do otherwise and survive. Oddly, critics rarely recognize this fact, nor do they even pause to explain just why it is wrong for colleges to offer vocational programs; the very mention of the term *vocational* is considered enough to demonstrate the unworthiness of the offending institutions. Such disdain has its roots in nineteenth-century England, at a time when influential writers, such as Cardinal Newman, championed a liberal education free of any practical vocational instruction, and the young gentlemen attending Oxford and Cambridge were not supposed to "go into trade."[34] Such attitudes have little relevance to present-day America, where college students know they will spend most of the waking hours of their adult lives at work and are naturally concerned about choosing a career and preparing themselves to get a job.

There is admittedly much more to college than acquiring occupational skills. Nevertheless, it is misleading to speak of students in vocational programs as if they study nothing but practical subjects. What a vocational B.A. typically means is

---

*The removal of occupational barriers that had hindered the entry of women into most professions also led to rapid growth in a number of vocational majors, notably business management. The net effect of this process is less striking, however, since much of the increase in the number of women entering business was offset by a decline in the number of women seeking degrees in education. Moreover, many of the the women seeking careers entered professions, such as law and medicine, that require a graduate degree normally preceded by a liberal arts concentration in college.

simply that a student has substituted a practical, job-oriented concentration for a major in a liberal arts discipline. The remaining courses in the undergraduate program (often more than half the total number required) are still available for general education and electives.[35] It may be that vocational majors do not offer the same benefits as a concentration in a traditional discipline or that some vocational majors have expanded to the point that they interfere with the general education program. But these are narrower arguments that call for discussion. Even if true, they suggest a need to revise vocational concentrations, not to abandon them entirely.

As for the overall quality of undergraduate teaching, there is little indication of a growing neglect on the part of college faculties. The widely publicized complaints are usually focused on the 125 research universities whose professors divide their attention among research, graduate instruction, and teaching undergraduates. Even within this restricted group of institutions, critics have leveled serious charges, but no one has offered convincing evidence that the quality of instruction was ever better than it is today. After castigating Harvard for failing to promote several popular younger faculty, Charles Sykes observes: "This [neglect of teaching] was, by no means, always the case at Harvard. At one time, Harvard boasted such brilliant scholar-teachers as Henry James, Irving Babbitt (a teacher of T. S. Eliot), George Santayana, Joseph Schumpeter, and William Ernest Hocking."[36] True enough, but it is also worth noting that, during the golden age to which Sykes refers, the Harvard College Committee on Instruction reported that "certain lecturers failed to interest, some were inaudible, and some wasted time dictating data or having it copied from the blackboard."[37] In this respect, Harvard was not unique. As Robert Angell of the University of Michigan observed in 1928, "No one can deny that professors are interested in their fields of study; but many believe that frequently they have little ability in, or enthusiasm for, imparting their knowledge and interest to immature undergraduates."[38] A perusal of student evaluations today at most major universities would tell much the same story, with many instructors receiving high praise along with others whose teaching could clearly stand improvement.[39]

History, then, offers weak support at best for the reports of a decline in the quality of undergraduate education. Loose allegations to that effect have little foundation in fact but instead rest on fanciful visions of some previous golden age.[40] Other charges alleging a growing neglect of teaching or the loss of some grand unifying purpose are likewise unsubstantiated. Even the recent growth of vocationalism is not unprecedented and results from underlying causes that most universities could not and should not ignore.

Although the prominent critics of undergraduate education may have an imperfect grasp of history, nothing that has been said proves that colleges are above reproach. It may well be that undergraduate education has not suffered any discernible decline in quality over the past 50 or 100 years. But is that really a satisfactory outcome? Most human enterprise improves with time and experience. That is certainly true of consumer goods, athletic performances, health care, the effectiveness of our armed forces, the speed of our transportation and communication systems, and much else. Given the vastly expanded resources colleges have acquired, thanks to growing private donations, steadily rising tuitions, and massive infusions of federal financial aid, isn't it fair to expect the quality of education to improve as well?

To be sure, the undergraduate enterprise has grown in several dimensions. Millions more students enter college today than half a century ago. Countless new buildings have been built; faculties have greatly increased in numbers; new courses of every kind fill college catalogues to overflowing. Undergraduates can now watch PowerPoint lectures, print out articles at their personal computers, and receive homework assignments via the Internet. But all these changes, however broad in scope, say very little about what is truly important. Has the quality of teaching improved? More important, are students learning more than they did in 1950? Can they write with greater style and grace? Do they speak foreign languages more fluently, read a text with greater comprehension, or analyze problems more rigorously?

The honest answer to these questions is that we do not know. In fact, we do not even have an informed guess that can command general agreement.

Colleges are not alone, of course, in finding it hard to demonstrate progress. Consumer products, medical treatments, and track and field performances may have improved demonstrably over the past 50 years, but there are plenty of activities besides undergraduate education for which it is difficult, even impossible, to render a convincing verdict. No clear consensus exists on whether the quality of architecture, poetry, or painting has improved since 1950, or whether lawyers are practicing their craft more skillfully or philosophers writing with greater insight.

This chapter ends, therefore, with an important question unresolved. Is it fair to judge the current state of undergraduate education as one might evaluate a consumer product, and ask for demonstrable improvements in quality? Or is the experience of college more like the writing of poetry and the practice of architecture, activities that normally defy such judgments, at least over periods of 50 or 100 years? This question will lurk beneath the surface of much that follows and will require at least a tentative answer before this book concludes.

2 | FACULTY ATTITUDES TOWARD UNDERGRADUATE EDUCATION

If history offers few clues for deciding whether the quality of undergraduate education has improved, is there any way to judge how well colleges are performing? This is a complicated question that can be approached from several different directions. A useful way to start is to examine the behavior of college professors, since they are the ones primarily responsible for the nature and content of what students learn in college.

Because faculties play such a prominent role, they are the principal target for much of the recent criticism leveled at undergraduate education. The most frequent complaint is that professors are so preoccupied with research and outside consulting that they neglect their teaching and ignore their students. There are undoubtedly individuals who fit this description, especially in the handful of leading research universities that preoccupy most of the critics who write about higher education. On close examination, however, the charge turns out to be a simplistic one that hardly gives an accurate description of the great majority of college professors.

Although research tends to be rewarded more generously than instruction, teaching has intrinsic satisfactions that cause most professors to work conscientiously at their classroom duties. According to the Department of Education, faculty members, on average, spend more than half their time on matters related to teaching and less than 20 percent on research.[1] Those who describe themselves as teachers and claim to care more about teaching than research greatly outnumber those who regard themselves primarily as researchers.[2] In fact, fewer than half of all professors publish as much as one article per year.[3] As for outside work, many members of the faculty do not consult at all. Very few spend as much as one day per week on such activities or earn as much as one-tenth of their income from outside pursuits. Those who do consult extensively usually teach as much as their less enterprising colleagues and receive better student evaluations.[4] Overall, then, there is no convincing evidence that faculty members frequently neglect their students. Undergraduates themselves do not consider their professors inaccessible; more than 75 percent claim to be "satisfied" with the opportunity to discuss questions about their courses with their professors.[5]

Although attacks on college professors seem clearly overblown, there is a subtler problem with faculty behavior that contributes to most of the shortcomings discussed in this book. However much professors care about their teaching, nothing forces them or their academic leaders to go beyond normal conscientiousness in fulfilling their classroom duties. There is no compelling necessity to reexamine familiar forms of instruction and experiment with new pedagogic methods in an effort to help their students accomplish more. The fundamental reason for the lack of such pressure is the difficulty of judging how successful colleges are in helping their students to learn and develop. No published reports exist that reveal how much undergraduates have progressed intellectually, let alone how such progress compares across colleges. In this respect, undergraduate education differs sharply from research. While there are no reliable methods for measuring the quality of a university's scholarly "output," the writings of its faculty are published in forums readily accessible to scholars and scientists everywhere. Through these publications, the faculty's research is constantly evaluated by other specialists. Gradually, reputations are built and consensus forms on the quality of scholarly work produced by the various departments and academic units in the university.

Reputations of this kind do not exist for the effectiveness of undergraduate education, because the quality of teaching and learning is all but unknown to persons outside the college in question. At best, there are perceived differences in the overall reputation of a college's faculty (based largely on its research), in the intellectual abilities of its students (based primarily on average SAT scores), and, to a lesser degree, in the excellence of its libraries, laboratories, and other facilities. As researchers have discovered, however, these characteristics say little about the quality of the education the college offers or about how much its students learn.

The factors that contribute to a college's reputation, however, do shape the priorities of academic leaders and their faculties. Much work is done to raise the standing of a college by trying to attract brighter students, upgrade facilities, and, in particular, recruit professors with more visible reputations for research. The desire to attract smarter students causes college authorities to provide better facilities, keep tuition levels in line with those of the competition, improve financial aid, and even institute particular academic programs that are thought to be especially appealing to prospective students, such as study abroad, honors classes, or popular vocational programs. None of this, however, necessarily improves student learning. Nor do other incentives exist that serve this purpose. As long as professors do not palpably neglect their students, colleges that do very little to increase the effectiveness of teaching and learning will not suffer a penalty, since the consequences of such inaction will normally be invisible. No one will know whether they are falling significantly behind rival institutions in developing the mind and character of their students, still less whether colleges as a whole are doing less than they might in these respects.

Thus the key problem is not that existing incentives divert professors from teaching or cause academic leaders not to care how much their students learn. Both faculties and their leaders normally have more than enough professional responsibility to avoid such neglect. What *is* true, however, is that neither faculties nor their deans and presidents feel especially pressed to search continuously for new and better ways of educating their students, nor do they feel compelled to offer the very best education possible in order to avoid losing large numbers of applicants or suffering other consequences that matter.

The net result is that faculties and their academic leaders have considerable freedom to shape undergraduate education and to teach their students as they choose. The manner in which they exercise their discretion and the values and attitudes they bring to the task have much to do with the quality of education students receive. As they carry out their responsibilities, at least six tendencies occur often enough and have sufficiently important (and often troubling) effects to warrant explicit attention.

DIFFERING PERSPECTIVES ON THE ROLE OF UNIVERSITIES

An initial source of difficulty resides in the divergent ways in which professors and students regard the role of the university and the proper domain of undergraduate education. The members of Arts and Sciences faculties have special values and priorities, like all professionals. Above all, they are preoccupied with the challenge of discovering and transmitting knowledge and ideas. To them, knowledge is not a means to other ends; it is an end in itself—indeed, the principal end of academic life. Most students, on the other hand, have different reasons for acquiring a college education. They tend to look upon knowledge and ideas less as ends in themselves and more as a means toward accomplishing other goals, such as becoming better, more mature human beings or achieving success in their careers.

These contrasting ways of valuing knowledge do not necessarily give rise to differences of opinion about the content of undergraduate education. Often they lead to the same result, albeit for different reasons. In some instances, however, the differing perspectives do have consequences for the curriculum. The most obvious example involves the place of skills. Professors who value knowledge for its own sake are not likely to attach the same importance to skills as undergraduates who have come to college seeking instruction that will help them succeed in their careers.

This difference should not be overstated. Arts and Sciences professors clearly acknowledge the value of certain skills, such as good writing, clear thinking, and competence in a foreign language—so much so, in fact, that they have long given them a prominent place in the curriculum. To the academic mind, however, skills as familiar as writing and logical thinking are still only a means to the creation and transmission of knowledge, and not the most important means at that. They lack the intellectual challenge of mastering a complex body of thought or discovering the answer to a difficult and intriguing problem. As a result, even when professors make room for a skill in the curriculum, they are often reluctant to teach the subject themselves, especially at the basic, introductory levels where most of the teaching takes place. At times, they delegate the task to others who are not part of the regular faculty (usually graduate students or part-time instructors), or, in the case of critical thinking, they persuade themselves that they are teaching a skill when they are often doing little more than summarizing and critiquing arguments in lectures delivered to a passive audience. In either case, the results usually suffer.

The differences between students and faculty in their attitudes toward knowledge have been gradually growing more obvious and more consequential. Undergraduates now place much greater importance on making money than they did 40 years ago. Students attending college for this reason are less likely to share a love of learning for its own sake and are more inclined to value education chiefly for its utility in achieving the material success they regard so highly. For such students, useful skills matter more than ever. This trend has been accompanied during the past few decades by advances in analyzing and teaching new competencies that were previously thought to be skills one either was born with or had to learn for oneself—skills such as facility in interpersonal relations, or the ability to communicate effectively across cultural boundaries, or techniques of mediation, negotiation, and leadership. As more becomes known about such competencies, students express interest in mastering them because of their value in helping to achieve a variety of desired ends—not only advancement in one's career but also success in community activities, in marriage, and even in such mundane tasks as bargaining over the price of a new car. Arts and Sciences professors, however, tend to be wary of these emerging subjects and often balk at including them in the curriculum. To many scholars, the newer competencies lack intellectual depth and call for a kind of cookbook training unsuitable for a proper university. If they do find their way into the curriculum, they are likely to be taught by instructors outside the regular faculty or consigned to departments that lack the status accorded to traditional Arts and Sciences disciplines.

The resistance of the faculty is not necessarily inappropriate. Students often think too highly of subjects that seem to have immediate utility. Given the chance, they could easily choose a course of study that included too many "practical" courses of ephemeral value even for their careers, let alone for other worthwhile ends of a well-rounded undergraduate education. Still, faculty preferences can also on occasion fail to produce optimum results. In some instances, the judgments of professors on what skills are fit for teaching in a university will be influenced less by an enlightened sense of what their undergraduates need than by their own professional interests and priorities masquerading as sound educational principles. On these occasions, faculty deliberations will not yield all that a college should provide in order to prepare its students for their future lives.

Another important difference between faculty and students has to do with the way in which they view the role of values in education. Most professors try to concern themselves only with provable knowledge—statements that can be verified by empirical demonstration, mathematics, or logic. In many disciplines, values are regarded with suspicion as mere matters of opinion; their validity cannot be established by the methods of scientists and scholars, and faculty members do not feel that they have special qualifications for teaching about them. Professors of this persuasion avoid using material on the ethical implications of their discipline or other questions of value that arise within the subjects they teach.[6]

To them, such topics are "soft." Raising them in class only invites windy exchanges of opinion at best, or at worst outright indoctrination.

Many students, on the other hand, are intensely interested in questions of this kind. According to a recent survey of more than 112,000 undergraduates, two-thirds of all freshmen consider it "essential" or "very important" that college help develop their personal values.[7] At this stage in their lives, students are often seeking to determine their identities —what they stand for, how they want to live their lives, what experiences hold the greatest meaning. They welcome discussions about these subjects, whether they take place in dormitory rooms or in meetings to protest the university's investment policies. Even young relativists, who shrink from passing judgment on the beliefs of others, can be deeply concerned with defining their own values.

Just as with skills, faculty attitudes toward values can have questionable effects on the curriculum. It is no accident that, among the traditional purposes of undergraduate education, the two that were most neglected during the past century— moral reasoning and civic education—are the two most heavily freighted with issues of value. One can appreciate the reluctance of the faculty to teach material in which the methods of analysis and validation are so subjective, material for which they claim no special expertise. Because so many professors avoid such subjects, however, most undergraduates get little help from formal coursework in attempting to formulate their own personal beliefs. Many gain more in developing their values and principles from bull sessions with friends and classmates than from the classes they attend. To this extent, they fail to gain as much enlightenment as they might about subjects that deservedly form a vital part of their development.

BARRIERS TO COLLABORATION

The second persistent problem in the work of faculties arises from the traditional independence of professors and their departments. In most colleges, debates over the curriculum are not a means of imposing order but a process for reaching a consensus among autonomous scholars. By common consent, no tenured professor should be forced to do anything. Very rarely is a department compelled to assume teaching responsibilities against its will. When the majority votes for specific requirements, it is often assumed that the necessary courses will all be staffed voluntarily, even if it means that someone else must be found to teach them.

This method of proceeding has a marked effect on the final result. Professors and departments are not obliged to cooperate with other units or individuals even when it might be educationally desirable for them to do so. As a result, interdisciplinary ventures must be voluntary. Programs that require collaboration across departmental lines, however valuable they may be, will only come into being if the prospective partners agree, which may not happen if the work involved does not serve their professional interests. Resourceful academic leaders can sometimes bring about cooperation, either by persuading all concerned that they will benefit as a result or by creating incentives that make it worthwhile to participate. Overall, however, the levels of cooperation will almost certainly be less than optimal, either because academic leaders sometimes fail to perceive the need for collaboration or because they cannot convince the parties that they ought to work together.

The fact that recalcitrant parties in a university can block useful collaborations does not mean that more prescriptive forms of governance would improve matters. A higher authority with power to compel collaboration might well make costly mistakes. Moreover, in higher education, as in other endeavors carried out by highly skilled professionals, solutions arrived at by compulsion are not likely to yield the best results. No one ever improved the quality of teaching by ordering professors to offer better courses. The existing methods of governance, for all their frustrations, may resemble Winston Churchill's democracy—the worst possible system . . . except for all the known alternatives. Yet, accurate as it may be, this sobering conclusion cannot obscure the fact that faculty autonomy often leads to unrealized opportunities and unsatisfactory results for want of voluntary cooperation. The undergraduate program that results is typically a whole that is smaller than the sum of its parts.

NEGLECTING PURPOSES

The third problem emerges when faculties sit down periodically to review and revise the curriculum. All too often on these occasions, the debate begins without the parties first having paid close enough attention to the objectives that a proper undergraduate education should pursue. Almost everyone agrees in principle that it is impossible to plan any human activity effectively without first forming a clear idea of what one wishes to accomplish. In practice, however, many faculties give this step only cursory attention before moving on to discuss the standard components of the undergraduate program—general education, the concentration, the advising system, and the like. Of late, to be sure, colleges have been reviewing the aims of their general education program and adding requirements to achieve new goals, such as understanding cultural diversity and globalization. But these ad hoc adjustments in one segment of the curriculum are hardly a substitute for a comprehensive review of all the ends that a four-year college ought to pursue.

Without a thorough consideration of purposes, discussions often proceed without attending to important threshold issues. For example, most colleges do not merely claim to train the minds of their students; they also promise to build their character. College brochures are filled with commitments to help develop such virtues as racial tolerance, honesty, and social responsibility. Some prominent professors, however, have publicly argued that colleges should occupy themselves solely with developing the knowledge and intellectual capabilities of their students and not attempt to foster values and behaviors.[8] Common sense suggests that no serious review of the undergraduate program can fully succeed without resolving this basic difference of opinion. Nevertheless, the issue is seldom raised in the course of faculty deliberations.

By not paying careful attention to purposes, faculties have also ignored important aims of undergraduate education over extended periods of time. For example, following the Civil War, most colleges (with the notable exception of church-related institutions) gradually withdrew from any attempt to teach their students to think about ethical questions of the kind that commonly arise in private and professional life. Fortunately, after an eclipse of almost a century, courses on moral reasoning have finally begun to make a modest comeback. Yet most students in America still graduate without taking any classes of this kind. Most colleges likewise fail to make any deliberate, collective effort to prepare their students to be active, knowledgeable citizens in a democracy, even though civic apathy and ignorance of public affairs are widely regarded as serious problems in America. Only a minority of undergraduates ever take a basic course on American government, while fewer than 10 percent complete a course on the perennial problems of social justice and political philosophy that underlie so many issues of government policy. Over the past century, then, two well-known educational goals with roots extending back to ancient Greece have been allowed to languish on most college campuses without much notice, let alone careful debate.

The failure to discuss purposes carefully has even wider consequences. Although most colleges periodically review their academic programs, no program can be evaluated properly without a common understanding of what it is supposed to achieve. Lacking agreement on this point, faculties find it difficult to arrive at reasoned decisions when questions arise about changes in undergraduate education. For example, on most campuses, concentrations are such a familiar part of the curriculum that their existence is taken for granted. No one remembers very clearly why they were invented in the first place or what purpose they were meant to serve. As a result, faculties are handicapped in deciding how to respond to the periodic requests to authorize new majors in emerging fields such as women's studies, conflict resolution, or environmental issues. They are likewise without a firm intellectual basis for reviewing existing concentrations in order to decide whether their requirements are well conceived, their teaching methods appropriate, or their means of evaluating students suitably designed.

An equally unfortunate consequence of treating purposes casually is a tendency to accept goals that seem important in theory without pausing to consider whether it is possible to achieve them within the time available in the curriculum. Teaching foreign languages illustrates the point. Many colleges require their students to study a foreign language, presumably to enable them at least to carry on a rudimentary conversation, read a newspaper, or comprehend a news broadcast. Yet very few faculties are willing to insist that students take the number of semester courses that such a goal requires. The usual result is an awkward compromise that demands enough language instruction to place a significant burden on the student but not enough to accomplish the desired result. ("Enough French to read the menu, not enough to compliment the chef," to borrow Dennis O'Brien's colorful description.)[9] Over the years, millions of undergraduates have taken two or three obligatory semesters of Spanish or French without coming away with the proficiency to fulfill any meaningful purpose.

Much the same problem arises in trying to give English majors, budding economists, or history concentrators an adequate grasp of science. The goal is widely accepted by college faculties for altogether admirable reasons. No one can deny the importance of science and technology in shaping the world in which we live, nor is it disputable that citizens in a democracy should ideally know enough about these subjects to understand debates about stem cell research, genetic engineering, global warming, and other important issues of public policy. But how can colleges accomplish this result without forcing students to spend inordinate amounts of time studying material from all the major branches of science? Some faculties may believe that they have found a convincing solution to this problem, but most pretty clearly have not.

I make this point with some embarrassment, recalling a moment during a faculty meeting on Harvard's curricular reforms in the 1970s when I was pointedly asked what I thought could be accomplished by including two yearlong science courses in Harvard's new core curriculum. Undismayed, I glibly replied that our aim should be to produce a level of scientific literacy sufficient to allow all our graduates to read and comprehend articles such as those appearing in *Science* or *Scientific American.* The faculty remained silent, though whether in acquiescence or stunned disbelief I cannot say. What I do remember is being approached after the meeting by Konrad Bloch, a kind and thoughtful man who had won the Nobel Prize in chemistry some years before. "Derek," Konrad began in his cultivated German accent, "*I* cannot understand all the articles in *Science* or *Scientific American.*"

Instead of acknowledging the underlying difficulty, countless colleges have simply forged ahead and forced their students to satisfy a science requirement by taking introductory biology or physics or chemistry, even though everyone knows that such courses cannot possibly make undergraduates "scientifically literate" in any meaningful sense or equip them to understand more than a very occasional issue of science policy. The results are often unfortunate. As a team of biologists admitted in their report to the Association of American Colleges, "Many students leave their one and only course in biology with a bad memory of that experience, wondering whether there is any connection between the plants and animals of the natural world and what they studied."[10] Once again, by failing to think about their purposes with sufficient care, faculties continue to impose requirements in pursuit of worthy goals without first figuring out whether they can possibly achieve their aim in the time realistically available.

A final example of treating purposes casually is the common practice whereby faculties set requirements in pursuit of widely accepted goals without being willing to teach the necessary courses themselves. This tendency occurs most often in the case of introductory classes intended to develop skills, such as expository writing and foreign languages, which are made obligatory but then turned over to a cadre of graduate students and part-time adjunct teachers distinguishable chiefly by meager compensation, loose supervision, and insufficient training for the task. It may be possible to achieve an important educational goal without the participation of regular professors, but it is folly to count on such success without making sure that the necessary courses will be competently taught and that the instructors clearly understand the underlying purposes. In all too many cases, these conditions are not met. Even so, required courses that lack competent instruction often remain in the catalogue for years with hardly a passing comment.

As these several examples make clear, reviews of undergraduate education frequently proceed in a haze of unwarranted optimism without a thorough discussion of ends and means. Requirements are adopted in the belief that hearing professors discuss great books and reading masterpieces of literature will develop caring, ethically discerning students or that taking a variety of courses—any courses—in several different fields of knowledge will be enough to produce broadly educated, intellectually curious adults. Faculty members talk as though a year or two studying a foreign language will convey an understanding of another culture and that merely listening to powerful minds lecture about serious issues will teach students to think critically. Rarely is any attempt made to approach these assumptions with anything like the care with which professors confront propositions in their own scholarly work. As a result, much of what emerges in the form of educational goals can be better thought of as a set of well-intentioned aspirations, possibly valid but often not, and rarely resting on a convincing body of evidence.

THE FIXATION ON GENERAL EDUCATION

A fourth problem in most debates on the curriculum is a tendency to spend almost all the time discussing the general education program, even though that program normally makes up only one-third or slightly more of the courses students take. The largest segment of the curriculum, amounting to between one-third and one-half of the total course load, is not general education but the concentration (or major). Yet concentrations rarely attract serious scrutiny from the faculty as a whole.

Making general education the focus of curricular debates does not serve it well. As new needs arise, more and more requirements are loaded into this one portion of the curriculum—learning to think carefully about moral issues, to understand different races and cultures, or to function in a more global society, to mention but a few recent examples. Eventually general education programs take on so many responsibilities that they cannot possibly do justice to them all.

Another problem with focusing so heavily on general education is that concentrations receive too little collective scrutiny. This neglect would be understandable if the concentration had achieved such perfection that it no longer needed attention. But that assumption is hardly warranted. According to a faculty task force reporting to the Association of American Colleges in 1985, "the major in most colleges is little more than a gathering of courses taken in the department, lacking structure and depth, as is often the case in the humanities, or emphasizing content to the neglect of the essential style of inquiry on which the content is based, as is too frequently true in the natural and physical sciences."[11] Despite these failings, faculties typically vote to continue the concentration requirement without extended debate, presumably because it is the segment of the curriculum most congenial to their scholarly and professional concerns. In pursuit of these interests, many departments have gradually expanded the number of courses required for concentrations. By now, some majors make such heavy demands that students and faculty are hard pressed to find enough room in the rest of the curriculum to accomplish all the other important purposes of a proper undergraduate education. Worse yet, under strict departmental control, concentrations often become so focused on covering their field of knowledge that they neglect or even undermine the teaching of good writing, critical thinking, and other important goals. These problems should be matters of concern to the entire faculty, yet they typically pass unnoticed in reviews of undergraduate education. By tacit consent, any serious review of the concentration is left on most campuses to the individual departments, where the professors involved will normally attend to the needs of their discipline with little regard to the other aims of a proper liberal education.

If any segment of the curriculum receives less attention than concentrations, it is the space reserved for electives. In most faculties, everyone agrees that students should have an ample opportunity to choose freely from the catalogue to explore special interests and satisfy individual needs. By convention, this portion of the curriculum is usually allotted approximately one-quarter of the total time available. Having decided to provide this measure of freedom and flexibility, faculties have typically let the matter rest. Rarely is any serious effort made to determine how the freedom is being used. Are students choosing electives to take easy courses that leave them more time for extracurricular pursuits? Are they using their freedom to explore new interests unrelated to their majors? Are they sampling a wide variety of subjects or massing their electives to complete a second major or to take more advanced, specialized courses in their fields of concentration? Looking back, do seniors value their electives more than courses in general education or their majors? One would think that answers to these questions would help faculties decide whether the elective portion of the curriculum should be expanded or contracted or shaped to encourage some uses over others. In practice, however, such inquiries are seldom made. Just as concentrations are left to the departments, so are electives abandoned to the students.

THE NEGLECT OF PEDAGOGY

The fifth problem common to most curricular reviews is the habit of spending almost the entire time discussing which courses should be offered or required while devoting little or no attention to the methods of teaching to be used. This approach is convenient for faculties. It allows them to argue over what every educated person ought to know while avoiding the touchier question of how to teach one's courses, a topic most professors would prefer to keep to themselves, beyond the collective scrutiny of their colleagues.

A critical weakness in focusing so heavily on subject matter requirements is the underlying assumption that students will remember most of what they learn. In fact, there are great differences in how well and for how long students will recall the material they study. For example, researchers find that memory of subject matter information tends to fade rapidly. By some calculations, the average student will be unable to recall most of the factual content of a typical lecture within fifteen minutes after the end of class.[12] In contrast, interests, values, and cognitive skills are all likely to last longer, as are concepts and knowledge that students have acquired not by passively reading or listening to lectures but through their own mental efforts.[13] Thus one cannot assume that students will retain most of what they are taught merely because they have taken a course, however important its content may be. Instead, the residue of knowledge and the habits of mind students take away from college are likely to be determined less by *which* courses they take than by *how* they are taught and *how well* they are taught. Yet reports on the curriculum are almost always bereft of any extended discussion of whether current teaching methods are well suited to the educational goals being pursued and, if they are not, how they might be improved.

The neglect of pedagogy in faculty debates is probably rooted in an instinct for self-protection. It is relatively easy to move courses around by changing curricular requirements. It is quite another matter to decide that methods of pedagogy should be altered. Reforms of the latter kind require much more effort. Instructors have to change long-standing habits and master new skills for which many of them have little preparation. To avoid such difficulties, faculties have taken the principle of academic freedom and stretched it well beyond its original meaning to gain immunity from interference with how their courses should be taught. In most institutions (other than small liberal arts colleges), teaching methods have become a personal prerogative of the instructor rather than a subject appropriate for collective deliberation. The result is to shield from faculty review one of the most important ingredients in undergraduate education.

The practice of concentrating on course requirements rather than teaching has consequences that go well beyond its effect on reviews of undergraduate education. It throws light on why the number and variety of courses on most campuses have changed much more than the methods by which the courses are taught. Similarly, it helps explain why the constant growth in the size of faculties invariably results in adding more and more subjects to swollen catalogues instead of having professors teach fewer classes but devote more individual attention to students and give closer supervision to the teaching assistants who conduct small discussion sections. In this way, subject matter triumphs over pedagogy and courses proliferate without demonstrable improvement in how much students learn.

Underlying the neglect of pedagogy is a studied disregard of the research on student development in college. By now, empirical papers on teaching undergraduates lie thick upon the ground. Scores of studies have been conducted on the single question of how courses on moral reasoning affect students' thought processes and behavior. Hundreds of papers exist on the effectiveness of group learning or the validity of student teaching evaluations. Occasionally monographs appear that relate existing research to the work of college teachers in language that everyone can understand.[14] Yet rarely does one discover a reference to this literature in the published reports by faculty committees reviewing their own colleges' curricula. Individual instructors do no better in their own teaching. In one faculty survey, only 8 percent of the respondents acknowledged taking any account of research on teaching and learning in preparing their classes, and many within this small minority referred to outmoded theories and conclusions.[15]

This neglect is curious, since curriculum debates are rife with unanswered questions and unproven hypotheses. When faculties assume that their general education programs will kindle lasting intellectual interests, that their mandatory courses in expository writing will yield clearer, more grammatical essays, or that their lectures will somehow improve the critical thinking of their students, they can hardly claim to base these suppositions on firm evidence. One would think, therefore, that they would welcome efforts to test these assumptions more scientifically. After all, many of them are familiar with the kinds of empirical methods used to investigate teaching and learning, and they constantly use these techniques to study other human activities and institutions. Admittedly much of the research on education reaches conflicting results or is subject to criticism on methodological grounds, but the same is true of empirical work on most questions involving social institutions or human behavior. Possibly professors doubt whether studies of teaching and learning in other universities can tell them much about the appropriate methods of instruction for *their* students and *their* colleges. But that cannot explain why they show so little interest in conducting serious research about educational practices in their own institutions.

The indifference to educational research is probably rooted in the same instincts for self-protection that resist collective debates about teaching. Studies of this kind can result in findings that call for wholesale reforms of familiar methods of teaching and examining students. Rather than risk such unsettling changes, better to ignore the research entirely, or, if others bring it up, dismiss it as inapposite or unreliable. Shielded in this way, even professors who devote their lives to research continue to ignore empirical work on teaching and learning when they prepare their own courses or meet with colleagues to review their educational programs.

THE NEGLECT OF THE EXTRACURRICULUM

The sixth and last recurring problem in debates over undergraduate education is the frequent failure to take careful account of activity outside the classroom. Most reviews devote almost all their attention to what professors do—giving courses, advising students, awarding grades. Yet studies repeatedly show that many undergraduates consider extracurricular life to be just as valuable as coursework to their overall college experience.[16] In fact, when students are asked to recall the defining moments in their college years, moments that led to real gains in understanding and self-knowledge, they are more likely to mention happenings outside class than memorable lectures or sudden insights in a seminar.[17]

Of course, the impact of the extracurriculum varies according to the nature of the college and its students. Full-time students who live in residences on campus are likely to be influenced most; part-time commuters who work at outside jobs more than 30 hours per week are probably affected least. Yet three-quarters of the students in four-year colleges attend full time, and those who live off campus can be encouraged to participate in athletics, student government, and other out-of-class activities. Thus the extracurriculum can be an important part of the college experience for the vast majority of undergraduates.

Common sense suggests why extracurricular activities often do more than coursework to stimulate several important forms of personal growth. Students are much more likely to learn about working effectively with others from playing on an athletic team, acting in a college play, or even belonging to a fraternity than from the solitary experience of attending classes and studying in the library. Many of them will gain a better understanding of people of different races and religions from living and working within a diverse student body than from taking courses on cultural differences or race relations. Many more will acquire greater empathy and stronger commitments to help the needy by assisting in a student-run homeless shelter than by listening to lectures about poverty. Extracurricular activities may include no formal learning. Even so, because they are more intense, more vivid, and more personal, they can easily make a deeper, longer-lasting impression than anything that occurs in the regular curriculum.

Faculty members who review the undergraduate program may concede all this but prefer to confine their deliberations to the formal educational program of the college, leaving the dean of students and other administrative officials to worry about the extracurriculum. This approach works well enough up to a point. Exercising their authority outside the classroom, administrators have initiated most of the important innovations in undergraduate education over the past few decades—the recruitment of more diverse student bodies, the growth of community service programs, the introduction of co-residential living units, even the creation of centers to help graduate students learn how to teach. In the end, however, simply handing over the extracurriculum to administrators is inadequate, because student experiences inside the classroom and out are often too closely intertwined to be kept separate in this way.[18] Preparing undergraduates for citizenship in a democracy—one of the oldest aims of education—occurs not only in courses on political science or American history but also in student government, dormitory elections, young Democrat and Republican clubs, and many other extracurricular settings. Learning to think more carefully and precisely about ethical questions can take place both in classes on moral reasoning and on athletic teams, community service projects, and honor code committees.

More important, what students study in class often affects the value of their extracurricular experience, which in turn can enhance what they learn in class. Undergraduates will understand a musical work more thoroughly if they have performed it themselves, just as they will play the piece with greater insight by having taken a course on composition. Students who volunteer to work with families in a local housing project will gain more from the experience if they have taken a course on poverty while also learning more in class for having worked closely with poor people. Because of this interdependence, any attempt to develop programs in civic education or the arts without considering the role of extracurricular activities runs the risk of being distorted and incomplete.

THE POPULAR CRITIQUES

It is interesting to note that none of the problems just described receives much attention in the well-publicized attacks on higher education that have appeared in the past 20 years. Reading these critiques, one soon discovers that, although they are much more polemical than the typical faculty curriculum report, they exhibit many of the same shortcomings. When the authors discuss the curriculum, they direct virtually all their attention to the general education program and rarely take up the other components that make up most of the academic program. In addressing the quality of education, they deride the flabby incoherence of current curricula, condemn the existence of trendy, leftist courses, or inveigh against the faculty for failing to integrate the disciplines, but they pay little or no attention to *how* classes should be taught. Although they often attack the senior faculty for caring only about research and refusing to give tenure to popular young instructors, they almost never discuss the teaching methods professors use, let alone look to existing research for suggestions of better ways to help students learn. As for what goes on outside class, the critics either ignore the subject altogether or content themselves with condemning undergraduates for their loose morals or their political correctness without considering how the extracurriculum could and should contribute to the serious purposes of undergraduate education.

The critical literature is especially deficient when it comes to suggesting specific reforms. The worst of the books cavalierly toss off remedies such as abolishing tenure or "vaporizing" three-quarters of all scholarly journals without bothering to consider the obvious practical problems that such suggestions would create. Other works, in varying degrees of detail, emphasize the need for a much more highly structured curriculum, often built around a study of the Great Books. While Allan Bloom merely mentions the idea in passing with very little discussion, William Bennett and Lynne Cheney offer detailed blueprints for curriculum planners.[19] What none of these authors do, however, is discuss with care the objections to their proposals, such as the difficulty of finding enough professors willing and able to teach such courses or the problem of attracting students to a college with such a curriculum. This oversight is odd, to say the least, since these objections have consistently kept the Great Books approach from taking hold in more than a tiny number of colleges since the idea was first proposed almost a century ago.*

---

*More recently, a few books have appeared that offer a larger vision to animate undergraduate education and unite professors from different disciplines. These essays are more thoughtful than the rest of the critical literature, and their treatment of faculty and students is more measured. However, they are also much less widely read, perhaps because the authors often pitch their discussion at a level of abstraction that makes them very hard to follow for anyone not steeped in the same intellectual broth. For example, according to one of these writers, "If we are to find some defining set of values for our social mission and if we are to forge a much-needed connection between matters of the mind, the demands of liberal democracy, and service to the economy, then we need to make sure that

Put bluntly, the widely publicized critiques of four-year colleges are largely a digression, diverting attention from questions of pedagogy, the college major, the neglect of moral development and civic education, and other truly serious educational problems. Rather than treat these issues, the authors prefer to focus on more arresting topics — on students (described as either neglected, promiscuous, politically correct, or excessively vocational); on faculty (treated as either trendy, radical, or obsessed with research and self-advancement); or on university officials (almost invariably pictured as permissive, timid, lacking in vision, or all of the above). These formulaic descriptions may contain a measure of truth (along with considerable exaggeration). Nevertheless, the professors who are quoted are seldom representative of the faculty as a whole, and the accounts of well-known controversies rarely reveal both sides of the dispute. Even the specific practices singled out for criticism, such as grade inflation, or political biases within the faculty, or the failure to promote popular lecturers, are seldom ones that have a demonstrable effect on how much students learn or how well equipped they are to live a full and successful life after they graduate.

---

somewhere, somehow, we address the question of how far we are enlightened and what constitutes our modernity" (Eric Gould, *The University in a Corporate Culture* [2003], p. 196).

Another author states: "my aim, then, is an anti-modernist rephrasing of teaching and writing as sites of obligation, as loci of *ethical practices*, rather than as a means for the transmission of scientific knowledge. Teaching thus becomes answerable to *the question of justice*, rather than to the criterion of truth. We must seek to do justice to teaching rather than to know what it is" (Bill Readings, *The University in Ruins* [1996], p. 154).

However earnestly set forth, such formulations offer but a faint and flickering light to the general reader or to those on campus trying to grope their way out of the darkness toward specific educational reforms.

In the end, therefore, the popular critiques offer a caricature rather than a useful and accurate picture of the contemporary American college. In trying so hard to identify culprits, the authors overlook the larger forces that have much more to do with shaping our system of higher education. The search for scapegoats is bound to leave out much of what most urgently needs attention. Although academe may have its share of human imperfections, the problems of our colleges are not so much the product of cautious, unimaginative leaders or radical, self-absorbed professors as the outgrowth of a system that lacks strong pressures to increase educational quality and that measures institutional progress by the average SAT scores of the students and the research reputation of the faculty. This system in turn is the product of many forces, some outside higher education and others inherent in the nature of the educational process. By ignoring these forces and concentrating instead on finding someone to blame, the critics miss the most serious problems of our colleges, which have to do less with decline and abuse than with unfulfilled promise and unrealized opportunities. That is why their books, for all their colorful rhetoric and acid commentary, have had very limited success in changing the nature of undergraduate education.

A better way to evaluate the strengths and weaknesses of our colleges is to begin—where all serious debates about education must—with a careful look at the purposes to be achieved. Once the aims of the enterprise are defined, we can examine each purpose in turn to determine how far our colleges have progressed toward accomplishing their goals. As we will discover, the problems identified in this chapter will reveal themselves at numerous points and leave their imprint on the quality of undergraduate education.

3 | PURPOSES

Any useful discussion of undergraduate education must begin by making clear what it is that colleges are trying to achieve. As W. B. Carnochan has observed, "Lacking adequate criteria of purpose, we do not know how well our higher education works in practice or even what working well would mean."[1] What, then, should colleges try to have their students take away after four years? How should they help young people to grow and develop during this formative period in their lives?

In pondering these questions, several critics of undergraduate education assume that there must be a *single* overarching purpose to college that faculties have somehow forgotten or willfully ignored. For Bruce Wilshire in *The Moral Collapse of the University*, it is to help students integrate fragmented, specialized fields of knowledge in order to address larger questions "about what we are and what we ought to be."[2] For Charles Anderson in *Prescribing the Life of the Mind*, it is "the cultivation of the skills of practical reason."[3] For Bill Readings in *The University in Ruins*, the unifying aim of a college education used to be the interpretation, advancement, and transmission of the "national culture," and it is the demise of this traditional purpose that has left the contemporary university "in ruins," bereft of any animating goal save the vapid claim of "excellence" in all it tries to do.[4]

Nowhere in their writings do the authors make clear why there should be only one dominant purpose for undergraduate education.

The very idea seems instantly suspect, since human beings develop intellectually in a number of different ways during their undergraduate years. It is especially implausible in the United States, for American colleges, at least those of the residential variety, to not merely offer courses but also undertake to organize the living arrangements, the recreational and extracurricular activities—indeed, virtually the whole environment in which their students spend four years of their lives. If colleges exercise such a pervasive influence, they should presumably try to help undergraduates develop in even more ways than those fostered by the curriculum alone. Anyone who tries to conflate these forms of growth into a single comprehensive goal is bound to suggest a purpose that is either far too narrow to capture all that colleges should accomplish or far too broad to convey much useful meaning.

Once college faculties look for a series of goals, they will quickly encounter an important threshold problem. According to a school of thought recently expressed by Stanley Fish, the only proper ends of the university are those that involve "the mastery of intellectual and scholarly skills."[5] Fish is not the only professor to hold this view, but his opinion is clearly at odds with the official position of many institutions. College catalogues regularly announce an intention to go beyond intellectual pursuits to nurture such behavioral traits as good moral character, racial tolerance, and a commitment to active citizenship.

Fish's principal argument against trying to develop character or prepare active citizens is that such goals are simply "unworkable." In his words, "There are just too many intervening variables, too many uncontrolled factors that mediate the relationship between what goes on in a classroom and the shape of what is finally a life."[6] Fish believes that universities should confine themselves to what they know how to do. He urges faculty members "to put your students in possession of a set of materials and equip them with a set of skills (interpretive, computational, laboratory, archival) and even perhaps (although this one is really iffy) instill in them the same love of the subject that inspires your pedagogical efforts."[7]

In making his argument, Fish commits one of the basic errors identified in the preceding chapter: he equates what an undergraduate education should accomplish with what professors can achieve in their classrooms. This is a cramped and excessively faculty-centered point of view. Colleges can hardly undertake to shape the environment in which their students live, in and out of the classroom, throughout four formative years and then insist that their aims are limited to the things their professors know how to do. By tailoring the role of the college to fit the capabilities and interests of its faculty rather than the needs of its students, Fish overlooks all that admissions policies, residential living arrangements, and extracurricular life can contribute to an undergraduate's development. There is much evidence that these aspects of college do have significant, reasonably foreseeable effects on the attitudes, the values, and even the behavior of students (including their moral and civic behavior). Rather than deal with these findings, Fish commits another error common to faculty debates about undergraduate education. He is content to rest his case on his own personal observations during 14 years on the Duke University faculty, pointing out that "While Duke is a first-rate institution with many virtues, I saw no evidence whatsoever that its graduates emerged with a highly developed sense of civic responsibility as they rushed off to enter top-10 law schools, medical schools, and business schools."[8]

In fact, researchers have shown that college graduates are much more active civically and politically than those who have not attended college (even after controlling for differences in intelligence, parental education, and socioeconomic background). In fact, political scientists find that formal education is the *most* important factor in explaining who does or does not go to the polls.[9] Several studies also suggest that certain courses and concentrations, notably in the social sciences, and certain outside activities, such as community service programs, have a positive effect on students' willingness to vote or to work to improve their communities following graduation.[10] Other large-scale studies have found that a variety of extracurricular experiences affect student values in consistent ways. For example, several researchers have concluded that efforts to admit a racially diverse student body and to promote interracial contact through policies on such matters as student living arrangements and racial awareness programs can build greater tolerance.[11] One can surely question such findings or disagree with the methods used in the studies. By ignoring the evidence entirely, however, and relying instead on casual, personal observations, Fish ultimately renders his arguments unconvincing.

Of course, one can accept the possibility of shaping student values and still balk at deliberate efforts to prepare active citizens, build stronger moral character, or promote greater racial tolerance. When colleges seek not merely to sharpen students' minds but also to improve their behavior, thoughtful faculty members may worry that such intentions smack of human engineering and raise the specter of indoctrination.

Anyone harboring such concerns would only be more troubled after reading essays from faculty members of the left, such as Henry Giroux, Frederic Jameson, or Frank

Lentricchia. These authors are explicit about their desire to transform undergraduates into citizens committed to fighting social injustice. Lentricchia plainly acknowledges that "I come down on the side of those who believe that our society is mainly unreasonable and that education should be one of the places where we can get involved in the process of changing it."[12] Literature professor Jameson announces that his purpose is to "make converts" and "form Marxists."[13] According to Giroux, professors should try to change society for the better by engaging their students with "critical pedagogy," that is, "pedagogical practices informed by an ethical stance that contests racism, sexism, class exploitation, and other dehumanizing and exploitative social relations . . . [and that] seeks to celebrate responsible action and strategic risk taking as part of an ongoing struggle to link citizenship to the notion of a democratic public community, civic courage to a shared conception of social justice."[14]

Many people would agree with Giroux's objectives, couched in these terms. Who could be against encouraging students to promote social justice and to oppose "dehumanizing and exploitative social relations"? Who is in favor of "racism, sexism, [and] class exploitation"? But problems start to emerge as one reads further. Behind the protective covering of "social justice" lies a distinct political view of society and a specific program of reform. There are official villains: "corporations have been given too much power in this society, and hence the need for educators and others to address the threat this poses to all facets of public life."[15] Giroux likewise has a specific political agenda: "progressive academics must take seriously the symbolic and pedagogic dimensions of struggle and be able to fight for public services and rights, especially the right to decent health care, education, housing, and work."[16] Apparently, then, faculty members must oppose corporations and promote a progressive welfare state agenda not only as private citizens but through their teaching as well.

Since these political goals are matters of legitimate debate, the vision of a university committed to promoting Giroux's agenda is deeply unsettling.* Could students who disagree with the agenda feel entirely free to express opposing views? Would appointments and promotions committees in Giroux's university evaluate faculty candidates on their intellectual merits or be swayed by how closely the candidates' teaching and writing conformed to his political vision? As Giroux has clearly stated, educators must regard "all calls to depoliticize pedagogy [and presumably scholarship as well] as simply a mask for domination."[17] What he seems to argue is that everything that goes on in a university is inescapably political, that all efforts at neutrality and objectivity are impossible and disingenuous, and that universities should therefore consciously adopt a political agenda and promote it through their teaching and writing.

To be sure, Giroux and others like him often add that students should be free to disagree with their professors. Still, in Giroux's university, one wonders whether undergraduates

---

*The problem of indoctrination is not limited to left-wing professors. Well-meaning programs sponsored by a university to improve race or gender relations can easily fall into the hands of officials who announce as fact to incoming freshmen such debatable propositions as "all institutions in America are deeply sexist" or "racism involves only acts of discrimination by whites against minorities." See, for example, Charles Alan Kors, "Bad Faith: The Politicization of the University *In Loco Parentis*," in Howard Dickman (ed.), *The Imperiled Academy* (1993), p. 153. Race and gender programs can be helpful when they allow open discussion of differences of opinion, potentially unfair practices, misunderstandings, and the like, but dogmatic assertions and indoctrination by persons in authority can be just as wrong in the context of promoting understanding among the races or between the sexes as in other academic settings.

concerned about their grade point averages will dare to differ with their instructors when they write their papers and take their exams. One also suspects that junior professors of different political persuasions will feel inclined to follow the prevailing party line in their teaching and writing, lest they be deemed expendable when they are considered for tenure. Since Giroux is not alone in his views, one can understand why some professors (and some others as well) might worry about proposals to shape the character and values of students.

Is there any way of promoting certain values and behaviors that does not amount to unacceptable indoctrination? Yes, but the limits need to be clearly defined and carefully circumscribed. Institutional efforts to build character or change behavior should include only goals with which no reasonable person is likely to disagree.* For example, virtually no one would quarrel with attempts to encourage students to be more honest, more scrupulous about keeping promises, more understanding of those of different races, backgrounds, and religions. Nor would anyone in a democracy oppose efforts encouraging undergraduates to vote, inform themselves about public issues, and participate in their communities. It is only when professors use their classrooms to influence *which* promises students keep, *how* they vote, or *what* kind of community programs they support that their teaching is open to criticism.

Even seemingly unexceptionable goals, of course, raise serious questions at the margin. There are surely *some* cases in which principled people can be excused for not telling the

---

*Exceptions may be made for private colleges, such as religiously affiliated institutions, that actively promote a set of special beliefs or behaviors, provided they make this clear to prospective students and their families.

truth or for refusing to vote. That being so, a student should always be free to question principles of behavior both in and out of class, no matter how correct they may seem. Although professors may disagree with students about their views on moral or civic questions, they must never use their power to suppress opposing opinions. Nor should the university use coercive authority to impose its moral or civic principles on its students except where necessary to maintain order, protect persons and property, or uphold the integrity of the academic process (e.g., by punishing cheating or plagiarism). In other words, attempts to shape behavior and character, even for widely accepted ends, should be carried out, insofar as possible, through argument, persuasion, and example, not by force or coercive authority.

Notwithstanding Professor Fish, it is perfectly possible to teach moral reasoning or prepare students to be enlightened citizens without having instructors impose their personal ideologies or policy views on their students. Of course, it is conceivable that instructors will abuse their authority in these ways. All manner of familiar subjects can and occasionally do degenerate into indoctrination in the hands of instructors intent on forcing their own beliefs on students.* Courses on American politics or political philosophy or international

---

*The meaning of indoctrination is not as obvious as it may seem. For example, teachers of "the dismal science" are sometimes accused of indoctrination because they accept the basic assumptions of neoclassical economics and do not devote class time to an in-depth discussion of possible alternatives. Similarly, professors of Constitutional law can be said to indoctrinate by refusing to entertain challenges to the legitimacy of the Constitution and the form of government it embodies. Nevertheless, there is a difference between these examples and, say, using a basic writing course to teach students how language is employed to oppress women, minorities, and the poor. In providing instruction on economics or Constitutional law, a college may well decide to offer elective courses in which

economics are obvious examples. Even required courses in English composition are sometimes used to promote a radical political agenda.[18] It would be folly to abolish all courses susceptible to such instruction. Such a response would decimate the curriculum. Rather, the proper course is surely to rally the entire faculty to consider their responsibilities as teachers and to discourage efforts by particular instructors to misuse their positions by trying to indoctrinate students.

To sum up, attempts to prescribe a single overriding aim or to limit the purposes of college to the realm of intellectual development take too narrow a view of the undergraduate experience and threaten to impose a moratorium on efforts to nurture some extremely important human qualities during four formative years of students' lives. Instead, colleges should pursue a variety of purposes, including a carefully circumscribed effort to foster generally accepted values and behaviors, such as honesty and racial tolerance. Within this ample mandate, several aims seem especially important.*

---

to consider alternative systems, but it is perfectly legitimate to refuse to use basic courses in these fields for this purpose. In such classes, as currently taught, instructors are not seeking to use the classroom to spread their own private set of controversial beliefs; they are making a commonsense judgment about how best to use scarce class time in a basic course to be of greatest use to the largest number of students. In the writing class, instructors cannot make this claim. Rather, they are taking a required course established for other purposes and deliberately using it to promote their personal political agendas.

*The list that follows does not attempt to include the multitude of purposes that might be appropriate for particular groups of students—learning Russian, for example, or writing poetry, playing football, or acquiring a knowledge of chemistry. The aims described here are those of broad enough applicability to be appropriate for virtually all undergraduates.

THE ABILITY TO COMMUNICATE

All undergraduates need to develop the capacity to communicate well with various audiences. The ability to write with precision and grace is the most familiar of these competencies, followed by an ability to speak clearly and persuasively. These skills are widely used by students both during college and after. They are essential in civic life and in almost all the careers that students are likely to enter. When asked what they look for in the college graduates they hire, employers repeatedly emphasize the importance of good writing and effective speaking.

Professors have long entertained the hope that students would acquire these skills *before* coming to college. Efforts were even made more than a century ago to force high schools to do a better job of teaching composition by introducing writing exams for students seeking admission to college.[19] Unfortunately, the wish has never been fulfilled. Freshmen have always arrived on campus deficient in their ability to communicate. They are especially likely to do so now that such a high proportion of young people come to college, often from mediocre schools and from families in which English is not commonly spoken. However welcome or unwelcome the task may be, colleges cannot escape the responsibility of preparing all their undergraduates to speak and write with reasonable precision, clarity, and style.

CRITICAL THINKING

Another aim basic to every college is to enhance the ability of students to think clearly and critically. The importance of this goal is so widely acknowledged that nationwide polls have found that more than 90 percent of faculty members in the United States consider it *the most* important purpose of undergraduate education.[20] In view of the wide variety of interests and backgrounds represented in a typical college faculty, such a strong consensus is impressive.

Defining what critical thinking actually entails, however, is more complicated than many people realize. Some psychologists have invoked a line of thought stretching back to Edward Thorndike's experiments at the beginning of the twentieth century and insisted that there is no such thing as "critical thinking," only an endless series of particular ways to reason about different kinds of problems.[21] There is clearly some truth to this observation. Many subjects are sufficiently complex and unique that no student can think about them productively without first mastering a body of specialized analytic methods and technical knowledge. If all thinking involved such methods, the scope for developing rigorous habits of thought in college would be severely limited, since few undergraduates could acquire enough of the necessary skills and knowledge to address more than a few of these subjects.

Fortunately, many problems arising in everyday life and experience do not require such highly specialized knowledge. Recent research suggests that certain familiar qualities of mind and habits of thought may help resolve such a wide range of problems that every student would benefit from acquiring them.[22] Among these qualities are an ability to recognize and define problems clearly, to identify the arguments and interests on all sides of an issue, to gather relevant facts and appreciate their relevance, to perceive as many plausible solutions as possible, and to exercise good judgment in choosing the best of these alternatives after considering the evidence and using inference, analogy, and other forms of ordinary reasoning to test the cogency of the arguments. These methods will not solve all problems; far from it. But they will solve many and clarify many more, enough to make proficiency in their use well worth the effort.

In addition to these habits of disciplined common sense, certain basic quantitative methods seem applicable to a wide enough range of situations to be valuable for almost all students. For example, a reasonable grasp of statistics and probability may prove useful in thinking about a host of familiar problems, from understanding newspaper articles about risks to personal safety and health to calculating the odds of getting into graduate school or understanding the reliability of opinion polls. A knowledge of mathematics accompanied by practice applying such knowledge to everyday problems and situations can likewise be helpful to students in completing their income tax forms, balancing their budgets, and thinking more rigorously about a variety of complicated subjects. A facility with computers can serve a wide and growing range of purposes in acquiring information and using it to solve problems.

Beyond these few examples, it is hard to think of general problem-solving skills that can be profitably used in enough situations to justify making their study mandatory. Formal logic and advanced calculus, for example, have not proved especially helpful except for solving a limited set of abstract problems.[23] As a result, courses on methods such as these should be available for those who need to learn them, but there is no compelling reason to force every student to master this material.

MORAL REASONING

A related but more controversial aim of college is to help students develop a clearer, stronger set of ethical principles. After decades of neglect, spurred by heated controversies in the

1960s over moral values in public and private life, universities began to offer courses challenging students to think about a variety of practical ethical problems. The growth of these new courses, however, has not persuaded all the skeptics in the faculty. "As for ethics," one sometimes hears, "by the time students begin college, they either have 'em or they don't." According to this line of thought, moral development is the responsibility of parents and schoolteachers, and universities that try to assume the task are destined not to succeed.

Comments of this kind reveal a failure to distinguish between two aspects of ethical behavior. One is the ability to think carefully about moral dilemmas, evaluate the arguments on all sides, and decide on the right thing to do. The other is the desire and self-discipline to put one's conclusions into practice. Parents may have the preeminent role in developing the desire and determination to act responsibly toward others, although, even here, experience teaches that other influences later in life can have an effect. However, when it comes to helping young people to identify ethical problems and to ponder them with care, colleges can certainly make a significant contribution, especially today, when so many students come to college with an easy relativism that clouds their ability to reason about many complex questions, ethical and otherwise.*

---

*Even those who understand the difference between moral reasoning and the will to act on one's beliefs sometimes dismiss the former as relatively unimportant. Gordon Marino, philosophy professor at Saint Olaf College, illustrates this tendency in a recent article in the *Chronicle of Higher Education.* "The fantasy," he declares, "seems to be that if up-and-coming accountants just knew a little more about ethics, then they would know better than to falsify their reports so as to drive up the value of company stock. But sheer ignorance is seldom the moral problem. More knowledge is not what is needed. Take it from Kierkegaard: The moral challenge is

Analyzing ethical issues, then, is a form of critical thinking much like other forms that faculties regularly teach. Learning to act on one's beliefs, on the other hand, presents a more formidable challenge that must await further discussion in Chapter 6. For now, the chance to help students learn to identify ethical issues and think about them rigorously is reason enough to include moral education among the aims of college, even if it is not clear whether students will act more ethically as a result. After all, business schools teach students to analyze issues confronting corporations, although one cannot be sure that graduates will have the resolve to act on what they have learned instead of using their powers of rationalization to justify a more expedient course of action. Law schools continue teaching how to reason about legal questions, although they know that students will sometimes ignore the proper an-

---

simply to abide by the knowledge we already have." Gordon Marino, "Before Teaching Ethics, Stop Kidding Yourself," *The Chronicle Review*, 50 *Chronicle of Higher Education* (Feb. 20, 2004), p. B5.

If Professor Marino were correct, one wonders why philosophers spent so much time in years past on practical moral issues. In fact, such questions are often not as simple as he suggests, and the problems have only grown more complicated in recent decades. Today, more than ever before, there is good reason for college graduates to know "a little more about ethics." Modern medicine has created a host of ethical problems that demand the most careful analysis: stem cell research and cloning, for example, not to mention the dilemmas doctors face in deciding whether to withhold the truth from patients or to test new drugs made by companies to which they have financial ties. Lawyers face vexing questions in reconciling their duties to a client with their obligations to court and society. Even accountants will often encounter difficult choices when they discover practices that seem to meet the letter of the accounting rules but arguably raise broader issues of public policy. In all these cases, students need to develop habits of thought that will help them to recognize moral problems when they arise and to reason about them carefully enough to arrive at thoughtful decisions on how to respond.

swer in order to tell important clients what they want to hear. Much of what faculties teach their undergraduates is conveyed in the faith that most students will use their knowledge and skills for proper ends. There is no reason why colleges should not make the same assumption when they teach students how to think carefully about moral issues.

PREPARING CITIZENS

Another widely neglected aim of liberal education is to prepare students to be informed and active participants in the process of democratic self-government.* Until the mid-twentieth century in America, educators believed that a sound liberal education would suffice to serve this purpose adequately. During the intervening decades, however, circumstances have changed in important ways that cast serious doubt on this assumption. For one thing, the amount of information citizens need to fulfill their civic duties has become far larger. To understand the broad array of important policy issues and make informed choices among rival candidates, today's voters would need a working knowledge of a vast agenda of complicated subjects, such as healthcare, social security, international relations, and global warming. It is impossible to familiarize students with all these issues, let

---

*Colleges do devote much attention to developing qualities of mind and spirit that can contribute to enlightened citizenship. Critical thinking, racial tolerance, general knowledge—indeed, almost everything a college tries to do—can be described as civic education in the broadest possible sense. For present purposes, however, the term *civic education* is used more narrowly to refer to efforts to give all students the essential knowledge that every citizen needs and to strengthen their commitment to participate effectively in the process of democratic self-government—as, for example, voters, candidates, public servants, commentators, campaign workers, or simply concerned citizens.

alone prepare them for the many new questions that will arise during their lifetimes. How to respond to this problem poses an extremely difficult challenge, but one cannot assume that it will be enough merely to offer a traditional liberal education.

In addition, prior to World War II, college students were a small elite, and educators could safely assume that they would take an active part in political and civic life. Now undergraduates in America make up a large share of a generation in which civic apathy is the norm. Young people vote less than any other age group and less than people of their age voted in generations past.[24] For the first time in modern memory, a majority of young Americans turning 18 will have grown up in a home in which no parent *has ever voted.* In such an environment, one cannot assume that graduates will even bother to go to the polls, let alone play an active part in their communities. Civic education is arguably no longer simply a matter of conveying the knowledge and skills to help students make enlightened judgments about politics and public affairs; colleges must consider whether there is anything they can do to imbue undergraduates with a stronger commitment to fulfill their civic responsibilities.

LIVING WITH DIVERSITY

Along with acquiring civic and moral responsibility, undergraduates need to learn to live and work effectively with other people and enter into fulfilling personal relationships. For generations, this part of growing up was taken for granted as a fact of life; it did not entail significant responsibilities for American colleges beyond enacting prohibitions against violence and theft and establishing parietal rules to limit contact between the sexes. In the aftermath of the civil rights revolution, however, blacks, Hispanics, and other minority groups began to enroll in growing numbers on predominantly white campuses, forcing universities to deal with a series of problems and controversies growing out of the troubled history of race in America. The feminist movement and the heightened awareness of subtle and not-so-subtle discriminations against women infused relationships between the sexes with new and urgently felt tensions. Gay rights activists began to assert themselves and urge college administrators to meet the needs of those with different sexual preferences.

Universities have not been the only institutions to experience these changes. All sorts of organizations find themselves employing a more diverse workforce and offering goods and services to a more heterogeneous set of publics. In this environment, with a population growing steadily more multiracial and a legal system bristling with safeguards for ethnic and religious groups, institutions of every kind expect colleges to prepare their students to work effectively with many different kinds of people. Meanwhile, some intellectuals worry whether a nation divided among so many ethnic and religious groups can hold together as a society, and they look to universities to do their part in fostering tolerance and understanding.

No college can sensibly refrain from doing what it can to help students learn to function successfully in this self-consciously diverse population. Failure to do so would not only seem insensitive to evident needs in the society and workforce; it would ignore deeply felt concerns that exist on every campus. When racial tensions flare, or women angrily protest against sexual violence, or gay students are openly persecuted, campus authorities must respond. They quickly find that merely enacting rules and meting out punishment will not suffice. In one way or another, every college must seek to apply the words of Martin Luther King Jr.: "We have inherited a large house, a great world house, in which we have to live together, black and white, Gentile and Jew, Catholic and Protestant, Moslem and Hindu, a family unduly separated in ideas, culture, and interest, who, because we can never again live apart, must learn somehow to live with each other in peace."[25] The challenge is to determine how to help students learn to live together with understanding and mutual respect while not appearing insensitive to the aggrieved, unfairly accusatory to the majority, or rigidly doctrinaire to the larger society.

LIVING IN A MORE GLOBAL SOCIETY

Americans increasingly find themselves affected by circumstances beyond our borders—by other governments, distant cultures, foreign nationals, international crises. Freer trade exposes American workers to overseas economies that can create new jobs or take them away. The lives of ordinary citizens are touched by distant wars, terrorist threats, Middle East oil shortages. Changing methods of communication and travel multiply opportunities for contact across national boundaries. Problems ranging from environmental dangers and narcotics trafficking to trade wars and nuclear weapons draw our government into new collaborative relationships with other nations. All these developments suggest that students today will need to know more than earlier generations of undergraduates about international affairs and about other countries and cultures.

Colleges must respond to these challenges, since their graduates are so likely to be involved with other nations and foreign nationals as business executives, public officials, lawyers, or simply citizens. Exactly how to prepare students for such a future, however, poses great difficulties. No one can hope to gain even a rudimentary knowledge of the many nations of the world, each with its own language and culture. Nor can undergraduates foresee in college just which cultures and languages will prove important to them after they graduate. No one can predict future events in the international arena with any certainty. Thus the peculiar challenge colleges face is how to construct a foundation of knowledge and understanding that will help their students adapt and respond effectively to whatever international problems and opportunities may confront them in their later lives. More than most of the aims that colleges pursue, this task is novel and remains clouded by uncertainty and confusion.

A BREADTH OF INTERESTS

Another, more traditional, aim of a college education is to give students the capabilities, knowledge, and breadth of interests to enable them to enjoy full and varied lives. Some of these interests may be intellectual—for example, in history or philosophy. Others may be artistic—understanding and enjoying music, poetry, and painting or actually practicing some form of art as an avocation. Still others may involve engaging in a lifetime sport, such as tennis, swimming, or running.

Such a variety of interests brings many blessings. It can help to avoid the dangers of excessive specialization by providing wider perspectives to enlighten judgment. It offers escape from a life too preoccupied with vocational concerns. It supplies the knowledge to understand more of what is occurring in the world, from global warming to presidential campaigns to chronic trade deficits. It furnishes the mind to contemplate the perennial human problems of good and evil, justice and injustice, war and peace. It affords a means for escaping boredom through all manner of absorbing private pursuits.

Although the case for acquiring a breadth of interests and knowledge seems compelling, it is hard to know exactly how colleges should respond. The task may seem manageable on first impression, but only so long as one assumes that students will remember most of what they are taught, especially in their general education classes. Unfortunately, this assumption is patently unrealistic. Most students retain only fragments, and even these will steadily disappear beyond recall if there is no occasion to use them.[26] The limitations of memory are an important reason why attempting to compile lists of essential facts and ideas that every student should know is likely to prove a fruitless enterprise. They also cast doubt on ambitious schemes to expose all students to a grand array of courses covering vast areas of human experience.

How, then, should colleges proceed? By trying to awaken interests that will inspire students to continue learning in a variety of fields throughout their lifetimes? By teaching undergraduates basic methods of inquiry that will enable them to explore subjects that might otherwise seem remote and impenetrable? By concentrating on a few fundamental ideas and texts in enough detail that students will conceivably remember much of what they have learned?

There are no easy answers to these questions. That is doubtless one reason why the subject of general education has attracted so much interest since its inception more than a century ago, and why it continues to provoke such heated debates.

PREPARING FOR WORK

A last, but still contested, aim of undergraduate education is to prepare students for a career. In his *Politics*, Aristotle asks, "should the useful in life, or should virtue, or should the higher knowledge be the aim of our training?"[27] Disagreement on this point persists to this day. Humanists have expressed special hostility toward attempts to dilute the liberal arts with courses that prepare students for work. To William Schaefer, former chair of the English department and an academic vice chancellor at the University of California, Los Angeles, "the most critical issue [is] purging the undergraduate curriculum of vocational training."[28] More than 30 years ago, philosopher Robert Paul Wolff also urged that all vocational courses be banished from the curriculum, arguing that such instruction inevitably diverted students from a pure desire to master a subject. Only through an effort to achieve such mastery, he believed, "sharply different from both the dilettante's superficiality and the professional's career commitment, can a young man discover who he is and whom he wants to be."[29]

These opinions seem strangely out of touch with the realities of contemporary American life. For the vast majority of college students, regardless of the college they attend, the undergraduate years are a time when they must choose a vocation. This decision will have a profound effect on their lives, and it is only natural that they should take it seriously and seek whatever help their college can give them. Indeed it is hard to know how any student could truly understand "whom [he wants] to be" *without* thinking carefully about what career to pursue. To make such choices wisely, students need to learn more about the role different professions play in society; the moral dilemmas their members commonly face; the social, psychological, and material rewards they can bring; and the mental, physical, and temporal demands they impose. Surely colleges should do something to help students acquire such knowledge so that they can make informed decisions about a question so vital to their future lives.

In most American colleges, a majority of undergraduates will not merely have to choose a vocation; they will move directly into the workforce and look for a job. For them, college is the last chance to prepare themselves for work by acquiring skills and knowledge of the kind best learned through formal education. Institutions with large numbers of such students can hardly deny them the opportunity. Colleges that did so would soon have to close their doors for lack of enough applicants, and deservedly so, since they might leave their students ill equipped to enter their chosen callings.

Preparing students for a career, of course, does not merely mean giving them the essential skills for their first or second jobs. Such a curriculum might have only temporary value and could easily crowd out other important purposes of undergraduate education. Devising a more appropriate preparation, however, presents a number of problems. How much time should faculties allot to the purpose in view of the other aims of a college education? How can vocational and liberal arts courses reinforce each other instead of existing in isolation, or even at cross-purposes with one another? Will vocational courses of the traditional kind actually help undergraduates to have a successful career, or will a solid grounding in the liberal arts accomplish more over the long run? These are questions that call for answers from any college with substantial numbers of students moving directly into the workforce. What is not justifiable—nor even practical—is to reject out of hand the very possibility of vocational courses or the legitimacy of preparing students for productive, satisfying careers.

This completes my list of the basic goals of undergraduate education. Although these aims have been treated separately for purposes of clarity, they interact and overlap in many important ways. Courses on moral reasoning help to develop skills in critical thinking and do so using problems that are especially interesting and provocative for many students. Classes in writing can also teach students to think critically and carefully. Courses that prepare students for enlightened citizenship can add breadth to their studies. Conversely, studying moral issues, or living with classmates of different races, or learning about globalization can all help develop more enlightened citizens. These reinforcing qualities do not constitute a problem but an advantage. If particular courses and activities can serve several purposes simultaneously, colleges are more likely to succeed in embracing a number of separate goals within a single four-year curriculum.

Despite the great variety of American four-year colleges, the aims described here seem suitable not only for all students but for all institutions as well. It is hard to imagine a college that would not want to improve the critical thinking of its undergraduates, enhance their communication skills, broaden their interests, and address in some manner their vocational needs. It is equally hard to understand why every college should not try to improve students' capacity to think carefully about moral questions and to fulfill their responsibilities as citizens. Naturally institutions will differ about how best to pursue these goals. Variations in student bodies, resources, and educational philosophy will dictate different choices. Yet the basic ends to which colleges should direct their efforts seem likely to be and to remain more or less the same.

After reflecting on the purposes just listed, some readers are bound to object that worthy goals have been omitted. How about nurturing powers of imagination and creativity? Fostering leadership ability? Developing judgment and wisdom? These are all valuable aims for any college that is able to pursue them. As the preceding chapter pointed out, however, many faculties have adopted impressive goals without knowing how to achieve them. Such quixotic efforts waste students' time and often leave them disappointed and disillusioned. These are consequences every college should try to avoid. With that cautionary note, the purposes described in this chapter are included not because they are the only important goals that human ingenuity can conceive, but because they are the only worthwhile aims for colleges to pursue that this author is able to recommend with enough confidence and understanding to warrant their inclusion.

4 | LEARNING TO COMMUNICATE

Almost everyone agrees on the need to communicate effectively. Curriculum committees regularly affirm the importance of expressing oneself with clarity, precision, and, if possible, style and grace. So do business executives, law partners, and other employers. Students, too, share this opinion. In Richard Light's lengthy interviews with 1,600 undergraduates, respondents mentioned improving their writing three times as often as any other educational goal.[1]

LEARNING TO WRITE

Freshmen have never arrived at college with impressive writing skills. Even in the 1890s, when only a tiny, privileged minority went to college, a distinguished visiting committee concluded that "about 25 percent of the students now admitted to Harvard are unable to write their mother-tongue with the ease and freedom absolutely necessary to enable them to proceed advantageously in any college course."[2] Since then, the problem has become more serious, as larger percentages of young people have enrolled in college, many of them from mediocre high schools and families in which English is not the native language. Even students from stronger schools may get little help with writing from teachers preoccupied with prepping their classes for high-stakes standardized tests.

Recognizing these deficiencies, university presidents and their faculties have long acknowledged a responsibility to teach students to

write well. Coursework in English composition was obligatory a century ago even in colleges with the most elective
curricula, and it remains so to this day in the vast majority of
American colleges. No other single course claims as large a
share of the time and attention of undergraduates. And yet,
when it comes to *implementing* the writing requirement, few
institutions have managed to do what is necessary to achieve
success.

While willing to force students to take freshman composition, senior faculty have long been reluctant to teach such
a course themselves. Professors in the sciences and social
sciences quickly referred the task to their colleagues in the
English department. Thereafter, in one college after another, the work was gradually handed down to lower and
lower levels of the academic hierarchy. By the early twentieth century, senior faculty were shifting the responsibility to
their younger, untenured colleagues. By the 1940s, junior
faculty were passing the baton to graduate students. As freshman enrollments rose rapidly during the decades after World
War II, English departments turned increasingly for their
staffing needs to part-time adjunct instructors (usually would-
be writers in need of income or Ph.D.s without a permanent
academic job). By the 1990s, more than 95 percent of all
compulsory writing classes in Ph.D.-granting English departments were taught by adjuncts or by graduate students.
Only in small liberal arts colleges was it common to find
such courses taught by tenured professors.

Teaching writing is hard, time-consuming work. As the
Conference on College Composition and Communication
has observed:

> The improvement of an individual student's writing requires
> persistent and frequent contact between teacher and stu-

dents both inside and outside the classroom. It requires assigning far more papers than are usually assigned in other college classrooms; it requires reading them and commenting on them not simply to justify a grade but to offer guidance and suggestions for improvement, and it requires spending a great deal of time with individual students, helping them not just to improve particular papers but to understand fundamental principles of effective writing that will enable them to continue learning throughout their lives.[3]

Unlike professors in typical lecture courses, who know next to nothing about how individual students are progressing, writing instructors are supposed to take an interest in the difficulties encountered by each and every member of their classes. While some students are a joy to teach and some even have a flair for writing, many have serious problems, not only in expressing their thoughts but also in their basic attitude toward learning. More than most college courses, freshman composition forces undergraduates to think for themselves and adjust to higher intellectual standards than they faced in high school. The challenge can be trying not only for students but for their composition teachers as well. The following description of a not-atypical freshman in a well-known state university gives a taste of the difficulties involved.

> [Darla] sat in the back of the classroom the first day and tried to keep her mouth shut. When I addressed a direct question, she looked at me with a fixed smile and shook her head, remaining silent. . . . Her writing was tortured and convoluted, and it worked as a smokescreen against anything she personally might have to say. She always came to my office when I asked her to, but *only* then, and she would do her best there to resist my attempts to find out more about the interesting hints of her ideas that had gotten through her self-censoring

mechanisms. "What am I supposed to write in my journal?" was one of her favorite questions. However, the answer, "what you think of the material, what strikes you, what questions do you have," left her confused. She wanted an assignment that had an answer she could look up in a book.[4]

It is hardly surprising that professors in English departments have shunned this kind of teaching. They are not hired to wrestle with such problems; their professional success depends on publishing works of literary criticism, and their pedagogic interests lie not in teaching composition but in lecturing on literature. Presidents and deans see little reason to deny them their wish, since graduate students and adjunct instructors can be hired to do the job for much less money.

The problem with this solution, of course, is that the quality of instruction often suffers. Most graduate students lack the experience to deal with the challenges of a basic composition course. Although they are more likely to receive some sort of training today than in years past, a week's orientation or, at best, a semester course on teaching composition is hardly preparation enough for the task of guiding freshmen coming from the overcrowded classrooms and indifferent instruction of many American high schools. Besides, graduate students have other concerns that matter to them more: finishing a thesis, mastering a specialty in English literature, finding a tenure-track job. Faculty advisors frequently warn them not to spend much time on their teaching lest they tarry too long before completing their degrees. Amid these competing pressures, freshmen in the writing course often lose out.

Adjunct lecturers bring problems of their own. Although some of them are accomplished writers and others have extensive teaching experience, many resent their low salaries and long hours and harbor little loyalty toward their employers. No wonder. They have little or no say in how their courses will be taught. Texts and syllabi are normally decided by others. They typically have no job security, no health benefits, not even an office in which to meet with students. They are the first to go when budgets must be cut. Often they are not even listed in college schedules by their own names but only by section numbers. Many of them—commonly known as "gypsies" or "freeway flyers"—can only make ends meet by holding down several part-time jobs at different universities, necessitating constant travel and causing even greater difficulties in giving individual attention to students. As one "freeway flyer" described her life in the early 1990s, "Typically, I taught sixteen hours per week—two semesters and the summer—averaging about $26,000 per year. I got incredibly burned out rushing from college to college, having to prepare anything up to five different courses per semester."[5]

Day-to-day supervision over the freshman writing program is normally given to a full-time director. Directors may be specialists with Ph.D.s in composition, but most do not have tenured faculty positions and feel undervalued as a result. Their position is often anomalous, belonging neither to the faculty nor to the administration. Whatever their status, their job is not an easy one. Although they must recruit, monitor, and train a large teaching staff, ultimate control over the program is usually lodged not with them but with the chair of the English department or with a faculty committee.[6] These professors often choose the texts and assign the graduate students to teach in the program, even though they do not teach composition themselves. Not surprisingly, this method of operation is keenly resented. As one director puts it: "The treatment of writing teachers in English departments has been a scandal for years, while the authority of composition directors has been consistently compromised to suit the interests of English graduate programs and faculty."[7]

Chafing under such arrangements, some composition heads have managed to break away to form separate free-standing writing programs. But this arrangement is rarely a panacea; it often merely substitutes one set of unsympathetic authorities (the dean's office) for another (the English department). In either case, most directors have to cope with constant staff turnover, low morale, sudden, unpredictable fluctuations in student numbers, insufficient resources, and an abiding sense of being marginalized by the faculty and administration despite performing functions that are both demanding and essential.

No single course, however ably staffed and amply financed, can transform undergraduates into skillful writers. In this respect, the required composition course resembles a set of introductory golf lessons. Such instruction can help beginners acquire a basic competence, foster their enthusiasm for the sport, and give them the know-how and helpful advice that will allow them to keep on learning and improving. Real proficiency, however, requires sustained practice. Similarly, undergraduates will never learn to write with clarity, precision, and grace unless they have repeated opportunities to keep on writing and get prompt feedback from the faculty. This commonsense conclusion has been confirmed by Alexander Astin's massive study of student progress through college. After controlling for differences in intelligence and other factors, Astin found that seniors who reported substantial improvement in their writing had usually been given a chance to write numerous papers and essay exams and to receive ample feedback from instructors.[8]

In recognition of these needs, many colleges in the 1970s began a new initiative called "Writing Across the Curriculum." Under these programs, faculty volunteers attend workshops on writing and agree to assign more papers in their undergraduate courses and to give special attention in grading them not only to their substantive content but also to the quality of the writing. Such efforts have undoubtedly improved the writing skills of many students. Unfortunately, however, they have never taken root in more than a minority of colleges. Their high-water mark came in the mid-1980s. Thereafter, financial pressures led to the abandonment of some programs and the scaling back of others. By now, formal programs of writing across the curriculum still exist in little more than one-third of all colleges.[9]

It is difficult to know what effect the teaching of composition—or the entire undergraduate experience—has had on the writing of college students. As veteran writing director Edward White acknowledges, "convincing empirical evidence of student improvement from composition instruction remains exceedingly rare."[10] Some early studies in individual universities found no improvement at all, but these investigations used crude and now-discredited methods of measurement, such as counting the number of errors in student essays according to standard rules of grammar and syntax. Arriving at generally accepted measures of progress is difficult, since composition teachers often disagree fundamentally on what they should be trying to achieve. An instructor trying to teach poorly educated students how to compose business letters in grammatical English will measure progress far differently than a teacher in an elite liberal arts college hoping to help freshmen write with style and flair by exposing them to the work of great essayists.

Notwithstanding these difficulties, a few researchers have tried to estimate the effects on writing of the entire undergraduate experience, using evaluations that purport to measure the organization, clarity, and persuasiveness of student essays. Pascarella and Terenzini estimate that writing skills improve on average by 19 percentile points during college.[11] (That is, seniors who entered with a proficiency in writing at the 50th percentile of their freshman cohort will reach a level equivalent to the 69th percentile of that cohort by the time they graduate.) It is not clear on what body of evidence this conclusion rests. One study, however, involving almost 3,000 students from 10 different colleges, compared the written and oral expressions of seniors and freshmen.[12] Seniors scored moderately higher than freshmen, recording gains of 19 percentile points above the average for entering students. Another study by Dean Whitla compared seniors with freshmen at a community college, a liberal arts college, and a major research university.[13] In all three institutions, after controlling for test scores and high school rank in class, seniors "composed more forceful and logical essays and made fewer syntactical mistakes than did freshmen." Interestingly, however, when Whitla broke down the results for the research university, he found that progress in writing was distributed most unevenly. Humanities majors made great progress, social science majors improved moderately, but students concentrating in science failed to improve or actually regressed.

Nancy Sommers has cast further light on the subject by studying the writings of some 400 Harvard undergraduates from their freshman through their senior years.[14] In keeping with Whitla's earlier observations, some students improved much more than others. By and large, progress seemed to depend most of all on how much writing students did, how much specific feedback they received, whether they wrote about something that they knew a lot about, and whether their subject let them bring their own intellectual interests into their compositions. A remarkable 86 percent of the seniors felt that completing a thesis in their major was the most important single experience in improving their writing. More than 80 percent agreed that giving more feedback was the most effective way to help students become better writers.

These findings help to explain why students in the humanities appear to make greater progress than science majors. At most colleges, humanities concentrators complete many more papers than their classmates majoring in the sciences. As undergraduates themselves confirm, nothing improves writing more than constant practice.

Studies such as those just described are open to dispute because of differences of opinion about the criteria used to measure proficiency. To avoid this difficulty, some researchers have simply asked recent graduates to give their own estimates of how much they have improved. In a study of more than 30,000 graduates of 26 selective colleges (both public and private as well as liberal arts colleges and research universities), William Bowen and I asked respondents to estimate the effects of college on a long list of capabilities. According to this survey (which was used for a study of race-sensitive admissions), 48 percent of black graduates and 40 percent of their white classmates felt that college had contributed "a great deal" to their "ability to write clearly and effectively."[15] In another study, covering 24,000 students from a more broadly representative sample of American colleges, only 27.6 percent of the respondents in their senior year felt that their writing skills were "much stronger" as a result of their undergraduate experience.[16] These results tend to confirm the observation that college helps some but by no means all students to improve their writing substantially.

However one chooses to interpret these findings, there is clearly much room for improvement. Employers grumble incessantly about the poor writing of the college graduates they hire, and "better communication skills" regularly tops the list of improvements firms would like to see among their new employees. Entire companies have been formed to serve large corporations by improving the writing of the recent college graduates they employ.

If writing is so important, why don't universities take greater pains to see that all students are well taught by competent, properly trained instructors? There are practical reasons, of course. Regular faculty have no professional interest in teaching composition courses and look upon them chiefly as a means to support their graduate students; presidents and deans save lots of money by using low-cost instructors; and freshmen are too new to the university to complain. These reasons tell part of the story. Nevertheless, the explanation is a bit too cynical. Surely faculty and administration must have *some* basis for thinking that the staffing policies they have adopted are reasonable.

The most likely explanation is that campus officials and even English departments think of teaching introductory composition as a relatively simple task to show students how to eliminate errors and careless habits so that they acquire sufficient competence to perform college-level work. If writing is merely a mechanical process of putting one's thoughts on paper, and if teaching composition is simply a matter of "purging students of bad habits," why not assign the task to graduate students and part-time adjuncts?

It is hardly surprising that deans and faculties think of composition in this way. Full-time composition specialists did much the same for many decades. Until the 1960s and 1970s, the dominant method for teaching writing focused on correcting mistakes.[17] Such research as there was on composition preoccupied itself almost entirely with searching for a truly objective, mechanical method for grading writing based on errors of spelling, grammar, sentence construction, and the like.

In recent decades, however, composition specialists have come to take a far different view of how writing should be taught.[18] Researchers find that simply emphasizing the correction of errors has no effect on improving writing and may even inhibit creativity and keep students from developing an authentic style.[19] Writing professionals no longer view composition as a mechanical process of turning previously formed ideas into suitable prose but as something inseparable from thinking itself. Undergraduates tend to agree, often looking upon their writing as a uniquely important stimulus to thought. As Marilyn Sternglass describes it: "Repeatedly, students [report] that reading alone or listening to lectures did not engage them deeply enough for them to remember facts and ideas nor to analyze them. Only through writing, perhaps through the condensation and analysis of classroom notes or through the writing of drafts of papers that required them to integrate theory with evidence, did they achieve the insights that moved them to complex reasoning about the topic under consideration."[20]

Nancy Sommers's study of undergraduates confirms and amplifies these observations. More than 70 percent of the seniors in her survey felt that writing had been either "important" or "very important" in helping them to synthesize ideas and information, to think critically, to gain in-depth knowledge of a field, and, of course, to express ideas effectively.

As professional compositionists began to regard thinking and writing as closely intertwined, they came to view teaching composition as a much more difficult task, especially with those students whose prior instruction was least adequate. No one described the challenge more eloquently than Mina Shaughnessy, drawing on many years of teaching writing to students at City College of New York. Far from a simple, mechanical process of eliminating errors, Shaughnessy found "such a complexity of problems and possible solutions (and such large territories of pedagogical ignorance) that a search for The Answer begins to seem an inefficient way to start thinking about a course (or courses) in basic writing. . . . Here the teacher, confronted by what at first appears to be a hopeless tangle of errors and inadequacies, must learn to see below the surface of these failures the intelligence and linguistic aptitudes of his students." In trying to do so, instructors must constantly grapple with "the reluctant, subtle phenomenon of the written language itself, which frequently evades our strictures, slips between our strategies, or grows in spite of them, defying us to explain precisely why a student fails or succeeds."[21]

Despite these difficulties, Shaughnessy insisted that there were patterns underlying student errors, patterns that could be analyzed and ultimately overcome. Her work gave impetus to researchers and thoughtful teachers and helped to professionalize the field. Soon books and articles on the teaching of writing proliferated, spurred by the appearance of graduate programs of communication and the accompanying growth of Ph.D.s in rhetoric and composition. Full-time specialists emerged and began to explore the "complexity of problems and possible solutions." Today the process of teaching composition is a topic bristling with controversy and debate, making the subject seem vastly more complicated and contested than it was only 30 years ago.

For decades, writing programs were split between those who conceived of writing as a practical skill for use in business and humanists who felt that students should learn to write by studying great works of literature. In the 1970s, however, new strategies began to appear. Chief among them was a shift from emphasizing "product" (i.e., finished papers) to encouraging "process"—the sequence of steps leading from first conceiving of a subject to developing it through a series of drafts to eventual completion.[22] Under the new approach, the writing teacher became less of a critic and proofreader and more of a coach or facilitator. Authenticity and invention took precedence over adherence to formal rules of discourse. Revision and more revision became the recommended path to a finished essay.[23]

The emphasis on process opened the door to a flock of new theories drawing on cognitive psychology, cultural studies, anthropology, linguistics, and other disciplines. Various teaching methods were proposed. Some compositionists thought instructors should assign paper topics; others believed that students should choose their own. Some favored exercises in "free writing"—overcoming inhibitions by putting down anything that came into one's head. Others experimented with group exercises in which students critiqued each other's work.[24]

Disagreements also arose over the proper goals of writing courses. Instructors continued to argue whether the aim should be to teach students to express themselves with grace and style or to help them learn to write business letters and other communications of a practical, vocational nature. Some urged that teachers emphasize argumentation and persuasion; others preferred having students learn to write for different academic disciplines. Some taught only writing, while others felt that composition courses should also cultivate the arts of oral expression and even listening.

As time went on, compositionists steeped in postmodern literary theory proposed even more ambitious goals. Feminist scholars spoke of developing an *écriture féminine* as a needed antidote to "patriarchal and phallocentric" prose. Theorists on the left saw in the required composition course an opportunity to educate students to be active, critical citizens by teaching them to recognize and resist the subtle efforts of the power structure to use language to make the public accept the oppression of women, minorities, poor people, and other exploited groups. As one such instructor put it, teaching writing should be "an active means to transform the existing social inequities of commodity capitalism."[25]

Unfortunately the proliferation of rival theories has not been accompanied by a corresponding effort to test how well the different methods work, nor do the theorists seem much interested in empirical work of this sort. Protesting this tendency, veteran compositionists Ray and Susan Wallace complain: "We have too many competing theories and not enough people sufficiently trained in research design actually trying to test these theories' hypotheses." As a result, the authors claim, "the chilling truth is that we are no closer to knowing how to teach writing than we were at the beginning of the process movement."[26]

What can one make of all the debate about teaching and administering college writing programs? It is easy to be distracted by the inflated rhetoric from some participants in the discussion, especially the postmodern theorists.* Yet such writings seem to have little practical effect on the daily

---

*For example, James Berlin characterizes the postmodern composition teacher as "a transformative intellectual . . . a force for progressive change everywhere in society"; *Rhetorics, Poetics, and Cultures* (1996), pp. 112–13. Patricia Bizzell adds that "our teaching task is not only to convey information but also to transform students' whole world view"; quoted in Elizabeth Sommers, "Political Impediments to Virtual Reality," in Gail E. Hawisher and Paul LeBlanc (eds.), *Reimagining Computers and Composition: Teaching and Research in the Virtual Age* (1992), pp. 3–4. To Susan Miller, the composition classroom is "an active existing site for dismantling particularly troublesome versions of hegemonic 'common sense'—particularly exclusivity, humiliation, repression, and injustice";

realities of classroom instruction around the country. Many writing teachers are probably unaware of the controversies that swirl around composition theory. Rather than take sides in the debate over emphasizing process or concentrating on the product, most instructors appear to do both. Some even continue stressing rules of spelling, grammar, and punctuation, even though this method has been widely discredited by researchers.

A more serious problem arises from the gulf that divides composition professionals, on the one hand, who see writing as a formidable pedagogical challenge involving "a critical substantive act of thinking and invention central to all fields," and those administrators and professors, on the other, who still tend to regard writing instruction as "a narrowly defined concern with punctuation, spelling, rules of grammar and mechanics."[27] Most people who have actually tried to teach writing skills to undergraduates would probably sympathize with the first formulation. Nevertheless, so long as the latter view remains, buoyed by its practical advantages both for administrators and for English departments, writing courses are unlikely to receive the support they need to contribute fully to a proper undergraduate education. Moreover, if most colleges do little to encourage good writing beyond the required, introductory course, large numbers of students will continue to graduate without being able to write much better than they did when they arrived as freshmen.

How can colleges improve their writing programs? A logical way to begin is to define as clearly as possible what the

---

Textual Carnivals: The Politics of Composition (1991), p. 187. Andrea Lunsford concludes by observing that compositionists "are dangerous precisely because we threaten the equilibrium, the status quo"; quoted in Sommers, p. 44.

college seeks to achieve. Although this point may seem too obvious to bear repeating, longtime composition professionals report that "most writing classes—even entire writing programs—rarely state clearly the outcomes for the course and then match course structure, assignment, and texts for the achievement of those outcomes."[28]

Defining goals is not as simple a matter as it might appear. As the previous discussion bears out, the differences of opinion on the subject are surprisingly wide. Objectives range from eliminating grammatical errors to inoculating students against the propaganda of an oppressive state. Choosing among these competing aims is not a task to be left to individual instructors, nor to writing program administrators, nor even to the English department. The entire college is responsible for the writing of its graduates, and every department has a stake in the results. Discussing the subject in a facultywide forum should curb the tendency of some instructors to adopt purposes of their own that almost certainly do not reflect the wishes of the faculty as a whole. It may also help professors and administrators to appreciate the difficulties involved in teaching undergraduates to write and thereby muster support for doing more to strengthen the quality of the composition program.

Once the goals are clearly defined, the next essential step is to assemble a competent staff of instructors for the basic course. Success does not necessarily require enlisting regular faculty members for the purpose. Professors of English are not trained to teach composition and would rarely throw themselves enthusiastically into the work even if they could be persuaded to take it on. Rather than trying to force reluctant scholars to accept responsibility, colleges can attempt to recruit first-rate, well-paid professional compositionists or experienced writers and intellectuals with a demonstrable ability to teach.

Ideally all teachers of basic writing would be full-time professionals. Because the course requires so many instructors, however, such a goal may be beyond the financial reach of many institutions, at least in the short run. Nevertheless every college can try to assemble a central core of experienced, properly compensated, full-time teachers to provide continuity and accumulate insight and skill that they can convey to the graduate students and adjunct professors recruited to the program. Whomever the college employs, teaching loads must be reasonable enough to allow sufficient time for meeting individually with students. In addition, all new instructors will need prior training in the objectives of the program, the methods and materials used to achieve these goals, and the pedagogical challenges involved. Once classes are under way, those in charge of the course can evaluate every section and weed out ineffective teachers, at least until they receive further training and improve enough to warrant another trial.

As previously mentioned, good writing—like critical thinking—will never be a skill that students can achieve or retain through a single course. However successful the basic program may become, sustained improvement will require repeated practice. Fortunately, for many students in the humanities—and often in the social sciences as well—practice is not a problem; they already have to write a number of essays and term papers. The same is not true for students in the sciences, however, who often find that good writing is not valued and that even expressing themselves in complete sentences wastes time that could be spent more profitably figuring out the answers to assigned problems. Insufficient practice is undoubtedly a major reason why undergraduates, especially in the sciences, often fail to improve their writing during their college years.

Even students who have many papers to write may make limited progress unless their instructors give them ample, timely feedback, not only on the substance of the papers but also on the quality of the writing. In an ideal world, professors would provide such comments as a matter of course. In reality, however, many professors do not pay close attention to student writing, nor are they necessarily trained to attend to the subtler problems of composition. Often they do not even read student papers themselves but leave the task to teaching assistants who are typically less qualified than they to evaluate student writing.

Adequate feedback will rarely come about through exhortation from on high; more substantial efforts are needed to engage faculty members from a variety of disciplines in reading and critiquing student papers. As a practical matter, few professors will accept this added responsibility for very long or perform it conscientiously and well unless they have adequate training and receive appropriate rewards in the form of extra salary or added teaching credit. Since competent writing is so important, the investment seems well worth the cost.*

Efforts to improve student writing are unlikely to make sustained progress unless campus officials can evaluate the

---

*Regardless of the success achieved by introductory courses and whatever the supplementary teaching received from other faculty members, some students will continue to experience writing problems. Thus a further step in constructing a proper program is the creation of a special office, or writing center, to which such students can repair to obtain individual assistance. No one should underestimate the difficulty of the work assigned to such centers. Diagnosing a student's problems and figuring out how to overcome them are functions that demand considerable insight, experience, and skill. They are tasks requiring well-trained specialists rather than graduate students in need of extra income or staff members with other responsibilities. Once again, the importance of effective writing justifies the necessary cost.

results on a regular basis. At present, few colleges know whether the instruction they provide actually changes student writing for the better. Few even know how much students write, department by department, throughout their undergraduate careers. Rather than remain in this state, faculties could determine how much writing students in different departments actually do, what sort of feedback they receive, and how much they improve during their four years of college. Having agreed on the goals they are trying to achieve, faculties could also start to evaluate the effects of different teaching methods. Already researchers have discovered that many writing instructors still teach in ways that have long since been shown to be less effective than other well-known methods. Rather than let outmoded practices continue, faculties could initiate a process of enlightened trial and error to test different methods on comparable groups of students in order to encourage those that work best and weed out those that are demonstrably ineffective.

The fact that so few faculties have taken the basic steps just described underscores the troubled state of student writing in America's colleges. While some programs are outstanding and some instructors work hard to help their students progress, the field as a whole suffers from widespread neglect. In the words of Edward White, "Responsible administration of a university writing program is a test of the institution's integrity, a test few institutions can pass at the minimum competency level."[29] Most deans, English departments, and senior faculties continue to underestimate the difficulty of teaching composition. As a result, they have consigned the task to graduate students and part-time teachers and let them function without clear goals, without adequate funding or proper training, and without determining whether their efforts are producing tangible results. In doing so, they illustrate the all-too-frequent tendency to pronounce a goal important enough to justify a required course without devoting the effort or the resources needed to make the enterprise a success.

ORAL COMMUNICATION

Rhetoric—the art of speaking effectively—has roots that extend even further back in history than writing. Oratory in ancient Greece was a vital part of civic life, and one that aspiring leaders had to master. Conceiving of public speaking chiefly as a means of persuasion, Aristotle codified the subject into a set of basic principles that still command attention today. The rhetorical tradition continued in Rome, where its definition was broadened beyond persuasion to become "the art of speaking well." With its stature burnished by noted orators, such as Cicero, Seneca, and Quintillian, rhetoric came to be included among the seven essential subjects of education (the "trivium" and "quadrivium"). The Renaissance brought renewed interest not merely in public speaking but in more intimate forms of conversation as well. Machiavelli wrote of the verbal tactics by which aspiring rulers might acquire and maintain power.[30] As time went on, other writers discussed the proper forms of communication at court, in the salon, and even at the banquet table. Still others explored the art of elocution, the "just and graceful management of the voice, countenance and gesture in speaking."[31]

Speaking in public was also central to undergraduate education in colonial America. Its importance came naturally to the earliest colleges that were founded with the express intent of supplying their surrounding communities with "teachers and preachers." In fact, undergraduates in the eighteenth century had much more practice speaking publicly than most college students today. Through repeated classroom recitations and disputations under the scrutiny of instructors, students in those early days grew accustomed to expressing and defending their ideas in front of others. Debating clubs and literary societies were also popular on many campuses, giving undergraduates added opportunities to hone their forensic skills.

Toward the end of the nineteenth century, public speaking received fresh intellectual energy from psychologists interested in using scientific methods to explore the impact of the spoken word on listening audiences. Researchers inspired by behaviorism began to study such questions as the effect on listeners of making threats and arousing fear or the degree to which the persuasiveness of speech might vary according to the order in which arguments were presented.

Shortly before World War I, seventeen teachers of public speaking broke off from the national association of English professors to form their own separate professional group. From this modest beginning, the field of oral communication gradually grew to embrace all manner of other subjects connected with speech. In some universities, entire schools of communication emerged to serve a wide variety of speech-related occupations, including radio, television, dramatic acting, even political consulting. As Brian Spitzberg and William Cupach declared triumphantly, "the relevant domain has extended from the traditional conception of persuasion to such divergent areas as mental disorder, problem-solving, relationship maintenance, and identity management."[32]

In the past 25 years, undergraduate enrollments in public speaking courses have enjoyed rapid growth, much of it in response to pressures from alumni and complaints from employers about the poor communication skills of many college graduates. In one survey of several hundred liberal arts institutions, 86 percent claimed to offer some form of communications studies.[33] The percentage of private four-year colleges requiring such instruction rose from 25 percent in 1975 to 40 percent in 2000.[34] One accrediting body, the Southern Association of Colleges and Schools, has made competence in speaking a requirement for all its member colleges.[35]

Notwithstanding its recent success, oral communication has not yet gained as prominent a place in the curriculum as writing has enjoyed. While the vast majority of colleges require at least a basic composition course, instruction in speech is still mandatory in fewer than half of all undergraduate institutions. It is not altogether clear why this should be so, since proficiency in oral discourse would seem to be as important to life and work as good writing, the more so now that speech is commonly defined to include interpersonal and small-group communication as well as public speaking. Perhaps the teaching of writing is accorded special importance in universities because students are graded on the basis of written papers and exams and rarely on their contributions in class. It is even more likely that writing takes precedence because it tends more than speech to require careful, probing thought, the process that always commands pride of place in the modern university.

Although the teaching of speech and writing would appear to have much in common, the two fields have developed in very different ways. Writing instructors emphasize the process of expressing one's thoughts and feelings in a clear, engaging, and authentic manner. Much emphasis is placed on conceiving what one wants to say and polishing the expression of these thoughts through the preparation of successive drafts. In contrast, since the early days of rhetoric in ancient Greece, instructors of speech have been much more concerned with the role of listeners and the way in which they react to various forms of oral expression. To a greater extent than writing, therefore, speech has been conceived of as an interactive process requiring not only clarity and eloquence but also sensitivity to one's audience, attentive listening, and continuous adaptation to verbal and nonverbal cues from those to whom one speaks. Thus, while teachers of written and oral communication have both come to regard their subject as a process, the former conceive it as a subjective process through which individuals develop their thoughts and convert them into writing while the latter view process as the interaction of the speaker with other people.

By emphasizing the relation between speakers and their audience, the study of speech has expanded its scope more widely than the field of writing. Since words enter into all manner of human encounters, almost anything in the realm of interpersonal relations can be included: racial problems, conflict resolution, negotiation, counseling, marital relations, and more. Gestures, facial expressions, and other forms of nonverbal expression have come to be legitimate subjects of study along with the spoken word. The use of social science methods to explore the effects of speech has added a further dimension to the field, giving it an empirical base for which there is no real counterpart in the typical writing program.

There is much variety in the role assigned to oral communication in college curricula. As Sherwyn Morreale and Philip Backlund have observed, "were you to ask a random sample of [communications] experts for a description of the ideal curriculum, you likely would get as many different responses as responses in your sample."[36] While many institutions require all students to take a basic course in the subject, others do not or require it only of communications majors. Some introductory courses focus almost entirely on public speaking, while others include interpersonal relations and attentive listening as well. As has been true of writing, a number of colleges have launched programs of "speaking across the curriculum," recognizing that the basic course needs reinforcement in other classes if its teachings are to take root and have lasting effect. In contrast to writing, however, some of these colleges have conceived of speaking across the curriculum not as a supplement to the basic course but as a substitute. This approach has understandably brought howls of protest from professors of communication, who point out that their subject requires highly qualified instructors and that no college would ever dream of instituting "chemistry across the curriculum" in place of courses taught by trained chemists.[37]

Instructors vary greatly in the ways in which they teach basic courses in speech. Some emphasize skills training, with much opportunity for practice and heavy use of audio- and videotaping; others treat the course as a study of rhetorical theory and research on the effects of various kinds of speech on listeners. Those with a more positivist bent approach the subject as a science, emphasizing the work of empirical researchers, while others from the rhetorical wing treat speaking humanistically, regarding it more as an art. Some believe in teaching public speaking "holistically," while others begin by breaking the process down into its constituent parts before trying to put them all together. Amid these differences, however, most basic courses in oral communication share one troubling feature with required courses in writing. In both cases, the bulk of instruction is carried out not by tenured professors but by graduate student assistants or by junior faculty.[38]

The effects of speech instruction are hard to gauge. Colleges and educational researchers have made even fewer efforts to measure the progress students make in public speaking than in assessing improvements in writing, perhaps because arriving at a convincing, objective test of speaking competence would be a formidable undertaking in itself. The most comprehensive study used the ACT College Outcome Measures Program to compare the speaking of 1,589 freshmen and 1,366 seniors at 10 different colleges. This study revealed a gain of 24.5 percentile points in speaking ability (i.e., an average senior will have raised his performance from the 50th to the 75th percentile of the entering freshman cohort).[39] A more subjective evaluation is contained in the finding by Alexander Astin and his colleagues comparing student surveys from the late 1980s and the late 1990s on how much seniors think they have changed during their college years. The results showed that 24.6 percent of the students reported substantial improvement in their public speaking ability and that the percentage rose more from the 1980s to the 1990s than for almost any other competence.[40] As far as one can tell, this surge reflected the rapid growth of enrollments in public speaking courses more than any dramatic improvement in the teaching methods used.

Despite its recent enrollment gains, the field of oral communication, like its sister program in writing, continues to occupy a lowly status on most university campuses. Why this should be so merits some explanation. After all, speaking articulately and persuasively has obvious value to students. One *Wall Street Journal* poll of large companies revealed that communication was the most important of all competencies to employers, who frequently complain about the inarticulateness of the college graduates they hire.[41] Surveys also reveal that fear of speaking in front of others is the single most prevalent form of anxiety among adults.[42] Since well-taught courses in oral communication can probably respond effectively both to student fears and to employer needs, one might have thought that instructors who could produce these results would enjoy greater respect on campus.[43] Yet respect from colleagues is precisely what professors of speech rarely receive in the United States.

One can only speculate on why the field of oral communication does not enjoy a higher status. The problem may stem from a perception that communication lacks a distinctive intellectual method or discipline of its own—a sense that its techniques are largely borrowed from psychology, linguistics, and other established disciplines and that its greatest intellectual advances have been made by professors from other departments. Part of the explanation may also lie in a suspicion that courses in oral communication lack rigor and intellectual substance, for though faculty publications in the field are packed with theory building and empirical testing, many of the basic texts and courses seem to rely more on simple common sense than on new knowledge and thought-provoking insights. Conceivably public speaking suffers from the fact that the most useful teaching involves the transmission of skills, a type of instruction too practical and too lacking in intellectual depth to command much respect in most academic circles. The situation is not helped by the annoying habit of some communications professors to label aspects of their subject using words such as "impression management," "relationship maintenance," and "conversation management," terms calculated to grate on the nerves of any self-respecting humanist.

In the end, therefore, despite its longer history, greater breadth of subject matter, and firmer empirical base, oral communication suffers from problems of academic status similar to those of its near relative, writing. Faculty members in both fields feel undervalued by other Arts and Sciences disciplines and victimized by a widespread impression that communication is a subject without much intellectual rigor and depth.[44] In both cases, they have responded by seeking independent status and developing ambitious programs of scholarship and research. In this respect, at least, communications professors have probably enjoyed more success than their writing colleagues. For both fields, however, the strategy has come at a cost to the quality of teaching. As professors of speech and writing have fled from basic courses to research and advanced seminars, most colleges have allowed budgetary pressures to override the interests of their students by entrusting introductory classes to a host of inexperienced, loosely supervised instructors.

This is a disappointing state of affairs and a shabby testament to the reigning priorities in the modern university. All undergraduates need to speak and write with confidence and style. Under competent guidance, almost every student can make substantial progress toward this goal. Indeed few courses in the college curriculum have as much potential to offer lasting benefits to so many undergraduates. For this reason, whether instructors in basic speech and composition courses are classified as professors or given some other title, they should be carefully selected, properly trained, generously compensated, and respected for the valuable work they do. Any colleges that can achieve this state will be much the better for it, especially if they are willing to experiment with new methods of instruction, assess the results, and gradually develop better ways of helping students to improve.

5 | LEARNING TO THINK

With all the controversy over the college curriculum, it is impressive to find faculty members agreeing almost unanimously that teaching students to think critically is the principal aim of undergraduate education.* The reasons for the consensus are quite clear. Merely accumulating information is of little value to students. Facts are soon forgotten, and the sheer volume of information has grown to the point that it is impossible to cover all the important material or even to agree on what is most essential. Concepts and theories have little value unless one can apply them to new situations. The ability to think critically—to ask pertinent questions, recognize and define problems, identify the arguments on all sides of an issue, search for and use relevant data, and arrive in the end at carefully reasoned judgments—is the indispensable means of making effective use of information and

*Unfortunately there is no universally accepted definition of "critical thinking." One of the more precise definitions is that of the American Philosophical Association: "Purposeful, self-regulatory judgment which results in interpretation, analysis, evaluation, and inference as well as explanation of the evidential, conceptual and methodological considerations on which a judgment is based"; *Critical Thinking: A Statement of Expert Consensus for Purposes of Educational Assessment and Instruction* (1990). Authors often use the term more loosely, however, to refer to analytical thinking, problem solving, reflective judgment, applied logic, or practical reasoning. Further complexity arises from the fact that there is no universal set of intellectual skills appropriate for thinking about all kinds of problems. Different subjects often have their own specialized methods of defining and analyzing problems, which may not be helpful in addressing problems in other fields.

knowledge, whether for practical or purely speculative purposes. What is remarkable, then, is not that professors place so high a value on critical thinking; the wonder, as we will soon discover, is that they do not do more to act on their belief. Ironically, the fact that college faculties rarely stop to consider what a full-blown commitment to critical thinking would entail may help to explain why they have been so quick to agree on its importance to the undergraduate program.

TEACHING CRITICAL THINKING

Of course, colleges do provide many ways for students to improve their critical thinking. Lectures and readings offer countless examples of how well-trained minds address difficult problems. Seminars give opportunities for participants to express their own thoughts on challenging questions and hear the reactions of professors and peers. Term papers and homework assignments invite students to think through problems carefully and have their work critiqued by knowledgeable instructors. Outside the classroom, undergraduates argue among themselves about problems raised in their readings, questions posed by their professors, and a host of other issues. Working on campus newspapers and literary magazines, on dormitory councils and debating teams, in political clubs and student senates, they are constantly involved in discussions that lead them to think for themselves and expose their thoughts to the criticism of others. In these encounters, the varied backgrounds, values, and perspectives represented in the typical student body challenge participants to examine their premises, confront novel arguments, and test their reasoning against new information and unexpected ideas.

Not surprisingly, researchers studying the effects of college find that these activities yield results; by all accounts, most undergraduates improve their critical thinking skills significantly by the time they graduate. After evaluating dozens of studies on the effects of undergraduate education, Ernest Pascarella and Patrick Terenzini conclude: "Compared to freshmen, seniors . . . are better abstract reasoners or critical thinkers, are more skilled at using reason and evidence to address ill-structured problems for which there are no verifiably correct answers, have greater intellectual flexibility in the sense that they are better able to understand more than one side of a complex issue, and develop more sophisticated abstract frameworks to deal with complexity."[1]

After reviewing the evidence, Pascarella and Terenzini find that the gains in critical thinking are approximately half of a standard deviation.[2] (More precisely, students beginning college with cognitive skills equal to the 50th percentile of a freshman cohort are likely to improve to a level equal to roughly the 69th percentile of that cohort by the time they graduate.) Many seniors looking back on their undergraduate experience also see improvement. In a study of 24,000 students from a large, representative sample of institutions, Alexander Astin found that 38.8 percent felt that they had become "much stronger" in critical thinking, while 32.5 percent believed that their analytic skills were "much stronger."[3] In an even larger study involving some 30,000 recent graduates of 26 academically selective institutions, almost half of the respondents felt that college had contributed "a great deal" to their analytical skills.*[4]

---

*A few investigators have found that the *kinds* of reasoning skills that students develop can be influenced by their choice of undergraduate major. According to these researchers, probabilistic reasoning (making judgments using estimates of risk or the likelihood of particular results occurring) improves substantially among students concentrating in the social sciences—where statistics is commonly taught and applied—but not

Cognitive skills are not all there is to thinking effectively.[5] Students must be sufficiently motivated to work hard to solve the problems they encounter in class, since added effort has a significant effect on progress in critical thinking.[6] This obvious proposition exposes a deeper problem confronting colleges across the United States. There is evidence that many undergraduates are not sufficiently engaged to work conscientiously at their studies and that their numbers are growing. According to information collected from several hundred colleges participating in the National Survey of Student Engagement, the average amount of time undergraduates spend studying for courses is far below the average of two hours per classroom hour recommended by the faculty.[7] Another national study in the 1990s found that 28 percent of college students are either wholly disengaged from the life of their institution or deeply involved in social and extracurricular activities at the expense of their coursework.[8] According to yet another study of undergraduates nationwide, time spent on homework declined from the late 1980s to the late 1990s, while hours devoted to watching television increased.[9] These two trends, both of which are associated with lower academic performance, are reinforced by the growing numbers of undergraduates who live off campus and have to work substantial numbers of hours each week.[10] As new, improved computer games, iPods, and other addictive distractions flood the campus, motivating students to work at problem-solving

among students in the humanities or natural sciences. Conditional reasoning (if *x* exists, then *y* follows) increases markedly among students majoring in the humanities and natural sciences but not among social science concentrators. See, for example, Darrin R. Lehman and Richard E. Nisbett, "A Longitudinal Study of the Effects of Undergraduate Education on Reasoning," 26 *Developmental Psychology* (1990), p. 952.

and other demanding assignments will be an even greater challenge for colleges trying to develop critical thinking skills.

The ability of students to think critically and solve problems is also affected by the epistemic assumptions they make in addressing the loosely structured problems, so common in real life, that have no demonstrably correct answers.[11] According to investigators, young people in early stages of development tend to think that all questions have definite answers. The way to find the answer is to ask the experts or consult some other authoritative source. As students advance to intermediate levels, they come to realize that many unstructured problems do not have certain solutions even for experts—only subjective opinions that reflect the respondent's values, experience, and beliefs. Undergraduates at these stages are naïve relativists; they think that different people have different views and that there is no valid basis for judging the opinions of others. At the highest levels of development, students continue to recognize that many questions cannot be answered with certainty, at least for the time being. Nevertheless, they realize that people must still make judgments, that those judgments can be evaluated, and that some are more persuasive and better reasoned than others based on available evidence. For students who have advanced to this level, even well-reasoned conclusions are best thought of as provisional, to be discarded if necessary when powerful contrary facts and arguments come to light.

Researchers have found links between epistemic stages and proficiency in critical thinking.[12] Students with weak critical thinking skills are almost always at an early epistemic stage and are invariably poor in arriving at thoughtful solutions to messy, loosely structured problems. As students progress to higher epistemic stages, their critical thinking tends to improve. Students at advanced epistemic stages who also have good critical thinking skills are almost always proficient in arriving at well-reasoned judgments about such problems.

The relationship between epistemic stages and critical thinking, however, is not perfectly symmetrical. Some individuals with strong critical thinking skills have not advanced to high epistemic stages. Students with these characteristics may be proficient at answering questions with definite answers, but they often fail to do as well at making reasoned judgments about messy, unstructured problems. One can readily understand why. Proficiency in critical thinking is a necessary but not a sufficient condition for making thoughtful judgments about problems that lack definite answers. Students also need to believe that critical thinking will be of genuine use in addressing questions of this kind. If they are naïve relativists, convinced that one person's answer is no better than anyone else's, they will presumably be less inclined to work at applying their thinking skills to arrive at well-reasoned judgments.

Using these epistemic stages, investigators have found that many entering freshmen arrive at college in a condition of "ignorant certainty," believing that most or all problems have definite answers, that ignorance may keep them from knowing the answer, but that the truth can be found by consulting the right expert.[13] During the college years, most students do make significant progress (from "ignorant certainty" to "intelligent confusion"), but large majorities remain in a naïve relativist state, persuaded that many problems have no single correct answer and that none of the possible answers is necessarily better than the others.[14] Only a small minority of seniors emerge convinced that ill-structured problems are susceptible to reasoned arguments based on evidence and that some answers are sounder than others.

Still other researchers have found that students are often unable to think effectively about material in a course or apply what they have learned to new problems and new situations because they have not truly understood the underlying concepts on which the course was based.[15] Some cannot grasp the concepts because they enter the course with faulty preconceptions that clash with the principles they are asked to learn. Others simply do not understand the basic principles. Many professors skip over these concepts too quickly, because they are so familiar with the ideas that they cannot appreciate how confusing this material can be to students or how often undergraduates come to the course with misunderstandings that actually make it harder for them to comprehend. In these circumstances, bright undergraduates frequently use rote learning to pass the course, without truly understanding the basic principles involved. So long as professors assign questions similar to those discussed in class, students can rely on their memory to find the right answers, and their instructors never realize how little understanding they possess.

In 1985, two professors, Ibrahim Halloun and David Hestenes, gave a vivid demonstration of this problem.[16] They administered a test measuring knowledge of the principles underlying Newtonian mechanics both to undergraduates who were about to take introductory physics and to a similar group that had successfully completed the course. The results showed that most students who had taken the course had gained very little understanding of the underlying principles and that what little they grasped was learned independently of the teachers. These students were able to use their memory to pass the exams but did not truly comprehend the underlying physics or know how to resolve even simple problems of applied mechanics that did not closely resemble those they had been given by the instructor.

Overall, therefore, while existing research gives clear evidence of progress in reasoning and problem-solving during the college years, the findings are not entirely reassuring. Undergraduates do seem, on average, to make significant progress in critical thinking. Still, the gains reported by Pascarella and Terenzini merely show that average seniors raise their ability from the 50th to the 69th percentile *of their entering freshman cohort.*[17] Equally worrisome is the fact that two-thirds of the students in Astin's national survey did *not* report substantial improvement in their analytic skills during college. Moreover, as Halloun and Hestenes so clearly demonstrated, students can pass courses and even earn high grades without truly understanding the material or how to apply it to problems different from those covered in class. More troubling still is the finding that large majorities of seniors appear to graduate without being convinced that it is possible to reach conclusions about messy, complex questions according to their "fit" with available facts and arguments. Most students at least understand that not all problems have simple right or wrong answers, but they do not see much utility in reasoning carefully about unstructured problems, nor are they convinced that one can critically evaluate the judgments of others.

Cognitive psychologists have an explanation for why colleges do not have greater success in improving the reasoning ability of undergraduates. Influenced by the work of Piaget, they affirm what many professional school faculty have long believed about how best to develop critical thinking. In their view, passive lecturing and drill can help students memorize rules and concepts and apply them to a limited range of problems similar to those covered in class, but they do little to equip undergraduates to apply their knowledge to new problems.[18] Merely inviting students to ask questions or allowing them to carry on a formless discussion among themselves is not much better. Instead, instructors need to create a process of active learning by posing problems, challenging student answers, and encouraging members of the class to apply the information and concepts in assigned readings to a variety of new situations.*

*According to one well-known survey of research results, "in those experiments involving measures of retention of information after the end of a course, measures of transfer of knowledge to new situations, or measures of problem-solving, thinking, attitude change, or motivation for further learning, the results show differences favoring discussion methods over lecture"; Wilbert J. McKeachie, Paul Patrick, Y. Guang Lin, and David A. F. Smith, *Teaching and Learning in the College Classroom: A Review of the Research Literature* (1986), p. 70. More recently, Ernest Pascarella and Patrick Terenzini report, on the basis of reliable studies: "we estimated that active learning approaches provide a learning advantage over passive approaches [i.e., lecturing] of about .25 of a standard deviation (10 percentile points)"; *How College Affects Students*, Vol. 2: *A Third Decade of Research* (2005), p. 102. On the other hand, empirical studies of the effects of teaching by active, problem-based discussion have not uniformly found that such methods do a better job than lecturing at developing critical thinking or a mastery of course material. See Michael Prince, "Does Active Learning Work? A Review of the Research," *Journal of Engineering Education* (July 2004), p. 223. While most studies reveal positive results, some investigators have found no difference in the outcomes for students taught by problem-based methods and classes taught by lecture. There are many reasons why such studies may not reach the same result. Instructors may not be adequately trained in teaching by discussion. The amount and duration of problem-based instruction may be too slight to produce positive results. There is some indication that students of low ability or inadequate prior preparation may not be receptive to active, problem-based teaching. The methods used to measure changes in critical thinking may be problematic; in fact, some studies comparing lectures with problem-based teaching do not measure critical thinking at all but instead test recall. The conflicts and weaknesses in existing studies should be neither a reason for ignoring research nor an excuse for continuing to teach by the lecture method. Rather they suggest a need for each institution to conduct its own carefully constructed studies to determine the effects of active, problem-based teaching on its students.

Active learning does not necessarily require a Socratic discussion led by the instructor. Many investigators have found that critical thinking and learning in general can be enhanced by giving students problems and having them teach each other by working together in groups.[19] Simply assigning tasks to groups, however, is not sufficient. For optimum results, participating students need to recognize that each depends on the others for a favorable result; collaboration must be face-to-face; each member of the group must be held accountable in some fashion (to avoid free riders); and members should periodically discuss how each has contributed to the final product and how each could help to make the group even more effective.[20] Where these conditions exist, the great majority of studies show that participating students make much greater gains (approximating half of a standard deviation) over those achieved by classmates studying individually or competing with one another for grades or other prizes.[21] Group learning has other benefits as well. It teaches students how to collaborate effectively. Where groups are mixed by race, it can reduce prejudice. It may even help integrate students into academic life and reduce attrition from college.

Teachers who focus attention on the process of problem-solving can also help their students. Researchers find that teaching students different strategies for solving problems can improve thinking.[22] More generally, encouraging students to reflect on their methods of reasoning and to try different approaches when initial efforts fail can significantly enhance performance.[23]

Finally, in addition to adapting their teaching to promote active learning, instructors need to give students frequent opportunities to test their cognitive skills and receive prompt feedback on the results.[24] Without periodic evaluation, undergraduates cannot know how well they are doing, what errors they are making, and what they need to do to improve. They can receive the necessary feedback in various ways— through periodic exams, student papers, or short quizzes in class. The essential point is to give tests or assign papers that call for the kinds of careful reasoning encouraged in class and then give a careful enough evaluation of the results that students can understand what they did wrong and where they still need to improve.

To sum up, instructors who do best at teaching critical thinking tend to follow a number of guiding principles. They begin not by deciding what material they ought to cover but by concentrating on what it is they want their students to learn—what reasoning skills they ought to master and what knowledge they need to absorb to deal with problems posed in the course. They devote much thought to how to awaken their students' curiosity and make them want to learn, not just to get a grade but out of intrinsic interest in the subject. They search for common misconceptions students bring to the course that interfere with their thinking and then look for ways to expose and ultimately overcome these mistaken beliefs. They encourage their students to think for themselves by challenging them with interesting questions and using class discussions, collaborative projects, and other forms of active learning to develop habits of critical thinking and respect for the power of careful reasoning and analysis. They evaluate their students through papers and tests closely tied to the objectives of the course in order to learn how well members of the class are progressing and give timely feedback to help students monitor their own progress and understand how they can improve their powers of reasoning and analysis. Finally, they try to convey high expectations for the class while giving students confidence that they can succeed.

Despite their overwhelming support for critical thinking as the primary goal of undergraduate education, most professors do not teach in the manner just described. Rather than discussing problems in class, or using group work to promote active learning, they spend almost the entire hour lecturing to a passive student audience. According to one survey of 1,800 instructors from a wide variety of institutions, between 73 and 83 percent of the faculty teach in this fashion.[25] Many studies of individual classrooms have confirmed this conclusion in both large universities and small liberal arts colleges. For example, a review of audiotapes made in 19 classes in diverse subjects at the University of Texas at Austin found that 88.5 percent of the available time was taken up by professors speaking with only 5 percent being used for talk by students.[26] Most of the few questions asked by professors were administrative in nature or asked students to recall factual information. Only rarely did professors challenge students with questions calling for higher-order reasoning.

There is some indication that more professors today are turning away from lectures as the sole or primary means of teaching their classes.[27] Even so, recent evidence suggests that "lecturing is still by far the modal instructional approach most often used" and that professors, on average, lecture more than two-thirds of the time, especially in the larger universities that most college students attend.[28] Even professors who allow student participation often do little more than invite members of the class to raise questions about the lecture or to repeat information contained in the assigned readings.

Methods of evaluating students are likewise open to criticism. It is well established that undergraduates study with an eye toward the kinds of questions they expect to see on their exams.[29] As a result, instructors need to reinforce the aims of their courses by taking care to construct exams that call for the very kinds of thinking that they most want to encourage. Using multiple-choice or short-answer questions, however, or having exams prepared by untrained graduate students all but guarantees that students will concentrate on rote learning rather than active reasoning. Added damage is done by giving students little or no timely feedback on their papers and tests or by relying almost entirely on a single final exam. Such grading practices have little educational value but merely rank students for the benefit of employers and graduate schools.

Despite these commonsense observations, most college examinations call for short answers or multiple-choice responses and test recall of information rather than analytical skills.[30] In reviewing examinations from 40 research universities of varying degrees of selectivity, John Braxton found that 36.98 percent of the questions merely asked for recall of information and 25.38 percent tested comprehension of course material, while only 17.71 percent called for critical thinking.[31] More-selective universities did not differ from less-selective institutions in this regard. Similarly, a survey of exams at the University of Illinois revealed that only 17 percent of the faculty used essay questions, while 82 percent of students reported that most of their grades were based on tests that mainly asked them to recall factual information.[32] Overall, according to a nationwide survey of college faculty, 26 percent of the respondents claim to use multiple-choice exams, while 35.2 percent employ short-answer tests.[33] Although 43.6 percent say that they use essay exams, this figure does not reveal how many of the essays call for critical thinking and how many simply require students to summarize factual material.

It is curious that faculty members rely so heavily on methods of teaching and assessment that seem ill suited for the goal they claim to value above all others. Why, for example, do so many college instructors continue to lecture long after most professional schools have drastically curtailed such methods in favor of more problem-based discussion? One can understand why a professor might wish to introduce a subject briefly by laying the groundwork for discussion or offer an occasional explanation to clarify a particularly troublesome point. But is there anything to be said for the hour-long lecture that is the standard bill of fare in most college courses?

Karl Jaspers offers a possible justification. For him, good lecturers have a unique capacity to inspire students by communicating a teacher's enthusiasm for the subject and giving students a sense of what a truly educated mind can achieve:

> The memory of outstanding scholars lecturing accompanies one through life. The printed lecture, perhaps even taken down word for word, is only a pale residue. True, what is of value in the lecture, its content, still communicates in written form. But the lecturer himself presents this content in such a way as to suggest the total context which motivates his scholarship. Through his tone, his gestures, the real presence of his thinking, the lecturer can unconsciously convey the "feel" of the subject.[34]

Jaspers is undoubtedly correct in describing the effect that a truly gifted lecturer can have on students. Nevertheless, countless college graduates would point out that many professors are not "outstanding scholars" in the sense Jaspers has in mind, and many of those who are do not lecture well enough to inspire their students. At most, therefore, his argument justifies a few hour-long lectures, or perhaps an occasional lecture course by a truly exceptional teacher; it scarcely warrants the heavy diet that most undergraduates receive today.

Many college professors seem to feel that lectures are needed to explain complex material or to cover large quantities of important information.* It is not clear, however, why such subject matter cannot be conveyed just as well in written form without using valuable class time for the purpose. Teachers who feel they must lecture to cover the necessary ground forget how little students retain of what they hear. Almost 150 years ago, in his inaugural address, President Charles W. Eliot of Harvard put it well: "The lecturer pumps laboriously into sieves. The water may be wholesome, but it runs through. A mind must work to grow."[35] Much empirical research confirms Eliot's point. One such study reports that students recall only 42 percent of the information in a lecture by the time it ends and only 20 percent one week later.[36] After a month or a year has passed, the residue is presumably even smaller.

Other studies have found that students retain material longer if they have acquired it through their own mental effort.[37] Hence students who have to use the concepts and information they acquire to solve problems tend to remember them longer than if they merely listen to lectures. Basic critical thinking skills are especially likely to remain when they are properly taught, because they are learned through re-

---

*"Observers have found that, even when instructors believe they should organize learning to achieve the goal of critical thinking, in actuality they organize it around field-related content"; Joan S. Stark and Lisa R. Latucca, *Shaping the College Curriculum: Academic Plans in Action* (1997), p. 147. The urge to cover material not only leads to lecturing; it interferes with cognitive growth by avoiding practice in applying concepts and reflecting on strategies for more effective problem-solving (metacognition).

peated practice and continually used and reused in everyday life after students graduate.[38]

Some professors defend their lecturing by pointing out that problem-based discussions are fine for seminars but impossible for large college courses. Nevertheless, the median class in many large universities has fewer than 20 or 30 students, providing plenty of opportunities for active discussion. Moreover, law schools have long since found that students can be taught effectively by the discussion method in courses of up to 150. True, most students in such classes can only participate vicariously in the discussion, but by raising provocative issues, asking questions that expose the weaknesses in student comments, and creating exams and assigning paper topics that demand careful reasoning, instructors can achieve much of what is attainable with smaller numbers of students.

The most persuasive explanation for the widespread use of lectures is simply that this method of teaching is the one most familiar to the faculty. Most professors were taught by lectures; lecturing is what they remember and feel they know how to do. Besides, Socratic teaching continues to take more time and effort than lecturing, even after professors have mastered the technique. Instructors cannot prepare for active student discussion merely by reviewing notes from previous classes or by making minor revisions to last year's typescripts. Because the conversation can move in unexpected directions and raise unanticipated points, professors must prepare anew for every class regardless of how long they have taught the course. Frequent papers and essay exams also mean more work, especially if students are to receive the prompt evaluation they need to gain full value from the exercise. While some of the assessment can be delegated to graduate students (in colleges where they are available), conscientious professors must still create exams that are aligned with the aims of the course and then prepare the teaching fellows and supervise their work to ensure that students are graded fairly and given useful feedback on their performance.

Teaching by discussion can also seem forbidding because it makes instructors uncomfortably aware of their shortcomings. Lecturers may delude themselves that their courses are going well, but discussion leaders know when their teaching is failing to rouse the students' interest by the indifferent quality of responses and the general torpor of the class. Trying to conduct a discussion with apathetic students is much like giving a bad dinner party. The very prospect of such an experience is enough to persuade even veteran Socratic instructors to spend ample time preparing. For faculty members unused to Socratic methods, the thought of teaching by discussion raises the specter of a long series of dull, dispiriting classes populated by sullen, unresponsive students.

Undergraduates too are often allies of the faculty in resisting active learning methods. Once they have grown used to problem-based discussions, they tend to value them more than lectures and are more motivated to prepare and participate in class.[39] Initially, however, they will often prefer lecturing. Lectures demand little of them except sitting still. No preparation for class is necessary. For students at primitive stages of epistemic development, it may be frustrating to have professors "waste time" encouraging debate instead of simply giving the class the correct answers.

Despite these inhibitions, the experience of many professional schools shows that it is possible for entire faculties to alter their teaching methods to help their students learn to think critically.[40] During the last quarter of the nineteenth century, as the laws in different states began to diverge more and more, law professors could not go on lecturing, since they could not possibly cover the different rules and procedures of all the states in which their students might practice. Instead the faculty shifted to Socratic discussions of actual legal opinions. In this way, they could concentrate on teaching the basic skills of legal reasoning and trust their students to look up the local law themselves. Several decades later, a number of leading business schools abandoned the effort to inform their students in detail about every important industry and started to conduct discussions aimed at teaching how to make decisions about real business problems. Later still, when biological research enlarged the store of knowledge about the human body beyond the capacity of students to absorb, medical schools felt impelled, much like their sister schools in business and law, to limit the number of lectures and adopt a problem-based curriculum that would prepare their students to reason about diagnosis and cure and to look up for themselves much of the knowledge they needed to treat their patients.

Most Arts and Sciences disciplines have not encountered intellectual pressures strong enough to force professors to move from conveying large quantities of material to teaching students to reason about a variety of problems. Still, the example set by professional schools of law, business, and medicine shows that it is possible for entire faculties to do so. The advantages of Socratic discussion, small-group instruction, and other forms of active learning are becoming widely enough recognized that even skeptical professors may have to change their ways eventually. Employers are increasingly calling for graduates with better, more adaptable problem-solving capabilities. The National Research Council has called on science professors to adopt more active methods of instruction.[41] University centers to improve teaching are beginning to emphasize discussion-based teaching. These mounting pressures give reason to hope that college faculties will eventually join their professional school colleagues in cutting back heavily on lectures and engaging their students more actively in learning how to use knowledge effectively to solve problems.

QUANTITATIVE REASONING

The kinds of critical thinking (or disciplined common sense) just described are not the only forms of reasoning needed in the contemporary world. Many problems call for more complicated forms of analysis that require special training. Most of these techniques are applicable to a sufficiently limited range of problems and are used by a sufficiently restricted group of people that it would hardly be fair to require all undergraduates to master them. Certain basic quantitative skills, however, are used extensively in enough situations and occupations that almost any graduates who lack them may find themselves at a disadvantage. Business executives have to work with spreadsheets, read balance sheets, and estimate profits and costs with great precision. Doctors need grounding in statistics to understand the risks of possible treatments or to evaluate clinical trials. Architects use computer graphics to design buildings. Farmers employ computers to locate markets and analyze soil conditions. Even baseball executives can benefit from the artful use of statistics, as Michael Lewis revealed in his best-selling book, *Moneyball*, describing the methods used by Billy Beane, general manager of the Oakland Athletics.[42]

Basic quantitative skills are also important for citizens if they want to understand public debates over tax policy, budget deficits, or balance of payments problems. Tourists must convert dollars into foreign currencies to figure out what they are spending. Even in their homes and private lives, individuals have to calculate the advantages of early retirement options, estimate the costs of various methods of financing homes and automobiles, compute their taxes, operate their computers, and understand the import of studies about the effects of personal behavior on their health.

What then do students need to learn? What mathematical, statistical, and computer skills are necessary to navigate the world they are likely to experience? A team of experts assembled by the National Council on Education and the Disciplines gave the following answer in stating the case for quantitative literacy.

- *Arithmetic:* Having facility with simple mental arithmetic; estimating arithmetic calculations; reasoning with proportions; counting by indirection (combinatories).
- *Data:* Using information conveyed as data graphs and charts; drawing inferences from data; recognizing disaggregation as a factor in interpreting data.
- *Computers:* Using spreadsheets, recording data, performing calculations, creating graphic displays, extrapolating, fitting lines on curves to data.
- *Modeling:* Formulating problems, seeking patterns, and drawing conclusions; recognizing interactions in complex systems; understanding linear, exponential, multivariate, and simulation models; understanding the impact of different rates of growth.
- *Statistics:* Understanding the importance of variability; recognizing the differences between correlation and causation; between randomized experiments and observational studies, between finding no effect and finding no statistically significant effect (especially with small samples), and between statistical significance and practical importance (especially with large samples).

- *Chance:* Recognizing that seemingly improbable coincidences are not uncommon; evaluating risks from available evidence; understanding the value of random samples.
- *Reasoning:* Using logical thinking; recognizing levels of rigor in methods of inference; checking hypotheses; exercising caution in making generalizations.[43]

All these skills are already widely used, and they promise to become even more so over the next few decades if past experience is any guide. By acquiring them in college and learning how to apply them to a variety of real-life problems, students are likely to overcome any resistance they may have toward numbers so that they can use them more effectively and master additional quantitative skills that prove to be necessary later on. Thus a strong case can be made that every student who lacks some or all of the basic techniques should learn them before graduating from college.

By the time freshmen arrive on campus, of course, they will normally have spent years in school studying mathematics. But mathematics in the traditional sense is different from quantitative reasoning. The typical school curriculum will concentrate on learning abstract mathematical rules without providing much practice in applying them to the ordinary problems of everyday life. Most students will respond by memorizing the rules without understanding the underlying concepts. As a result, they are likely to be at a loss to know how to use mathematics in practical situations. They are also unlikely to have had much exposure to statistics or to problems of estimation, and even their facility with computer games and e-mail may not extend to using spreadsheets, performing complex calculations, or accessing databases for research.[44]

The weaknesses in high school math were clearly revealed in a 1995 international test (Trends in International Mathematics and Science Study or TIMSS) designed "to see how well students could apply what they had learned in mathematics and science to situations likely to occur in their everyday lives."[45] The test was administered to 500,000 students from 40 countries who were in the third and fourth grades, the seventh and eighth grades, and the senior year in high school. American students performed reasonably well in the earliest grades, came close to the average for seventh and eighth grades, but did worse than students in every participating country but Cyprus and South Africa in the senior year. These results are not merely the consequence of failing urban schools. Comparisons limited to the top 5 percent and 10 percent of the seniors in these countries did not alter America's position near the bottom of the rankings.

Once in college, freshmen are unlikely to find a program in quantitative reasoning that includes the application of mathematical skills. Many undergraduates in the humanities and social sciences do not take any mathematics courses at all. Their quantitative skills generally fail to improve and may even decline during college.[46] Students interested in subjects such as medicine, science, or engineering usually take a basic mathematics course, typically algebra or basic calculus, but the teaching is likely to emphasize memorizing abstract rules, employed in formal, abstract ways, with little opportunity to consider applications to real life. Mathematician Bernard Madison described such courses as "an enormously inefficient and ineffective system of introductory college mathematics." In his words:

> The [usual] sequence, driven by the needs of scientists and engineers, controls the system, but the system now serves— or more accurately disserves—a much larger population. In the interests of efficiency, we have gathered together largely

uninspiring algebraic methods and created courses with a singular dominating goal of preparation for calculus, the gateway to the use and further study of mathematics. Those who do not survive are left on the side of this narrow road with fragmented and often useless methodological skills. The system produces millions of such students every year, at least three of every four entering college students.[47]

Undergraduates who take quantitative courses taught in conventional ways often find the work difficult and do not understand the underlying mathematical concepts well enough to apply them successfully. Concerned by this tendency in his basic calculus course, a Berkeley instructor, Uri Treisman, set about investigating the problem in interesting and ultimately successful ways.[48] What troubled Treisman most was the high rate of failure among black students in his class. Accordingly he decided to compare the study habits of blacks with those of Asian Americans, who were unusually successful in the course.

Treisman soon discovered a clear difference. Whereas black students studied alone, Asian Americans worked in groups. When blacks could not solve a problem, they did not seek help, often became discouraged, did not hand in their homework, and fell further and further behind. When Asian Americans had difficulty, other members of their group helped them to understand where they had gone wrong. In the process, everyone in the group benefited. Those who were confused learned what their difficulty was and how to overcome it. Those who helped them benefited as well, since the process of explaining the problem clarified their own thinking and allowed them to understand the material even better.

Having discovered this difference, Treisman organized the black students into groups and encouraged them to work together. The results were dramatic. The grades of black students improved; their dropout rate fell substantially; and many more than usual went on to major in science and math. Since then, many professors have adopted his methods and reported similar results in teaching a variety of subjects.

Other instructors have discovered that students who succeed in using quantitative methods to solve the problems given them in class may still not understand the underlying concepts well enough to answer even simple questions that arise in contexts different from those they have studied. One such teacher was Harvard physicist Eric Mazur.[49] For several years, Mazur taught his quantitatively oriented introductory physics course in the manner common to most beginning science classes. He delivered lectures, distributed lecture notes, and left the students to clear up remaining ambiguities by reading from the prescribed textbook. His student evaluations were strong and everything seemed to be going well until he came across the article by Halloun and Hestenes describing how a simple test had shown that undergraduates in a similar physics course relied on memory to solve the problems assigned them without truly understanding the underlying scientific principles.

Mazur's immediate reaction was to doubt the results, or at least to question whether they were applicable to *his* students. Still, something led him to give the same test to his physics class. To his surprise, the results were very disappointing, so much so that he decided to alter his way of teaching fundamentally.

The strategy he developed departed radically from his previous method. Instead of allowing students to read the text *after* the lecture, he required them all to submit a short paper a day or two prior to each lecture answering two problems based on the text assignment and identifying any portions of the readings that they found particularly hard to understand. In this way, Mazur not only made certain that students completed the readings and thought about them in advance, he also discovered points he needed to emphasize in class to ensure that everyone understood the material.

In the classes themselves, Mazur no longer lectured for 60 minutes. Instead, he would talk for 10 or 15 minutes and then give students a multiple-choice question on the meaning of the underlying physics concepts. After a brief period, he invited the students to record their answers electronically. At this point, he would ask students to discuss their answers in small groups so that those with different answers could try to persuade one another why their solution was correct. After several minutes of animated discussion, students would again record their answers. If a large percentage reached the correct response, Mazur would explain the result briefly and move on. If a substantial number still had the wrong answer, he would spend more time trying to explain the underlying principle. During the course of a single hour, students might have to respond in this way to three different questions. Weekly sections taught by teaching assistants were devoted to further discussion and small-group problem-solving.

To evaluate his new method, Mazur compared the performance of his students with that of other undergraduates who had been taught the same material in the traditional way. As predicted, the students taught by the new method made twice as much progress in grasping the underlying physics as well as substantially outperforming their classmates in solving the quantitative problems common to most introductory physics courses.[50]

The reasons for this success seem clear enough. The papers students prepared in advance of each class allowed Mazur to adjust his teaching to the needs of the students by addressing common confusions and misconceptions that distorted their understanding of physics. The problems discussed during class forced students to think further about the underlying scientific principles. The small-group discussions worked well not only because the many separate groups could adapt better to the varying difficulties encountered by different students but also because students with correct answers had a better intuitive sense than Mazur of why their classmates were having difficulty and hence were more effective in helping them understand the error of their ways.

Once Mazur began to publish accounts of his new approach in academic journals, interest in his methods quickly spread, not only among physics teachers but also among professors in other fields, such as chemistry and astronomy. Several hundred instructors have now adopted his methods. Even so, his techniques have yet to penetrate more than a small fraction of the quantitative science courses across the country, leaving most students still at risk of getting through by memorizing material they do not truly understand.

Like learning to write well or speaking a foreign language, numeracy is not something mastered in a single course. The ability to apply quantitative methods to real-world problems requires a facility and an insight and intuition that can be developed only through repeated practice. Thus quantitative material needs to permeate the curriculum, not only in the sciences but also in the social sciences and, in appropriate cases, in the humanities, so that students have opportunities to practice their skills and see how useful they can be in understanding a wide range of problems. In this way, quantitative reasoning can become a centerpiece of interdisciplinary learning, linking a wide range of subjects to a common methodological framework rooted in mathematics.

In principle, at least, it should not be too difficult to achieve the necessary reinforcement for quantitative skills. Professors of economics or physics or sociology should have no qualms about evaluating student papers and exams that make use of quantitative methods. The application of these skills is an integral part of the research carried out in many disciplines and imposes no extra burdens or unfamiliar responsibilities on instructors. Thus it should be relatively simple for professors in various departments to make sure that quantitative applications are included in their course materials and in the examinations and paper topics given to students. If anything, the existence of a required course in quantitative reasoning and the chance to use quantitative methods in other classes ought to make life easier for professors by allowing them to teach at a more advanced level without worrying that some of their students will not understand the material.

In practice, however, spreading quantitative reasoning to other courses turns out to be difficult. Professors in other fields sometimes worry whether they will be capable of teaching quantitative methods or balk at the prospect of taking time away from covering important subject matter in their courses. Many classes must be altered to include appropriate quantitative problems, requiring the cooperation of a substantial number of professors. A consensus has to emerge on what quantitative reasoning means, why it is important, and how it differs from conventional college courses in mathematics. Mathematics professors may resist, fearing a dilution of their discipline or the loss of students from more traditional courses in college algebra or calculus. Even if opposition does not materialize, several departments—statistics, computer science, and mathematics—must be persuaded to collaborate to create the newly required quantitative courses.

None of this will come easily. In the long run, however, professional organizations will continue to urge reform. The practical needs of employers will give new impetus for faculties to impart the necessary skills. These pressures have already led to change on a number of campuses. Such progress will undoubtedly continue. The critical question in the end, therefore, may not be whether quantitative reasoning courses spread, but whether the courses will be taught by competent instructors or delegated, like other introductory offerings in the curriculum, to graduate students and part-time lecturers who carry on with little supervision, few rewards, and no continuing process of experimentation and assessment to improve the quality of teaching and learning.

THE CONCENTRATION (MAJOR)

Educators have long understood that part of learning to think carefully and solve problems is having to delve deeply into complicated subjects to analyze problems and arrive at well-reasoned explanations. By the early twentieth century, therefore, more and more colleges required undergraduates to choose a certain number of units in a single field or discipline so that they could explore a subject in depth instead of merely taking a scattershot assortment of introductory courses. Originally students had to complete only a few courses in their chosen field of concentration. Over time, as faculties grew in size and disciplines acquired more and more subspecialties, requirements for the major expanded to occupy one-third or even one-half of all the classes students were required to take in order to graduate.

By now, the concentration is such a familiar part of the curriculum—and so closely aligned with the intellectual interests of the faculty—that its value is simply taken for granted.

In the curriculum reviews that every college conducts from time to time, faculties typically endorse a continuation of the major with only perfunctory discussion. In many institutions, no one remembers very clearly what concentrations are supposed to achieve or what criteria should govern proposals to create new ones.

The original aim in requiring a major was to give undergraduates the experience of pursuing a subject in depth by developing capacities for thinking and problem-solving not readily taught in isolated courses—for example, acquiring a substantial body of knowledge about a particular field, learning special techniques to search for information and analyze it in illuminating ways, and, ultimately, using these methods to address problems of substantial complexity. Thus conceived, the major promised to develop habits of thought that almost any student could use with profit in later life.

To accomplish this purpose, a major ought to satisfy four criteria.[51] Students should acquire a body of knowledge relevant to some significant subject or field. They should learn the standard methods of inquiry that scholars in the field employ to obtain relevant information. They need to master the most useful methods of analysis that will help them utilize knowledge to answer typical questions in the field. And finally, they should have opportunities to test their ability to work in depth through a series of tasks of increasing complexity, culminating, ideally, in some final project or inquiry that will allow them to demonstrate such mastery of the subject as they have achieved.*

---

*Some writers have proposed other criteria for concentrations, such as acquainting students with the ethical problems arising in the field. But many departments lack members with the knowledge or training to teach such a course well. Moreover, it is not clear that a knowledge of ethical problems will be necessary in order to achieve the central purpose of the con-

It is sometimes said that every major should be arranged sequentially so that each course builds on those that have come before in such a way as to provide increasing levels of sophistication and complexity. Not all disciplines, however, lend themselves to ordering of this kind.[52] Still, even those that don't can usually offer some reasonable form of progression. An introductory course can acquaint students with the principal subfields of the discipline and the basic concepts and ideas that distinguish the field. Intermediate courses can acquaint students with the methods of the discipline for acquiring and analyzing information. More advanced courses can then apply what has been learned to important problems in the field. Finally, a culminating experience—normally a substantial research paper—will allow students to draw on previous courses and readings to gather and analyze information and ultimately produce a piece of work of their own that demonstrates their ability to explore a problem in depth.

With these guidelines in mind, what conclusions can one draw about the growth of new interdisciplinary majors in subjects ranging from Latin America to women, world peace, and environmental issues? On reflection, there is no obvious reason why the aim of the concentration cannot be achieved by focusing on subjects that combine more than one discipline. In fact, such majors may bring added value by teaching students how different disciplines can relate to one another and what the limits of a single discipline are in understanding important problems in real life. Interestingly, several studies have even found that interdisciplinary programs can produce greater gains in critical thinking than an equivalent number of courses in a single discipline.[53] Achieving these effects,

---

centration requirement. Thus it may be wiser to leave moral reasoning to other professors who are better qualified to teach it.

however, calls for more than merely aggregating courses from two or more disciplines. Students must engage in the hard work of integrating material from different fields to throw fresh light on a common problem.

What is important for a proper interdisciplinary major is that the different parts relate to one another in such a way that each new course deepens students' understanding of other courses in the concentration or strengthens their capacity to use knowledge to analyze problems in the field. Thus a faculty might reasonably reject a proposal for a major in baseball studies made up of courses on such topics as the physics of the curve ball, the psychology of base-stealing, the economics of ticket pricing and stadium construction, and the use of statistics in making player trades. In such a concentration, learning the material in any one course would be of limited value for understanding other subjects or analyzing other problems. In contrast, courses in an environmental studies major could well complement each other; for example, material in environmental science would be highly relevant to a study of environmental policy.

Whether majors are traditional or interdisciplinary, many departments do not arrange the required work in a manner that builds on prior knowledge to reach higher levels of complexity and sophistication. In some cases, students can complete the requirements merely by passing a requisite number of courses offered by the sponsoring department. In others, they must gain a broad familiarity with the field by taking at least one course in several different specialized subjects within the discipline but need not acquire a thorough knowledge of any particular area. Such a requirement may be justified as a foundation for students planning to obtain a Ph.D. in the discipline; it is hardly appropriate for all concentrators since only a small fraction normally go on to obtain an advanced degree in the field.* Even more worrisome is the willingness of most departments to allow students to fulfill their major without successfully completing a substantial inquiry or project. For example, the Association of American Colleges has reported that only 7 percent of economics departments require a substantial research paper.[54] This practice is hard to justify, since a demanding research project seems essential to give students the very experience of exploring a subject in depth that justifies requiring a concentration.

The weaknesses just described may help to explain what investigators have discovered about the effects of the major in developing cognitive skills. According to this research, students do acquire a store of information relating to their field of concentration and perform better than other students on tests about solving problems closely related to the discipline. But these gains are beneficial chiefly for the minority of concentrators who go on to take an advanced degree in the field. There is scant indication of wider benefits. After reviewing numerous studies, Ernest Pascarella and Patrick Terenzini report that "we found little consistent evidence that one's major has more than a trivial net impact on one's general level of intellectual or cognitive outcomes."[55] Most of the progress in critical thinking—the skill so rightly prized by faculty—seems to take place during the first two years of college, before many students even start their concentration.[56] Moreover, despite much folk wisdom to the contrary, researchers do not find that some majors, such as philosophy or mathematics, produce greater gains in critical thinking than others, once proper allowance is made for initial differences in ability among the students.[57]

---

*For example, only 3 percent of economics concentrators pursue an economics Ph.D. Even in physics, no more than one-third of the concentrators seek a doctorate.

Investigators have also discovered that many concentrations have unintended effects on other important aims of undergraduate education. Ideally, well-constructed majors would be taught in ways that furthered these purposes. For example, at least some professors teaching courses in a concentration would emphasize good writing. Within the sciences and social sciences, teachers would provide abundant opportunities for students to apply their quantitative skills. Offerings in humanities and social science concentrations would include comparative material not only to enrich the readings but also to advance the college's efforts to prepare students for a more interdependent world.

Unfortunately, far from reinforcing other aims of undergraduate education, many concentrations appear to have the opposite effect. Thus Alexander Astin's study of 24,000 undergraduates revealed that majoring in engineering was associated with *declines* in writing ability, cultural awareness, political participation, and a commitment to improving racial understanding. Majoring in education proved to be negatively associated with self-reported growth in analytical and problem-solving skills, critical thinking, public speaking, and general knowledge. Other concentrations were associated with declines in critical thinking (fine arts) or civic engagement (science) or writing ability (science).[58]

These findings should be matters of concern to the entire faculty. While only the sponsoring department can make decisions about imparting the specialized knowledge of a major, some degree of overall faculty supervision is needed to ensure that concentrations do not interfere with other important aims of undergraduate education. In most universities, however, no such oversight occurs, and concentrations remain the exclusive concern of the sponsoring departments.

Still another problem with the contemporary liberal arts major is the tendency of some departments to require more courses than are actually needed to give students the experience of pursuing a subject with rigor and depth. This goal can almost certainly be achieved in most fields with little more than the equivalent of a year's study. Yet majors in many colleges insist on much more. Such heavy requirements may please department faculty by justifying more courses of the kind they like to teach and by helping make certain that concentrators who eventually apply for a Ph.D. are well prepared. But the heavy demands involved not only keep many students from choosing other courses they would rather take, they also make it difficult to find room in the curriculum for other important aims of undergraduate education, such as preparing students as citizens, providing for their moral development, or ensuring adequate breadth of study.

Faculty members may respond that courses in the concentration are the most appreciated of all college offerings, not just by professors but by students as well. True enough, undergraduates tend to rate courses in their major more highly than courses outside the major.[59] But that is not a sufficient reason for leaving too little room in the curriculum to accomplish other valuable educational purposes, especially when empirical evidence suggests that the typical concentration actually yields such limited cognitive gains. If students want to take more than the minimum course load in their major field, they can use their electives to do so. Undergraduates who plan to pursue a Ph.D. will presumably take this option. What is hard to justify is a requirement that forces all concentrators to use more than, say, one-third of their entire program to fulfill an educational goal that could be achieved with fewer courses.

In spite of these concerns, the aim of having students explore a problem in depth continues to hold great intuitive appeal.

If properly constructed, a major can deepen a student's power of inquiry and analysis, contribute to greater proficiency in writing and research, and add substantially to a student's store of knowledge. It may even lay the foundation for a long-term engagement with a particular field, either vocationally, as the prelude to a Ph.D. and a subsequent scholarly career, or simply as an important avocational interest to enrich one's future life.

While these contributions justify the concentration, too many faculties have lost sight of the purpose that gave rise to the requirement in the first place. As a result, concentrations frequently impose demands that are either too limited, in failing to require the substantial intellectual tasks that develop a capacity to think deeply about a subject, or too expansive, by forcing students to take more courses than are truly needed to accomplish the purpose that gave rise to concentrations. All too often, the result is that particular majors are linked to declines in writing, civic responsibility, and other important aims of a rounded liberal education. These weaknesses make a persuasive case for reform. Departments need to review the structure of their major to ensure that it is well designed to help students learn what it means to explore a problem in depth. Entire faculties should take collective responsibility for making certain that no concentration demands more time than is necessary or works at cross purposes with other important educational goals.

Unfortunately the prospects for such changes are cloudy at best. The firm tradition of departmental autonomy coupled with the satisfaction of most students with the courses in their major make concentrations more resistant to substantial change than any other part of the academic program. Be that as it may, few improvements would do more to strengthen undergraduate education than a willingness on the part of faculties as a whole to engage in constructive dialogue with individual departments over how each concentration can most appropriately serve all the ends of a sound undergraduate education.

A MATTER OF PERSPECTIVE

The most striking aspect of the treatment of cognitive skills in college is the gap between the behavior of instructors, on the one hand, and the findings of educational researchers, on the other. Although almost all faculty members claim to give highest priority to helping students learn to think critically, they spend most of the time in their curricular reviews arguing over which courses to offer and which to require. Researchers, in contrast, find that the arrangement of courses per se has little effect on the development of critical thinking. What matters more is the way in which courses are taught and the effort students and faculty devote to the educational process.

Most studies show that improvement in critical thinking varies directly with the time students spend studying, the extent to which they participate actively in class, and the amount of discussion they have on intellectual matters outside class, both with faculty and with classmates, especially those with views and backgrounds different from their own.[60] As for the role of professors, the aspects of teaching that matter most to student learning are the extent to which instructors prepare for class and organize their material well, the degree to which they encourage active, problem-based discussion in class, the way they construct their exams, their willingness to offer prompt feedback on student work, and the amount of informal discussion they have with undergraduates outside class on academic or intellectual matters.[61] None of these behaviors receives much attention, if any, in the typical faculty review of the undergraduate program.

In considering how best to improve critical thinking, researchers are likely to be more reliable guides than the faculty. They can draw on dozens of studies that measure the growth of cognitive skills during college. In contrast, most professors have an imperfect understanding at best of the progress their students make in critical thinking and know little or nothing of the research on the subject. Lacking such information, they rely on anecdotal evidence and personal impressions when they plan their courses and review the curriculum, and many of the conclusions they draw seem suspiciously self-serving.

One can always scoff at educational research or dismiss existing studies that involve institutions and students different from one's own. Rather than carp at research, however, faculties would do better to support careful studies of critical reasoning within their own college. In the short term, such inquiries could help them decide which methods of teaching and learning are most appropriate and effective. In the longer run, research could explore the next great pedagogic frontier and help instructors understand how to evaluate individual students and adjust their methods of teaching to fit the varying cognitive styles, preconceptions, and epistemic assumptions that undergraduates bring to the classroom.[62] So long as work of this kind remains undone, colleges run the risk of continuing to rely on familiar methods of instruction and curricular policies that do far less than they should to develop the very cognitive abilities that faculties endorse so strongly as the principal aim of a college education.

6 | BUILDING CHARACTER

"Highly educated young people are tutored, taught and monitored in all aspects of their lives, except the most important, which is character building. When it comes to this, most universities leave them alone. And they find themselves in a world of unprecedented ambiguity, where it's not clear . . . if anything can be said to be absolutely true."[1] This sweeping verdict was announced by David Brooks on the editorial pages of the *New York Times*. What can we make of his conclusion? Is he reasonably accurate in his assessment of universities, or is there more going on than he knows to help students become moral human beings?

In one respect, at least, colleges have relaxed their efforts to build good character. There are fewer regulations governing student behavior today than there were 50 years ago, and the penalties seem less severe. For those who believe that character and morals are best developed through clear rules and stiff, swift punishment, colleges appear to have slipped. Their record over the past half-century continues a gradual retreat from the stern regimes of the eighteenth century, when students were subject to elaborate codes of conduct enforced by the entire faculty.

In another respect, however, Brooks is on shaky ground. Following decades of omission and neglect, university faculties are currently offering many more courses on moral issues than they did 50 or 100 years ago.[2] These new courses are quite different from the lectures on ethics that college presidents gave to their seniors prior to the Civil War. Instead of delivering authoritative answers to moral and political questions of the day, professors try to teach their students to think more carefully about ethical problems by having them discuss dilemmas that arise frequently in personal and professional life. By now, thousands of these courses have appeared across the country. Entire departments, centers, and programs on applied ethics have sprung up in medical schools, law schools, business schools, and other parts of the university.

One stimulus for the growth of these courses was the angry controversy in the 1960s over moral issues, such as racial integration, abortion, and women's rights. Another contributing cause was the rising public concern over ethical standards in the country following a series of troubling events ranging from Watergate, urban riots, and anti-busing violence to mounting drug use and a host of countercultural assaults against traditional values. Whether or not lying, cheating, and disrespect for law were actually on the rise in America, many believed they were. As Americans are wont to do, people looked to educational institutions for a remedy. Bar associations, business school alumni, and other influential groups began to press universities, and their professional schools in particular, to give the teaching of ethics a prominent place in the curriculum.

The practical ethics movement has taken firmer root in professional schools than in the colleges. By now, every self-respecting school of business, law, or medicine has courses on moral questions, and often they are required. At the undergraduate level, the situation is less clear. Although offerings on applied ethics are common, they are seldom required. Many of the instructors who teach these courses rely heavily on lecturing rather than discussion and use moral dilemmas more to test ethical theories than to resolve the problems themselves. Within the faculty as a whole, questions still linger about whether education of this kind is necessary or even appropriate.

Such doubts seem curious in light of the evidence on the moral standards of young people coming to college. Teenagers seem to be smoking less than they did 20 years ago, and fewer admit to using drugs. But 80 percent of high school seniors with "A" averages acknowledge having committed some form of academic dishonesty, and cheating among all high school students seems to have risen substantially in the 1990s.[3] According to a survey by the Josephson Institute, 43 percent of high school students agreed in 2002 that "a person has to lie and cheat sometimes in order to succeed" (up from 34 percent in 2000).[4] Nearly 40 percent of the students in the same survey admitted that they were willing to lie or cheat to get a good job.[5] By all accounts, many applicants do employ dubious tactics, such as having others write (or heavily rewrite) their personal essays or submitting false claims of disability to gain more time to complete their SAT exams.

Surveys of high school students also indicate considerable confusion in thinking about ethical questions. For example, a 2004 survey of almost 25,000 students revealed that more than 90 percent were satisfied with their own ethical standards and 98 percent felt that being a person of good character was important, even though 82 percent admitted having lied to a parent about something significant, 62 percent admitted lying to a teacher, 62 percent admitted cheating on a test, 22 percent admitted stealing something from a relative, 27 percent admitted stealing something from a store, and 54 percent acknowledged having hit someone "because I was angry," all within the past 12 months.[6] Although the survey did not separate out college-bound students, it is significant that the percentages did not vary appreciably between public high schools, private religious high schools, and private nonreligious high schools.

It would be rash to assume that these problems disappear once students enroll in college. Surveys have found that large majorities of undergraduates acknowledge having cheated while at college.[7] Moreover, one series of surveys measuring undergraduate cheating on the same set of campuses in 1962–63, 1990–91, and 1995–96 suggests that the problem has grown substantially worse in recent decades.[8]

As David Callahan points out in his recent book *The Cheating Culture*, the world of work has also changed in ways that increase incentives for students to behave unethically after they graduate.[9] The huge rewards currently given to top managers create stronger temptations for younger executives to cut corners to get promoted. Intense competition also pushes people to cheat to get ahead. Greater insecurity and diminished employee loyalty in an age of corporate downsizing weaken the resolve to maintain high ethical standards. At the same time, cuts in funding for government enforcement agencies lower the risk of getting caught.* The cumulative effect of these trends is substantial. One study by the accounting firm Ernst & Young has estimated that companies lose $600 billion every year from employee fraud and theft.[10]

---

*Callahan presents considerable anecdotal evidence to suggest that white-collar crimes (of the kind typically committed by college graduates) have been increasing. Recent corporate scandals offer widely publicized examples, and there are many others as well. "Lawyers are overbilling as they've been pushed to bring in more money for the firm and as it's gotten to be harder to make partner. Doctors are accepting bribes from drugmakers as HMOs have squeezed their incomes" (p. 20). In the past decade, newspapers have reported more than the usual number of journalists fabricating newspaper stories and authors plagiarizing other sources. While instances of this kind are suggestive, reliable evidence of trends in white-collar crime is still lacking.

Under these conditions, colleges can hardly claim that the moral development of undergraduates is unimportant. Indeed instruction in ethics is needed all the more today, since students appear to be much less influenced by parents, churches, or other external sources in developing their own moral beliefs. After interviewing hundreds of people in a broad sample of communities, Alan Wolfe has aptly described a new attitude toward ethics that he finds throughout the country:

> Contemporary Americans find answers to the perennial questions asked by theologians and moral philosophers, not by conforming to strictures handed down by God or nature, but by considering who they are, what others require, and what consequences follow from acting one way rather than another. . . . The defining characteristic of the moral philosophy of the Americans can therefore be described as the principle of moral freedom. Moral freedom means that individuals should determine for themselves what it means to lead a good and virtuous life.[11]

If young people do not look elsewhere for ethical rules but instead prefer to develop their own standards of behavior, they deserve the most helpful readings and the most stimulating opportunities for moral reflection that human ingenuity can devise. It is not the place of faculty members to prescribe what undergraduates ought to consider virtuous. But surely faculties should do whatever they can to prepare their students to arrive at thoughtful judgments of their own.

TEACHING MORAL REASONING

Until quite recently, most educators seemed to believe that a good liberal arts education with a solid grounding in the humanities was enough to accomplish this purpose. For example, Harvard's much-discussed report of 1945, *General Education in a Free Society*, suggested that "the best way to infect the student with a zest for intellectual integrity is to put him near a teacher who is himself selflessly devoted to the truth."[12] The report went on to conclude that the college could instill "a proper discrimination of values" by simply giving its students a broad exposure to the humanities, social sciences, and sciences and trusting to "the Socratic dictum that knowledge of the good will lead to a commitment to the good."[13]

Although these words seem overly optimistic, the traditional liberal arts curriculum, bereft as it was of any courses on moral deliberation, did serve in various ways to prepare students to address ethical issues more perceptively. As Chapter 5 pointed out, the college experience helped undergraduates to analyze complex problems, ethical and other-wise. Reading great literature raised serious moral questions and heightened awareness of the needs and feelings of others. Courses on ethics and the history of philosophy acquainted students with the ideas of moral thinkers from Plato to modern times. Exposure to a diversity of views, both in and out of the classroom, challenged undergraduates to abandon easy dogmatism and rethink previous ethical positions.

These contributions to moral reasoning, however, were incidental by-products of a curriculum largely designed for other purposes. Except in Catholic colleges and other church-affiliated institutions, professors rarely assigned readings explicitly dealing with ethical dilemmas that students might encounter in their personal and professional lives. Rarer still were opportunities in class to engage in serious discussion of the moral questions embedded in courses on subjects ranging from literature to the sciences. It is this void that the newer courses try to fill.* In doing so, they offer several benefits.

To begin with, through discussions of moral dilemmas in private or professional life, the new courses can teach undergraduates to recognize such problems more quickly, when it is often easier and less costly to respond appropriately. One has only to read the newspapers to learn of individuals in public and professional life who fail to perceive ethical problems until they have become much harder to resolve. At this late stage, perpetrators are more likely to resort to lies, cover-ups, and other evasive actions that only compound the difficulty.

Another benefit of the newer courses is that they acquaint students with philosophical writings that bear directly on the kinds of moral dilemmas that arise in daily life. Most traditional courses on ethics or the history of philosophy are quite abstract and organized around a different set of questions. Students in these classes may never have a chance to connect the readings to an ethical issue in their own lives — or to any concrete problem, for that matter. In contrast, the whole point of the newer courses is to draw from philosophy to help students to think more deeply about practical moral issues — about the reasons to be concerned, the responses one might make, the arguments for and against each alternative action,

*Some authors oppose classes on applied ethics and argue instead for including ethical issues in courses throughout the curriculum. The problem with this approach is that professors in other disciplines are not trained in ethics and are consequently reluctant to discuss such questions in class. Thus, while embedding ethics throughout the curriculum has often been advocated, the strategy has rarely succeeded in practice. If the approach is ever to work, it will probably need to be combined with courses on applied ethics taught by well-trained ethicists, so that faculty members will at least have knowledgeable colleagues to whom they can turn for advice and encouragement.

and the consequences involved for other people. By showing how careful analysis can clarify issues and how some arguments are more persuasive than others, capable instructors can help students develop and deepen their better instincts to offer a more thoughtful, principled response to moral problems.

Since ethical issues ultimately rest on values rather than provable facts, not all moral questions have definite answers. Still, all societies and major religions share certain basic moral beliefs, such as a general disapproval of lying, cheating, breaking promises, and using violence against others. With the help of these common values, careful analysis can often lead to reasonably clear conclusions. Even when moral disagreements seem insoluble, further thought can sometimes produce an imaginative course of action that will avoid the ethical difficulties while still achieving the ends of everyone involved.

Moral disagreements do occur in which all attempts at reason fail to yield an acceptable result. Classes devoted exclusively to such problems could actually discourage students from thinking carefully about ethical questions by persuading them that all moral arguments are inconclusive. But a well-constructed course can easily avoid this result if instructors make sure to include moral dilemmas of varying degrees of difficulty. Even when truly intractable issues arise, close analysis can at least dispose of much shoddy thinking and thereby clarify the nature of the underlying dispute. Students can gradually overcome the easy relativism that often characterizes undergraduate discussions of ethical questions as they come to observe that some arguments are more firmly grounded in fact and reason than others. In this way, they may gain in understanding even when they cannot ultimately agree on the solution.

By now, much empirical work has accumulated to document the effects of moral reasoning courses (and the entire college experience) on the thinking and behavior of undergraduates. In contrast to the results just a generation or two ago, the findings from more recent work are at least moderately encouraging. In commenting on studies from the 1930s, 1940s, and 1950s, before the recent growth in the number of courses on applied ethics, Howard Bowen remarked, "It is worth noting that the things for which the impact of college appears to be 'negative change,' 'no change,' [or] 'not ascertainable' are precisely the dimensions usually associated with excellence of personal character."[14] Subsequent research, however, has found that improvements in students' capacity for moral reasoning are now among the largest of the changes that have been measured by researchers.[15] Investigators have also found that the gains from college in principled moral reasoning "do not diminish over time but tend to increase."

While the improvement in moral reasoning cannot be attributed solely to courses on applied ethics, researchers have concluded that much of the gain is due to college, rather than simple maturation.[16] Moreover "the findings do suggest that purposefully designed curricular or course interventions can have positive, if modest, effects on the development of principled moral judgment during college."[17] In this regard, several studies have found that classes devoted to active discussions of moral dilemmas are much more effective than traditional lecture courses in improving moral reasoning.[18] Interestingly, however, research suggests that the courses with the greatest impact are those that combine discussions of moral dilemmas with more didactic expositions of underlying ethical theories.[19]

Of course, it is one thing to show that well-taught courses can improve moral reasoning and heighten awareness of ethical problems and quite another to prove that such gains change the *behavior* of students and make them better human beings. Everyday experience suggests that knowing the right thing to do is quite different from actually doing it. All manner of fears, temptations, and personal weaknesses can lead people to ignore their better judgment and behave improperly. As Portia observes in *The Merchant of Venice*, "If to do were as easy as to know what were good to do, chapels had been churches, and poor men's cottages prince's palaces. . . . I can easier teach twenty what were good to be done, than to be one of the twenty to follow mine own teaching. The brain may devise laws for the blood, but a hot temper leaps over a cold decree."[20]

One can think of several reasons, however, why improved powers of moral reasoning and greater moral awareness ought to have *some* positive effect on behavior. Most undergraduates are still trying to define their identity and find the level of integrity at which they wish to lead their lives. They are likely to place a higher value on acting ethically if they have had a chance to reflect at length on the reasons for doing so, or been asked to imagine themselves in the place of those who are the victims of a morally questionable act, or considered what life would be like if everyone felt free to behave in particular self-serving ways. After engaging in rigorous discussions of ethical dilemmas, students may find it harder to resort to the spurious rationalizations they might otherwise have used to justify unethical behavior. By thinking about ethical dilemmas in the sheltering environment of the classroom, where nothing of consequence rides on the result, they may also be better prepared to act morally than they would if they encountered such problems for the first time at work, early in their careers, when they are particularly vulnerable to pressure from clients and superiors to forget their moral concerns and wink at unethical behavior.

Individuals will often do the wrong thing not because they are amoral or weak willed but simply because they fail to perceive that their situation presents an ethical problem or because they do not fully understand the reasons for acting ethically or the consequences of failing to do so. For example, a *Wall Street Journal* article described one class in a leading university in which students were asked whether or not it was ethically permissible to lie to a member of Congress to forestall a poor piece of legislation. According to the instructor, the students seemed "to see things essentially in cost-benefit terms. Is [the lie] for a good policy? What are your chances of getting caught? If you get caught, how much will it hurt you?"[21] Many students who argue in this way would presumably change their position if they had to think more carefully about a world in which all government officials felt free to lie on behalf of their own private notions of the public good. And once they recognized the drawbacks of such a world, one would suppose that at least some of them would alter their behavior accordingly.

Similar benefits are likely to flow from analyzing other reasons commonly used to justify unethical behavior. Students often claim that they have to cheat because "everyone else is doing it." Accountants regularly steal small sums of money, explaining that their actions are trivial compared with the amounts top executives receive by ripping off the company with huge salaries. Doctors connive in cheating insurance companies on the ground that they are only trying to help their patients. Justifications of this kind, which can seem persuasive to those who talk only to themselves, often take on a different hue when subjected to open discussion and analysis. Students will learn to examine such rationalizations from wider perspectives than the immediate situation of the individual involved. "Would I want to live in a community where everyone acted in this way?" "Would I feel confident if I had to justify my action publicly to a group of people I respected?" Once again, it is only reasonable to suppose that at least *some* students will modify their behavior once they ask such questions and come to recognize the flaws in many of the common excuses for violating basic ethical rules.

It may be that a few students are so utterly lacking in moral scruples that they will resort to unethical behavior whenever they believe that they can get ahead or benefit in some other way from doing so. Courses in ethics may even make such students cleverer at finding reasons to justify their irresponsible behavior. But it is highly unlikely that individuals of this kind make up anything close to a majority of college students. Indeed investigators find that just the opposite is true.[22] So long as most undergraduates want to act ethically (at least, if doing so does not require too much trouble or sacrifice), a clearer understanding of ethical issues and arguments should lead, on balance, to better behavior. At the very least, courses in moral reasoning can improve their capacity to think of alternative solutions, when the nature of the problem permits, that will allow them to avoid ethical difficulties without interfering with what they are trying to accomplish.

In sum, although nothing professors do can *guarantee* that students who improve their powers of moral reasoning and moral awareness will act morally, there are grounds for believing that well-taught courses in practical ethics will tend to have at least a modest effect on behavior. That is pretty much what investigators have concluded after exploring the link between moral reasoning and moral conduct. Summarizing several hundred studies using a variety of research methods, Ernest Pascarella and Patrick Terenzini conclude that "there is an impressive body of evidence to suggest positive, systematic links between principled moral reasoning and what might be considered moral behavior among college students."[23] But the links they describe are generally weak, accounting for something on the order of 10–15 percent of the variance in the behavior of students confronted with a moral dilemma.[24]

STRENGTHENING THE WILL TO ACT MORALLY

With such limited gains, few parents who care about the ethical standards of their children will feel that universities have done enough by giving courses in moral reasoning. William Bennett, during his term as secretary of education, voiced this concern in typically blunt fashion during a campus talk in 1986. "Where are our colleges and universities," he asked, "on the issue of their responsibility to foster moral discernment in their students?" When reminded of the college's requirement that all undergraduates take a course in moral reasoning, he replied, "That's about [ethical] dilemmas, lifeboat stuff. I meant getting drugs off campus."[25]

Bennett may have been too quick to dismiss classes on moral reasoning and too glib in ignoring the practical problems of banishing drugs from campus. Still, his reference to drugs suggests a useful point. Courses in practical ethics may not be the only means of raising standards of behavior. It is conceivable that universities can find ways outside the classroom to foster concern among students for the needs of others and to strengthen their commitment to do what they think is right.

Moral will—the desire to act in accordance with ethical principles—can develop in any of several closely related ways.[26] One can act morally, first of all, because of empathy—a feeling of genuine concern for the needs and feelings and sufferings of others. Such empathy involves a capacity to shift perspectives and see a situation through the eyes of others—"to feel their pain," in the words of President Bill Clinton.

Another source of moral will is the desire not to incur the disapproval of people whose good opinion matters. Parents are the obvious example of persons who inspire such feelings. Peers can be another example, although they are often a contributing cause of immoral behavior as well.

A final reason to act morally is to avoid violating one's own standards of behavior, one's inner sense of the kind of person one wants to be. For example, when a well-dressed gentleman accidentally drops a $10 bill in an upscale restaurant, some diners will hurry after him and return the money even though no one else has noticed the bill and the gentleman will almost certainly never miss it. Such individuals have acquired an identity in which pocketing money that does not belong to them, or merely failing to return it to its rightful owner, will cause them personal discomfort, even though they can perceive no adverse consequences from such behavior.

Depending upon their nature, educational institutions have varying amounts of power to shape the environment in ways that can strengthen the sources of moral will. A boys' boarding school will be able to exert more influence than a liberal arts college, which in turn will have more influence than a large urban university filled with part-time, commuting students. Still, every college has at least some opportunity to strengthen (or weaken) the tendencies of its students to act morally.

To begin with, those in positions of authority in universities can try to set examples that will encourage, or at least reinforce, the development of a personal identity that places a high value on moral conduct. To this end, university presidents, campus ministers, deans, and other officials should (and often do) try to set a proper tone for the institution and its students by speaking out on the importance of developing strong ethical principles and concern for the welfare of others. Welcoming speeches to students when they arrive and graduation addresses when they leave are favorite occasions for such remarks. But words alone can only accomplish so much. They will have an effect only insofar as students respect the speaker. Uplifting remarks from a president or dean may have no impact or even cause disillusionment if they are belied by the policies and practices of the institution.

The university reveals its own ethical standards in many ways, including its scrupulousness in upholding academic standards, its decency and fairness in dealing with students and employees, and its sensitivity in relating to the community in which it resides. Talk is cheap, and undergraduates will be most impressed when they observe university officials making sacrifices for what they believe — refusing donations that have questionable strings attached or resisting outside pressure in order to protect academic values. Conversely they may cease to pay heed to a president who lectures them about high academic standards while condoning the admission of students who would clearly be rejected were it not for their athletic ability or the fact that their parents occupy a high position or promise to make the institution a substantial gift.

In addition to making sure that their practices are ethically defensible, campus officials can take care to explain the reasons for actions that are likely to be challenged by others. In some cases, of course, such explanations are not possible. Presidents may be locked into questionable athletic practices that, as a practical matter, they can do very little to change. Administrators may be unable to explain the true reasons for controversial disciplinary actions because of an overriding duty to maintain confidentiality. Still, campus officials should be able to explain their actions satisfactorily most of the time. By doing so, they not only offer a form of ethical instruction of their own, they also increase their moral authority and set a valuable example of moral seriousness for their students.

At times, a dean or president can turn a seeming conflict between principle and practice into a valuable teaching opportunity, not by explaining why a controversial practice is justified but by demonstrating a willingness to change the practice when closer examination reveals that it is not supportable. When President Charles Vest of MIT admitted publicly after studying a report from women faculty that the university's policies were discriminatory, he won immediate respect. When he proceeded to take firm action to remedy the problem, he left a lasting, positive example for students and faculty.

Setting a high moral standard goes well beyond maintaining and justifying ethically sound institutional policies. A university communicates its values in countless smaller ways by the actions of financial aid officers, the behavior of dormitory proctors, the decisions of student affairs officials, and many others. Often impressions gained through encounters such as these transmit a stronger sense of institutional values than declarations of university policy announced from on high.

Consider, for example, the role of athletic coaches. Student athletes are likely to be especially attentive to their coaches because of their intense desire to improve their performance and receive as much playing time as possible. Coaches in turn have many opportunities either to act as role models and set a high moral example or to engage in weak, evasive, or even contemptible behavior. What to do with the star player who flouts important team regulations? Whether to break NCAA rules in order to recruit a highly valued prospect? How to respond to a team captain who suggests holding "voluntary" practices before the official starting date in order to gain a competitive edge? University presidents may not even be aware of all these issues, let alone know how they are resolved. Nevertheless the values and guiding principles communicated by top university officials and, in turn, the work of athletic directors in choosing and supervising coaches can do much to ensure that decisions are made in a principled fashion. If coaches feel they are rewarded or fired primarily for their won-and-lost record or if their year-end evaluations focus entirely on the revenues their teams bring in and never on the example they set for their players, no one should be surprised when they do whatever it takes to win, including bending and breaking the rules.

Disciplinary rules and their enforcement are not only a means of keeping order and upholding academic integrity, they are also a way of transmitting the standards and values of the institution and persuading students of their importance. Presidents and deans can hardly know about all the individual cases that come before campus disciplinary bodies, let alone keep track of how each dispute is eventually resolved. Once again, however, there are actions they can take that will increase the chances that rules of behavior and disciplinary proceedings help to enhance respect for ethical standards rather than the reverse.

An initial step is to accompany written regulations with an explanation of their rationale, at least for rules whose purpose is not self-evident. This extra effort serves several purposes. It helps those who must interpret the rules to apply them correctly in specific cases in which their application is not obvious. It allows administrators to identify rules that no longer serve a useful purpose. Most important, it helps persuade students that rules are not merely arbitrary commands handed down from above but considered restraints that help maintain a decent community for the benefit of all its members.

In addition to explaining rules, colleges must clearly do their best to enforce them fairly and conscientiously. This simple proposition is sometimes harder to live up to than one might think. Laws prohibiting under-age drinking and drug use, for example, present a peculiarly difficult problem because they are hard to enforce, widely disliked by students, and not rules the university itself has imposed. Even so, the way in which the institution responds can send a powerful message to students. The university cannot and should not establish a police state by subjecting undergraduates to constant surveillance in an effort to root out violations. Such policies would destroy the trust and confidence of students and drive a wedge between them and the administration. But if campus authorities are seen to avoid even reasonable efforts at enforcement and to wink at obvious violations, students are bound to gain the impression that it is legitimate to ignore laws they consider unnecessary or inconvenient.

An even more serious error is to refrain from imposing the usual penalty when rules are violated by faculty members, star running backs, or others deemed to have special importance to the institution. Unfortunately such instances are probably quite common. Athletes are quietly forgiven after engaging in behavior that would cause an ordinary freshman to be suspended; tenured professors guilty of sexual harassment receive a milder punishment than the penalties regularly meted out to graduate student instructors. Nothing could be more damaging to the respect for law and the concern for justice that campus officials should try to engender in their students.

Colleges have fewer opportunities to generate peer pressure in support of moral behavior, but examples are not unknown. Some institutions have enlisted student leaders to work with campus officials to combat racism. Others have formed student organizations to counteract male attitudes associated with sexual aggression. Such efforts may seem to have only temporary value, since the peer pressure will disappear with graduation. Still, habits formed by parental discipline and other transitory experiences often take root and endure in adult life.

The most intriguing possibility for building constructive peer pressure involves the effort to prevent cheating on exams. Most universities rely on proctors to deter cheating and detect infractions. The usual reason institutions give for using proctors is that they are the most effective means available. With the intense competition to gain admission to graduate and professional schools, students themselves often prefer careful monitoring of exams to ensure fairness for everyone. Curiously, however, researchers find that using conventional methods that rely on proctors tends to result in *more* dishonesty than introducing honor codes.[27] Apparently honor codes themselves are not as important as the efforts accompanying them to create a supportive peer environment that affirms honesty and discourages cheating of any kind.* Campuswide discussions about the responsibilities of students not only help to create such an environment, they also provide valuable opportunities for undergraduates to reflect on their moral obligation to obey legitimate rules and observe high standards of integrity.

Whether or not colleges choose to adopt honor codes, they should at least respond to infractions conscientiously and evenhandedly. Although this admonition seems too obvious to bear repeating, faculty surveys suggest that enforcement on many campuses is deplorably lax and haphazard. One study of faculty responses to cheating at 16 colleges and universities found that fewer than half the respondents would report an incident of cheating to the appropriate college authority: 31 percent would give the student a failing grade on the test, 9 percent would merely issue a warning, 9 percent would give a failing grade for the course, and 1 percent would do nothing.[28] A similar study found that no more than 20 percent of the faculty respondents would comply with the official college procedures and that 8 percent would do nothing.[29] According to the leading researcher on the subject, such widespread disregard of established procedures has a direct effect on the incidence of cheating, since many students are influenced in their behavior by their estimates of what will happen to them if they are caught.[30]

These findings suggest that the most important question confronting college authorities is not whether to adopt an honor code but whether to seek higher standards of compliance and ethical conduct by encouraging discussion about

---

*Another plausible possibility, suggested to me by Michael McPherson, is that students look upon cheating differently when they are asked on their honor to act responsibly than when they are being watched over by proctors.

cheating and other aspects of campus discipline among both students and faculty. Without a serious effort to make students understand everyone's stake in obeying the rules, cheating will spread despite the use of proctors. Without a conscientious effort to educate the faculty, many professors may refuse to enforce disciplinary rules conscientiously in accordance with established procedures. In either case, the result must surely be to foster cynicism, create haphazard penalties for violators, and undermine compliance by damaging the climate of respect for basic rules that ensure fairness and decency for all members of the community.

Apart from setting positive examples and enforcing rules evenhandedly, universities can try to foster ethical behavior by helping students develop greater concern for the needs of others. Empathy supplies the most powerful motive for acting ethically. As Sissela Bok points out, "Empathy and fellow feeling form the very basis of morality, as philosophers such as Mencius and Immanuel Kant have maintained. Without some rudimentary perception of the needs and feelings of others, there can be no beginnings of felt responsibility toward them."[31]

Concern for the interests and needs of others can grow during college for a multitude of reasons ranging from reading great works of literature to observing the serious illness of a roommate. While most of these experiences are unplanned, colleges can and do design programs to increase empathy and extend its scope to embrace broader and broader groups of people. Classes and workshops on diversity (discussed in greater detail in Chapter 8) are probably the most common example. The central point of these classes is to help students see the world through the eyes of those who belong to another group and thus acquire a more sympathetic appreciation of their situation. Studies have indicated that participating in such discussions does in fact tend to extend students' moral awareness.[32]

Imaginative college officials can think of all sorts of additional ways to increase sensitivity to others. For example, on one campus (and doubtless on countless others), a number of undergraduates departed for summer vacation leaving their dorm rooms in a chaotic state. An alert official took color photographs of the worst rooms and sent them to the occupants with a polite note explaining that they might be interested to see the conditions they had left for student dorm crews to clean up. The response was immediate and telling. Many students wrote anguished letters of apology. Some enclosed money to distribute to the luckless dorm crews. In this case, certainly, a picture was worth a thousand words in teaching students to care about the effects of their behavior on others.

The most common example of a program designed to extend student empathy is community service. The intention is to give students a vivid appreciation of the plight of others less fortunate than themselves by encouraging them to take care of the homeless, tutor underprivileged children, or visit the aged and infirm. By all accounts, the effort succeeds. For example, in one survey of 1,100 undergraduates engaged in community service projects, 57 percent replied that "coming to appreciate the rewards of serving others" was among the most important things they learned; 85 percent said that it was at least a "very important" part of their experience.[33]

Although the number of community service programs in colleges and universities has increased considerably in recent decades, much room remains for further growth. According to one large-scale study, the percentage of students who participate "frequently" in service activities during high school drops by more than half in college, while the percentage who never participate more than doubles. Two in five frequent participants in high school service activities do not participate at all in college.[34]

University officials can do much to encourage community work on their campuses and to enhance the value of the experience. By merely speaking out periodically about the importance of service and giving seed money to initiate new programs, presidents and deans can substantially increase the number of student participants. Equally modest steps can improve the quality of the experience. Taking care that projects do not simply provide make-work but allow students to make meaningful contributions and work directly with people in need will enrich the program and increase student concern for others. Appointing experienced adults to give advice and offer feedback will help students gain more from the experience. So will opportunities for students to reflect on what they have learned by discussing their work with others or through integrating service with regular courses. When all these features are in place, the results can be impressive. One large survey showed substantial numbers of undergraduates claiming that community service caused them "to see social problems in a new way."[35] In another massive survey of college students in the 1980s, the authors found that, after controlling for other variables, students participating in community service became more committed to volunteer to help others and "more committed to personally effecting social change."[36]

Although moral reasoning and the will to act ethically have been treated separately in this chapter, they are closely interconnected. The empathy and sense of fairness that are formed in early life provide the motive power that can overcome self-serving inclinations and nurture a desire to act morally. Education in turn can guide empathic motives with reason and expand their reach. Through discussions and readings, coursework can supply the arguments for behaving ethically and convey the knowledge and understanding of others that will extend empathic concern beyond family and friends to embrace more distant and dissimilar groups. In these ways, moral reasoning and empathy reinforce one another to help bring about more principled behavior.

Over the past three decades, universities have moved in various ways to capitalize on these opportunities. Hundreds of courses on practical ethics and moral reasoning have found their way into college catalogues. Community service programs have flourished, and more and more undergraduates are participating. Many institutions have begun to link service programs to courses in the curriculum. Evidence from scores of research studies indicates that efforts of this kind have an effect on how undergraduates think about ethical problems and how aware and concerned they are about those less fortunate than themselves.

To this extent, therefore, David Brooks is clearly wrong when he asserts that universities are doing nothing to build the character of their students. Far too much is going on to warrant such a statement, and persuasive evidence exists that these efforts have beneficial effects on the moral awareness and behavior of students. At the same time, it is equally clear that academic leaders and their faculties could be doing a great deal more. Large majorities of students are still graduating without having taken a course in moral reasoning. Only a minority of undergraduates nationwide participate in community service programs, and many of the programs that exist have too little supervision, too little opportunity for careful reflection on the experience, and too little connection with the curriculum. As for the moral example colleges set for their students, it is impossible to generalize, but such evidence as one can glean from studies of athletic programs, student reports of cheating, and accounts of lax enforcement of underage drinking laws suggests that much room remains for improvement.

All in all, it is fair to say that moral development exists in most colleges today as one among many options that interested students can pursue. They can sign up for a course in moral reasoning or volunteer for a community service program, but they need not do so if they are not so inclined. (Unfortunately one suspects that those who decline these opportunities will often be the ones who need them most.) Colleges too have options. For example, they can try hard to avoid compromising admissions and academic standards in order to win on the athletic field, refrain from investing in tobacco stocks, or insist on strong conflict-of-interest rules that prohibit their professors from launching clinical trials to test the products of companies in which they hold financial interests. But measures such as these are only options. Colleges need not do any of these things if they decide that the risks of losing money, upsetting alumni, or angering some professors make such action seem imprudent from a cost-benefit point of view.

Under these conditions, the most important issue is not whether to introduce new courses in ethics or add more community service programs but to decide what place moral development ought to have in a rounded liberal education. On this point, the views of the faculty are divided (at least outside the church-affiliated colleges). Only a slight majority of professors nationwide (55.5 percent) think it "very important" or "essential" for a college "to develop moral character."[37] Academic leaders would probably express stronger support, but many fewer seem prepared to display much initiative in attempting to move their institutions in this direction.

There is a threshold question, then, that every college needs to debate. Should moral development be merely an option for students who are interested (and for college authorities when it is not too costly or controversial)? Or should it be an integral part of undergraduate education for all students and a goal demanding attention, effort, and, on occasion, even a bit of courage and sacrifice from every level of the college administration? After so many years of ambivalence and neglect, surely it is time to address this question with the care and deliberation it deserves.

7 | PREPARATION FOR CITIZENSHIP

From the time of Thomas Jefferson to the present day, leaders in America have pointed to education as the key to a healthy democracy. And for good reason. Civic responsibility must be learned, for it is neither natural nor effortless. It takes work to inform oneself sufficiently to cast an intelligent vote, let alone equip oneself to make wise decisions as an elected public official. It takes a sense of civic duty and an understanding of the importance of elections in a democracy merely to cast a ballot at all. After all, to borrow an observation attributed to Edward Banfield, voting is irrational from a purely self-interested point of view, since the odds that any single person will affect the outcome of an election are lower than the risk that he will be hit by a truck on the way to the polls. Education is the obvious means to foster the civic commitment and intellectual competence that citizens need to participate effectively in public life. That must be what John Dewey had in mind when he declared, "Democracy has to be born anew every generation, and education is its midwife."[1]

THE CHALLENGE OF CIVIC APATHY

Preparing citizens has taken on new urgency given the long slide in civic participation over the past 40 years. From the early 1960s to 2000, voting rates in presidential elections fell from almost 65 percent to barely 50 percent, a drop of roughly 25 percent.[2] In off-year elections for Congress and for governorships, participation sagged from 48 to 36 percent.[3] Similar declines have occurred in all active forms of civic engagement, such as working for a political party, attending meetings on town or school affairs, signing a petition, or attending political rallies and speeches.[4]

Political participation is especially weak among younger citizens. Their voting rates are well below those of older age groups. The percentage of Americans between the ages of 18 and 24 who cast a ballot in presidential elections fell below 40 percent before rebounding in 2004.[5] Of course, younger people have always been less inclined to vote than their elders. Still, turnout among 18- to 24-year-olds has been dropping with every succeeding generation for decades—in presidential elections, from more than 50 percent in the early 1970s to less than 40 percent in 2000; in alternate-year elections, from almost 30 percent in the early 1970s to less than 20 percent in 1998.[6] Other forms of civic and political participation also show greater declines among younger people than among their elders.[7] Since new cohorts of young Americans will steadily take the place of citizens currently over 65, who have the highest voting rates of any age group, participation seems likely to erode further unless something happens to reverse the long-term decline.

Not only do young people vote less than their parents and grandparents, they know less about public affairs. In the 1960s, Americans aged 18–29 read newspaper articles about national elections at the same rate as those over 65. By 2000, the percentage of young people reading newspapers about political campaigns plummeted to a level less than half that of senior citizens.[8] Knowledge of politics followed the same pattern. In National Election Study tests, Americans under 30 scored about as high in the 1960s as people over 65. By 2000, young people did only two-thirds as well as seniors.[9]

How concerned should one be about these trends? Why worry if a young New Hampshire woman tells a reporter on national television that she is not planning to vote in the upcoming national primary because "politics isn't one of my hobbies"? After all, won't election turnouts as low as one-half or even one-third of the potential voters still bring many millions to the polls and keep officials responsive to the will of the people?

On closer inspection, citizen apathy turns out to be a more serious problem than this question would suggest. In fact, it has something to do with almost all the features of American politics that trouble people most. Failure to vote does not occur randomly throughout the population. Those who are more extreme in their liberal or their conservative views are generally more zealous and hence more likely to continue voting; it is the moderates who stay away from the polls. Hence low turnouts cause politics to become more polarized, more partisan, less amenable to compromise, and less civil. Declining interest in politics also forces the media to struggle to retain their audience by cutting back on hard news about public affairs in favor of stories of violence, personal tragedy, and other forms of "infotainment." Similarly, apathy invites the use of widely disliked campaign tactics, such as attack ads, that are designed not to build support for a candidate but to discourage supporters of opposing candidates from voting at all. Low turnouts also weaken the influence of poor people, who vote least, while giving undue influence to well-organized groups, such as the National Rifle Association, that are adept at getting their members to the polls. When few people vote, such groups can easily exert an influence far beyond their actual numbers, especially in primary elections in which only 15–20 percent of potential voters normally bother to cast a ballot. In fact, civic apathy helps special-interest lobbyists even more by making it harder for citizen groups to rouse enough grass-roots opposition to defeat efforts to push through self-serving legislation.

After many years of neglect, writers on American government have finally begun to pay more attention to the problem of civic engagement. As William Galston points out, "Compared with previous generations, scholars today are more likely to agree that well-designed institutions are not enough, that a well-organized polity requires citizens with the appropriate knowledge, skills, and traits of character."[10] The American Political Science Association Task Force on Civic Education (made up of professors of political science) has declared it "axiomatic that current levels of political knowledge, political engagement, and political enthusiasm are so low as to threaten the vitality and stability of democratic politics in the United States."[11]

Fortunately recent events give some hope of reawakening a stronger sense of civic engagement among Americans of all ages. In the wake of the close 2000 presidential race and stepped-up efforts by political parties to get their supporters to the polls, voting rates turned sharply upward in the election of 2004.[12] Citizens under 30 joined the surge, increasing their voting from 16.3 million in 2000 to 20.9 million in 2004.[13] By all accounts, college students shared fully in the larger turnout, offering universities a chance to build on this resurgence so that it can continue and increase.

Schools and universities have a special responsibility to take citizenship seriously because of the close connection between education and political engagement.[14] Studies consistently show that years of education are the strongest factor in explaining voter turnout, and several analysts have found that the civic attitudes young people acquire tend to persist through adult life.[15] Knowledge of government and public affairs also contributes to more enlightened voting that reflects more accurately the interests and preferences of those casting ballots.* Investigators even find that people with a greater knowledge of politics are less distrustful of government, more likely to support democratic values, more willing to tolerate differing views, and more inclined to vote. As Sam Popkin and Michael A. Dimock have concluded, "the dominant feature of nonvoting in America is lack of knowledge about government; not distrust of government, lack of interest in politics, lack of media exposure to politics, or feelings of inefficacy."[16]

Since most young people will eventually be eligible to vote, the best place to offer a proper civic education is in the schools. Unfortunately public schools have not done much to overcome the ignorance and apathy their pupils display toward government and public affairs.[17] On the contrary, declining interest in politics has been matched by diminished concern for teaching civics, as education officials have turned their attention increasingly to training the workforce to function well in a global economy. Although more than 40 states require course work in civics, at least as one part of a social studies course, the emphasis is typically on memorizing facts about political institutions and processes rather than acquiring real understanding of how our government works and why it matters. The most positive development

---

*See generally Michael X. Delli Carpini and Scott Keeter, *What Americans Know about Politics and Why It Matters* (1996). Contrary to the claims of some political scientists, citizens who vote in ignorance of the issues do not necessarily cancel each other out, since neither ignorance itself nor the errors that it produces are distributed randomly throughout the population. This point is explained at greater length in Derek Bok, *The Trouble with Government* (2001), pp. 378–81.

has been the growth of community service programs, which now exist in half the nation's public high schools, although even here the quality of the programs is uneven.[18]

With civics courses in a weakened state, test scores measuring the political knowledge of high school students appear to have dropped during the past few decades.[19] Interest in public affairs has also dwindled. According to the annual survey of entering college freshmen, the proportion keeping up with politics fell from 58 percent in the mid-1960s to 26 percent in 2000, while the proportion who claim to discuss politics frequently dropped from 29 percent in 1968 to 14 percent 30 years later.[20] Since 2000, fortunately, these figures have finally turned upward, but the percentage who think it important to "keep up to date with political affairs" has still regained only a quarter of the ground lost since the 1960s.[21]

THE RESPONSE OF THE COLLEGES

Since the public schools are unlikely in the foreseeable future to prepare students adequately for citizenship, the role of colleges has taken on a special significance. Not only will college graduates continue to vote more frequently; since they are better informed than those with less education, their influence on the outcome will be greater. As in the past, they will likewise make up the vast majority of all public officials, elected or appointed. All these factors make their preparation for enlightened citizenship especially important to the nation.

Oddly, however, despite frequent references to citizenship in college brochures, faculties have paid little attention to the subject. Here and there, a college announces a full-blown commitment to civic education backed by appropriate courses and a variety of supporting extracurricular programs.[22] But these instances are extremely rare. Very seldom does a faculty give any explicit consideration to civic education in their periodic reviews of the undergraduate curriculum. The president of the Association of American Colleges and Universities, Carol Schneider, has even reported that, after "five years of active discussions on dozens of campuses, . . . I have been persuaded that there is not just a neglect of but a resistance to college-level study of United States democratic principles."[23]

Why have universities shown so little interest in civic education? Decades ago, perhaps, faculties could believe that a sound liberal education was all that was needed to prepare students for a role in politics and public life. Whatever the apathy in the electorate as a whole, most colleges could count on their alumni to vote and participate in local affairs at a time when fewer than 5 percent of the population graduated from college and those that did were natural leaders in their communities.

After World War II, the situation changed dramatically. Once a majority of young people began attending college, one could no longer assume that undergraduates were immune from the apathy that affected the public as a whole. Informing oneself about civic and political issues became a more formidable task as the government assumed greater responsibilities at home and overseas. At that point, surely, civic education became a subject deserving explicit attention from the faculty. Before colleges had much opportunity to respond, however, they were engulfed by the struggles of the 1960s. Students rebelled against authority, defied long-standing conventions, and mocked their elders for their tolerance of racism, poverty, and discrimination against women. In such an atmosphere, civic apathy hardly seemed a problem. Instead, with undergraduates inflamed by an unpopular war in Vietnam, patriotism and citizenship became suspect words on campus, associated with swaggering militarism and mindless obedience to country "right or wrong."

One must still ask, however, why colleges have continued to neglect civic education 30 years after the era of campus turmoil came to an end. While some faculty members are still suspicious of civic education, surveys show that substantial majorities of the nation's professors agree that "[preparing] students for responsible citizenship is an 'essential' or at least a 'very important' aim of a college education."[24] Apparently, then, many faculty members continue to believe that a normal undergraduate program, by itself, will suffice to serve the civic purpose.*

This view is not entirely without substance. After all, almost every generally accepted aim of undergraduate education—critical thinking, moral development, racial tolerance, communication skills, global understanding, breadth of learning—can be thought to contribute to good citizenship, generously defined. Beyond the classroom, extra-curricular experiences in student government and other undergraduate organizations offer training in democratic procedures. Democratic and Republican clubs provide forums in which to discuss politics and talk with public offi-

---

*Some faculties may avoid paying explicit attention to civic education because the subject seems so contentious. Opinions are divided on whether such education should emphasize rights or duties, whether to stress national or world citizenship, and whether to try to foster loyalty to the country and its system of government or mobilize students to be activists in a struggle against the oppression of minorities, women, and poor people. While these disagreements may explain the reluctance to address the subject, they do not justify it. Differences of opinion surround most important educational issues, but the differences are normally faced and eventually resolved.

cials. Working as a volunteer in housing projects and home-less shelters instills a greater awareness of human needs and the inadequacies of laws and policies that affect the poor. When so much in the college experience seems relevant to responsible citizenship, it is easy to conclude that nothing further needs to be done.

Moreover, the findings of researchers indicate that colleges do produce significant results in preparing students as citizens. According to Ernest Pascarella and Patrick Terenzini, studies "almost invariably indicate changes during the college years in students' political attitudes and values toward . . . greater interest in social and political issues and greater interest in and involvement in the political process."[25] More precisely, the same authors concluded that "net of other factors, including prior levels of involvement, individuals with a bachelor's degree (compared to those with only a high school diploma) were 1.8 times more likely to be frequently involved in political activities, 2.4 times more likely to be involved in community welfare groups, 1.5 times more likely to be highly committed to community leadership, and 2.5 times more likely to vote in a national, state, or local election."[26] In recent years, the growth of community service programs has helped to increase civic engagement even further. Linda Sax and Alexander Astin analyzed the responses from 24,000 students attending college from 1985 to 1989 and determined that "controlling for students' pre-college disposition toward service, students who spend time volunteering during college, compared to those who do not volunteer, become more convinced that individuals can change society, feel more committed to personally effecting social change, and develop stronger leadership skills."[27] Since almost half of all students in four-year colleges now spend time volunteering, these findings bode well for democracy.

Another study by William Knox, Paul Lindsay, and Mary Kolb has shown how the civic contributions of college continue on in adult life by tracing the political and civic involvement of 5,409 individuals who graduated from high school 14 years before. The authors found that the percentages voting, volunteering in the community, and frequently discussing politics all rose steadily with higher levels of educational attainment. These effects persisted strongly even after introducing controls for differences in wealth, parental education, and other characteristics of respondents when they graduated from high school.[28] Still another study involving the 1988 presidential election found that the amount of formal education citizens received had much to do with how much they knew about the candidates and the positions candidates took on the issues.[29]

These findings are encouraging. Still, as with so many other aims of undergraduate education, a closer look at the evidence suggests that colleges could be accomplishing a great deal more to prepare their students as citizens. Rarely does a faculty adopt course requirements to reflect its conviction that certain bodies of knowledge are essential to enlightened, responsible citizenship. Outside the curriculum, student government and Democratic and Republican clubs generally exist but attract only a limited number of participants. Even community service programs, for all their recent popularity, enroll fewer than half of all undergraduates.

The fact that so few institutions pay any explicit attention to civic education seems to have had an effect on students. In 2004, the Association of American Colleges and Universities conducted a series of focus groups among undergraduates (and college-bound high school students) to explore their attitudes toward preparing themselves as citizens. In every group, civic involvement was regarded as the least or next to the least important reason for attending college. "Collectively, these students had no developed conception whatsoever of the role their education might play in preparing them to work on significant social questions confronting their democracy or the larger world. Indeed, it was clear from the conversation that civic responsibility was not really a part of their vocabulary at all."[30]

The attitudes just described are reflected quite clearly in the choices students make about which courses to take. It is obvious (as political scientists increasingly emphasize) that citizens need to have a basic knowledge of government, politics, and public affairs in order to vote intelligently, let alone carry out other civic responsibilities. There is clear evidence, however, that many students graduate from college without taking even the most basic courses they need to prepare themselves for these functions. According to Department of Education statistics, barely one-third of undergraduates ever complete an introductory course in American government and politics. Fewer than one in ten study political philosophy or international affairs. More than 40 percent do not even take a basic course in economics.[31] Although college graduates do score much higher on tests of political knowledge than those with only a high school degree, researchers estimate that college-educated students today possess only approximately the same levels of political knowledge as high school graduates achieved in the late 1940s.[32]

Recent research by Norman Nie and Sunshine Hillygus has also reached the surprising conclusion that several subjects that are popular with students actually tend to discourage active citizenship.[33] The more undergraduates study social science, the more likely they are to vote and participate in community activities. In sharp contrast, however, the more courses they take in science or engineering, the less they participate politically. More striking still, the more courses they take in business, the most popular of all majors, the less they engage in community service, the less they vote, and the less they feel inclined to try to have an influence on the political process (even after controlling for prior grades, test scores, parental education, race, gender, and other variables). On second thought, perhaps these results are not so surprising after all. In most colleges, many students who major in science or in some form of vocational program graduate without taking any course that might awaken an interest in public life or convey some knowledge of the institutions and procedures of government.

Even community service work may not do all that one might think to promote habits of civic responsibility. It is true that participants are more likely to get involved in politics than classmates with no community service. Nevertheless surveys show that most volunteers come to community service not as a stepping-stone to civic engagement but as an *alternative* to politics and government.[34] To many of these young people, politics is unsavory, politicians hopeless, and petitioning the government a waste of time. Serving in homeless shelters or tutoring poor children emerges in their mind as the *only* effective way of doing something about social problems.

Such attitudes seem plainly shortsighted. Feeding the homeless is laudable and even essential as a stopgap measure, but it is hardly a cure for the conditions that give rise to widespread homelessness in the wealthiest nation on earth. While the reasons for this condition are complex, the fact that many participating undergraduates do not see a connection between homelessness and government policies toward mental health, poverty, affordable housing, and the like demonstrates a failure of education. The same is true of their mistaken belief that no useful results ever come from citizen efforts to persuade the government to respond to social needs. By itself, therefore, community service, however laudable, cannot provide an adequate civic education. On the contrary, it underscores the need to pay more attention to educating students about the role of government and the importance of civic participation to our democracy.

Once students graduate, of course, they do participate more actively in civic affairs than their fellow citizens who did not go to college. Still, their levels of involvement are far from optimal in absolute terms. Over the past 40 years, college graduates have shared in the decline in civic participation throughout the population as a whole.[35] Moreover, according to Knox, Lindsay, and Kolb, while civic participation among recipients of B.A. degrees 14 years out of high school was above the levels of those without a college degree, fewer than 10 percent of the graduates were active in political campaigns or participating in community groups or volunteer work, and fewer than half reported engaging frequently in discussions of political issues.[36]

The failure to mount a deliberate program of civic education not only gives students inadequate preparation to participate effectively in government and community. Together with the precarious state of practical ethics, it also leaves undergraduate education largely bereft of a compelling public purpose. Most people today think of college primarily as a stepping-stone to well-paid careers but not as a vital means for achieving better government or stronger communities. At best, undergraduate education provides the human capital to build a stronger economy, but that is a benefit for which students receive an ample private reward and not something most people think of as a valuable public service. Since universities receive tax exemptions, financial aid, and many other direct and indirect subsidies, they have an obligation to use their educational resources to meet legitimate public needs. To the extent they fail to do so, they can hardly complain when state legislators shift more and more of the financial burden of attending college from taxpayers to parents and students. After all, the more colleges neglect the task of preparing moral human beings and active, enlightened citizens, the more their education resembles a private investment rather than a public good.

TOWARD A MORE DELIBERATE
PROGRAM OF CIVIC EDUCATION

How, then, should a college go about trying to prepare its students as citizens? The first step, surely, is to agree in general terms on what colleges can appropriately seek to accomplish. For reasons already explained, no institution should try to indoctrinate students to embrace a particular political agenda. Where issues of policy are concerned, the role of the faculty is to raise questions, not impose answers. At the same time, the need for political neutrality does not excuse universities from their responsibility to prepare students as citizens. How to vote and what causes to support are matters that students must decide for themselves. But the need to vote and the importance of becoming informed and active citizens are values so widely recognized and so fundamental to our system of government that no university oversteps the bounds by endorsing them.

The least that colleges can do to fulfill this responsibility is to offer their students an intellectual foundation that will enable them to vote and participate in public life as wisely and thoughtfully as possible. Such an effort clearly encompasses most of the familiar aims of undergraduate education—

enhancing students' analytical and problem-solving abilities, developing their ethical awareness and powers of moral reasoning, and enhancing their tolerance and respect for other points of view. These qualities, however, are not uniquely relevant to citizenship; they would be important even if students had no responsibility toward their government. The distinctive role of civic education is to give students enough knowledge to make the thoughtful, informed choices that enlightened citizenship requires.* As William Galston observes, after summarizing a variety of recent studies, "competent democratic citizens need not be policy experts, but there is a level of basic knowledge below which the ability to make a full range of reasoned civic judgments is impaired."[37]

Defining the content of this basic core of knowledge is admittedly a difficult process. The possibilities are endless, since government enters into almost every facet of American

---

*Some authors have argued that people should be taught to be citizens of the world more than citizens of a particular country; see, for example, Martha Nussbaum, *For Love of Country: Debating the Limits of Patriotism* (1996). While it is important to prepare students to live and work in a more interdependent, or global, economy (see Chapter 9), such an aim should not be equated with developing *citizens*. It cannot replace the need to prepare students to vote and participate actively and knowledgeably in the civic life of their own country. The United States and its various subdivisions will almost certainly remain the most important units of democratic government for the vast majority of undergraduates during their lifetimes. In contrast, the family of nations, in its current and foreseeable form, offers many fewer and less consequential opportunities for individuals to participate in multinational governance by helping to influence policies or to choose political leaders. International relations and other nations and cultures are undoubtedly among the areas of knowledge that citizens of the United States should know something about. But educating students to be active, enlightened citizens of *this* country remains the most important civic goal for American universities to pursue.

life from science and medicine to crime, education, and the arts. It is clearly not feasible to acquaint every college student with all the information required merely to understand the most important policy problems confronting the government. Even if it were possible to do so, faculties have no way of anticipating the issues that will prove most pressing over the lifetimes of today's undergraduates.

Certain bodies of knowledge, however, have such enduring importance for active citizenship that every student should be acquainted with them. Four subjects arguably qualify on these grounds. One is an introduction to American democracy that goes well beyond the typical high school civics class to combine a basic understanding of our institutions of government, our rights, and our freedoms with a realistic appreciation of the way in which policies are actually made, including the role of public opinion, the media, interest groups, party politics, campaign financing, and judicial review. Such a course should convey not only a sense of the strengths of our democracy but also an awareness of its persistent problems, such as the influence of money in politics, the political weakness of low- and moderate-income groups, and the diminishing number of truly competitive elections for national and state legislatures. Another important subject is political philosophy, including such fundamental normative issues as the nature of a legislator's duty to represent constituents; the meaning of the claims of equality, equal opportunity, and social justice; and the arguments over redistribution, civil liberties, and minority rights, among others. The third important area of knowledge includes the basic elements of economics, since issues such as unemployment, growth, inflation, and trade are so important to citizens and public policy and because the government itself is so constrained by economic considerations, such as budget deficits, trade balances, and fluctuations in the value of the currency. The last component is a knowledge of America's engagement in world affairs—its role as a military and economic power, the international institutions and arrangements through which it interacts with other countries, and the dilemmas it confronts in fields ranging from combating terrorism to promoting trade interests to global warming and other international environmental issues.

How a faculty should combine elements of political science, economics, political philosophy, and international affairs and how much space in the curriculum they should receive are questions best left to each individual institution. What is hard to justify, however, is the decision to keep these subjects optional, as they are at present in the vast majority of colleges. Citizenship is *not* just another option for students to pursue or not as they choose. Virtually all American undergraduates will be eligible to vote, and society has a compelling interest in having them sufficiently informed to do so thoughtfully. It is surely odd to require all students to take courses in the sciences or study a foreign language while taking no steps to ensure that they have enough knowledge to understand the basic problems and processes of their democracy. Many graduates will go through life never using the language they studied in college, and even more will make only occasional use of the scraps of knowledge they recall from their course in introductory chemistry, biology, or physics. But very few will escape the responsibility of being a citizen and having to understand something about the operation of their government and the major recurring issues that every modern democracy confronts.

Preparing citizens involves more than imparting relevant knowledge, more even than developing the cognitive qualities required for enlightened political participation. As in building good character, students must not only gain the knowledge and intellectual competence to make enlightened choices, they must develop a sense of responsibility to fulfill the basic obligations of citizenship and participate in civic life. For some undergraduates, such commitments may be forged by serving in student government or by working in a political campaign. Only a few students, however, will enjoy these experiences in the normal course of events. Most will arrive at college affected to some degree by the civic apathy that pervades the population as a whole. Thus colleges need to consider taking affirmative steps to nurture a stronger sense of the responsibilities of citizens in a democracy.

There is recent evidence that professors who try to encourage civic participation can increase the interest and commitment of their students in becoming involved with politics and public issues. Investigators examined the results of 21 courses given on a variety of campuses. Although the classes were on different subjects, all included some attempt to stimulate civic engagement. Half of the students in the study were already very interested in politics, but the other half were politically disengaged and took the courses to fulfill a college requirement or for some other extraneous reason. Surveys taken before after the students completed the courses showed that disengaged students became significantly more interested in politics, more committed to involving themselves in politics and civic affairs, and more confident of their political skills. In view of the concerns of some skeptics about the risk of indoctrination, it is interesting to note that participants did not change their political orientation or party allegiance as a result of taking the courses.[38]

In recent decades, many campus leaders, aided by organizations such as Campus Compact, have helped to encourage civic commitment by expanding and improving community service programs. Researchers confirm that partici- pating in such activities has positive effects on civic involve- ment. For example, Linda Sax and Alexander Astin con- cluded from an extensive study of college students in the late 1980s that, after controlling for initial differences in attitude and personality, community service had a substantial effect "on students' lifelong commitment to volunteerism and community activism."[39]

Academic leaders can take various steps to expand and im- prove service programs. Merely expressing support for these activities will signal their importance and encourage more students to participate. Limited amounts of seed money can launch new programs and pay for experienced advisors to help participants perform more effectively and derive added benefit from their experience. Equally important is an effort to link community service more closely to related studies of government policy and politics by providing a background course on poverty or incorporating a service component within regular courses on subjects such as health care, hous- ing, and welfare policy.[40] Fortunately initiatives of this kind have multiplied in recent years. In addition to giving stu- dents a broader perspective on their service experience, such linkages can help to counter the all-too-prevalent notion that community service and political involvement are alterna- tives rather than complementary pursuits.

University officials can also foster active citizenship by en- couraging the growth of student government and the use of democratic processes in all extracurricular organizations. Some form of student government exists in almost every uni- versity, but its importance varies widely from one campus to another. At some colleges, holding elected office is a mark of great prestige and carries considerable responsibility; at others, it is something of a joke. Unfortunately indifference seems to be winning out. According to surveys conducted by Arthur Levine and Jeannette Cureton, the percentage of students voting in campus elections dropped by more than half from 1978 to 1997 to a range of 11–15 percent.[41]

While attitudes toward student government are not entirely within the university's control, much can turn on the responsibilities entrusted to the undergraduates involved. Where student representatives can only give advice (which frequently goes unheeded), their work will hardly amount to much in the eyes of other undergraduates. But if a student senate administers a budget and has significant functions to perform, it will normally enjoy a higher status, and its members will derive more value from the experience of serving. This is not to say that undergraduates should sit on tenure committees or assume other tasks for which they lack the necessary experience. Yet many issues of importance to students, such as those affecting living arrangements, intramural athletics, and other social and extracurricular activities, are well within their capabilities and can lend substance to the work of student leaders. By trusting them with such functions, a university can accomplish more than one might think. According to Sidney Verba, Kay Schlozman, and Henry Brady, participation in democratically run student organizations is a more powerful predictor of future political participation than taking courses in American politics or political science.[42]

Finally, university presidents can offer leadership by making clear in words and actions that they consider voting an important obligation for every citizen. Of course, campus officials must take great care not to act in any way that could be construed as politically partisan. But it is surely appropriate for universities to enlist student volunteers to encourage all undergraduates to register and vote, and to acquaint them with the procedures in their home state for voting by absentee ballot. A widely overlooked provision in the Higher Education Act requires universities receiving benefits under the act to obtain registration forms at least 120 days prior to a federal election and to distribute them to all students enrolled in regular academic programs.[43] According to a 2004 national survey, only 17 percent of colleges responding to the poll were in full compliance with the law.[44] One-third had not even taken steps to secure registration forms or to organize any kind of registration drive on campus. Another 19 percent were "not sure." Surely colleges can make a better showing than that.

College officials can also stimulate interest in forthcoming elections and foster knowledge of the issues involved by organizing debates, candidate visits, mock conventions, and other similar activities. They can try to establish a polling place on the campus instead of forcing students to hunt for somewhere to vote in the neighboring town or city. They can actively oppose efforts by local officials to inhibit students from registering and voting. They can even encourage undergraduates to play a role in the surrounding community by working in nearby high schools to register 18-year-olds or by serving as poll watchers on election day. In all these ways, universities signal to their students the importance of citizen involvement and help build habits of civic responsibility that will persist after graduation.

The steps outlined in the preceding pages are neither especially novel nor unusually difficult. The fact that they are so often lacking on American campuses suggests that the principal challenge in civic education is not deciding how to take constructive action. Rather the challenge is to persuade college faculties and their leaders that educating citizens and strengthening their sense of civic responsibility are important tasks for a college to perform and that a traditional liberal arts education is not sufficient in itself to impart either the knowledge of public affairs or the sense of civic obligation that a vibrant democracy requires.

It is strange that universities should need convincing of this fact. After all, developing citizens is not only one of the oldest educational goals but a goal of great significance for educators themselves. Universities are peculiarly dependent on an active, flourishing democracy, since no institution of learning can expect to prosper under an authoritarian regime. As Robert Hutchins once remarked, "the death of democracy is not likely to be an assassination from ambush. It will be a slow extinction from apathy, indifference, and undernourishment."[45] At a time when the quality of American public life is jeopardized by ignorance and apathy, it is an act of self-interest, as well as a civic duty, for educators to do whatever they can to address the problem.

8 | LIVING WITH DIVERSITY

College yearbooks have a different look today than they did a century ago. In yearbooks from 1906, the pictures of graduating seniors seem strikingly homogeneous. White faces predominate — "a parade of Anglo-Saxon names and pale, freshly scrubbed faces," to quote Laurence Veysey.[1] Women appear quite frequently, but not in the books from leading private colleges. Immigrants, Catholics, and Jews are included in modest but growing numbers. Only rarely can a black or Asian American face be seen, and few, if any, Hispanic names appear.

Over the past century, however, and especially during the past 40 years, the earlier homogeneity has vanished. Student bodies have become far more diverse in race, religion, gender, and nationality. More than half of America's undergraduates are women. Approximately 10 percent are black, 8 percent are Asian or Asian American, 7 percent are Hispanic, and almost 3 percent come from outside the United States.

As women and minorities have grown more numerous, they have become quite vocal in articulating their special needs. The feminist movement has encouraged women to stand up for their equal right to an education and an equal chance to compete for a professional career. Blacks, Hispanics, and Asian Americans have pressed for greater minority representation in the faculty and more courses in the curriculum on non-Western cultures and the experience of minorities in the United States. All these groups are quick to protest any attempt to demean them or deny them equal treatment.

These developments have added variety and intensity to campus debates, making the college environment at once more stimulating and more disputatious than it was throughout the first two-thirds of the twentieth century. The resulting differences sometimes cause controversy and inflict pain, but they pay educational dividends as well. Researchers find that encountering diversity not only broadens experience but also helps students improve their powers of critical thinking by challenging them to respond to different values and perspectives.[2] Other scholars report (after controlling for initial differences in background and belief) that students experiencing the most contact across racial lines become more civically active, more inclined to help others, and more committed to improving their communities than their classmates.[3]

Society too has much to gain from having students from diverse backgrounds learn to live and work together on campus. A successful democracy demands tolerance and mutual respect from different groups within its citizenry in order to contain the religious and ethnic tensions that have riven so many countries around the world. Employers, conscious of the growing numbers of immigrants and minorities, look for college graduates who can work effectively with diverse groups of employees and customers. (This need doubtless helps to explain why so many Fortune 500 companies filed amicus briefs on behalf of the University of Michigan when it was challenged in the federal courts for using race-based admissions policies to enroll a more diverse entering class.)

A century ago, students managed to coexist with little help from campus officials. Colleges enforced basic rules against violence and theft and tried to protect women by imposing detailed parietal regulations to restrict contact with men. Beyond these simple steps, however, colleges were generally content to let students learn for themselves how to get along with one another by living together in campus residences, playing together on athletic fields, and working together in a host of extracurricular activities.

In recent decades, however, as undergraduates have become more diverse and more and more student groups have begun to assert their special interests and insist on their rights, colleges have found it impossible to continue playing such a passive role. Racial slurs, anti-gay discrimination, and acts of sexual harassment have aroused hostility on many campuses, provoking protests from victims along with demands for punishment and better protection. In response, college authorities have felt impelled to work proactively to encourage students to be more understanding of the differences they meet among their fellow undergraduates. In doing so, officials have encountered a minefield of human emotions requiring exceptional sensitivity and skill in striving to create an environment in which everyone can feel welcome and respected.

With so many forms of diversity on today's college campus, it is impossible in these pages to treat every group and relationship that can give rise to significant problems. Two types of interaction, however, seem especially instructive. The first involves blacks and whites, a relationship that has the most troubled history and touches the rawest nerves of any in our universities. The second relationship involves men and women, the oldest of human encounters but one that has undergone especially rapid and far-reaching changes during the past few decades.

BLACKS AND WHITES

In the 1960s, as one college after another began reaching out to enroll larger numbers of African American students, many college officials believed that their only challenge was to find enough blacks capable of doing college work and to give them the academic and financial support they needed to remain in school. These early illusions quickly vanished. Rather than expressing gratitude for having been admitted and given financial aid, the new arrivals soon began to protest on various grounds. Why were there not *more* black students? More black faculty? More black employees? Why were there no courses on black history and black culture? Why no Third World social center where blacks could relax, hear their own music, and get away from the slights and condescensions they endured every day from white students?

Demands for Third World centers underscored the fact that merely creating a diverse student body did not mean that blacks and whites would automatically live together harmoniously. Members of both races often came to college having had little experience with other ethnic groups. To this day, 90 percent of white students at the University of Michigan come from racially homogeneous schools and neighborhoods, as do 50 percent of their black classmates, and those who have attended racially mixed public high schools often have unpleasant memories of their encounters with diversity.[4] When blacks first came to colleges in numbers during the 1970s, a decade scarred by racial protests and white backlash, the two groups seemed to coexist like oil and water. As inquiring reporters soon discovered, African American students frequently sat together at all-black tables in the dining halls, pressed for separate residence units (or created them de facto), and organized their own social events.

White students did not always help to make the campus welcoming. Some uttered racial slurs or urged blacks to leave. Fraternities frequently excluded minorities and occasionally gave offense by parodying African American culture. Even well-meaning whites, trying to be friendly, often seemed condescending by talking only about minority issues or black entertainers and sports stars, as if their darker-skinned classmates could have no interests unconnected with race.

Faced with such conflicts and misunderstandings, college faculties and administrators could not sit idly by. They responded in a variety of ways. Most colleges introduced new courses or entire departments in Afro-American studies and searched for black faculty to staff them. Other black adults quickly appeared on campus as assistants to the president for minority issues or associate deans for student affairs. Well-known African Americans came to speak or to accept honorary degrees.

These early responses were only partially successful and soon gave rise to further steps to improve relations between the races. Dismayed by signs reading "Niggers Go Home" and similar blatant expressions of insensitivity and bigotry, a number of colleges enacted speech codes making racially demeaning statements a punishable offense. Such measures, however, proved too crude to be effective and, in any case, were eventually struck down by judges for interfering with the right of free speech.[5] Other steps seemed more promising. Campus officials began to organize racial awareness programs for incoming freshmen in an effort to promote understanding and encourage greater sensitivity to the subtler forms of racial discrimination. A few colleges launched experiments to bring together white and black volunteers to live in residential units featuring African culture or periodic readings and discussions about America's race problems. Faculties even approved mandatory courses on diversity. Some of these offerings emphasized the history of different races in America and the nature of their different cultures.

Others dwelt on problems of discrimination and inequality involving racial minorities and other oppressed groups. Still others combined readings on race in America with material on foreign cultures. By 2004, almost two-thirds of all colleges either required a course on diversity or were in the process of developing one.[6]

How well have colleges succeeded in their efforts to achieve greater racial understanding? Opinions on this score are badly split. According to college authorities and others who champion diversity, the numbers of black tables and other signs of racial separateness are diminishing. Racial awareness programs and courses on diversity have allegedly increased tolerance and cultural awareness. With the numbers of minority students continuing to rise, blacks are said to feel less like strangers in a foreign land. Overall, proponents claim, rather than merely assimilating minority students into white society, colleges are creating greater understanding among the races while enhancing respect and appreciation for America's different cultures among all undergraduates.[7]

Others are not at all convinced by this positive account of campus race relations. In their view, racial hostility is still widespread, black tables have not disappeared, and voluntary segregation continues.[8] After visiting many colleges, Arthur Levine and Jeannette Cureton reported in 1998 that "multiculturalism remains the most unresolved issue on campus today."[9] In the words of a black clinical psychologist,

> whether it is the loneliness of being routinely overlooked as a lab partner in science courses, the irritation of being continually asked by curious classmates about Black hairstyles, the discomfort of being singled out by a professor to give the "black perspective" in class discussion, the pain of racist graf-

fiti scrawled on dormitory room doors, the insult of racist jokes circulated through campus e-mail, or the injury inflicted by racial epithets (and sometimes beer bottles) hurled from a passing car, Black students on predominantly white college campuses must cope with ongoing affronts to their racial identity.[10]

In response, many whites assert that black students exaggerate their problems and are too quick to interpret ambiguous incidents as racially inspired. Amid such tensions, skeptics insist that any periods of calm that may exist on campuses at a given moment merely reflect a stifling political correctness, reinforced by racial awareness programs, that imposes a kind of thought control to mask the animosities and suspicions that bubble beneath the surface.

Where does the truth lie? No categorical answer is possible. A poll of 550 student newspaper editors in the 1990s suggested that many college campuses in America resemble the optimistic picture painted by diversity proponents, while many others confirmed the gloomier version portrayed by the doubters.[11] Enough evidence has accumulated, however, to allow at least some informed guesses about the overall condition of race relations on American campuses.

Several investigators have tried to discover whether the college experience tends to encourage greater tolerance among students. The results are not always the same. A few researchers studying single campuses have found that attitudes toward other races have deteriorated from freshman year to senior year.[12] Overall, however, as Pascarella and Terenzini have declared after analyzing a long list of studies, "the more recent evidence seems conclusive in indicating that college attendance, independent of numerous other factors, promotes racial understanding and openness to diversity as well as the belief that racism remains a social problem.[13]

Unfortunately, Pascarella and Terenzini go on to report that improvements in racial understanding seem to be quite modest, perhaps amounting to only a few percentage points.[14] Alexander Astin has reached a similar conclusion based on large-scale student surveys, adding that the gains during college in racial attitudes, as reported by students, were not as large in the 1990s as they were a decade earlier.[15]

In our own book on race-based college admissions, William Bowen and I inquired more specifically into relations between blacks and whites by surveying some 60,000 students who had enrolled in 26 selective colleges, half of them in 1976 and half in 1989.[16] These data, covering a variety of selective institutions with race-based admissions policies ranging from small liberal arts colleges to major research universities, gave a more positive view of race relations and minority feelings on these campuses. Large majorities of both races supported university policies aimed at creating a racially diverse student body. More than 90 percent of both blacks and whites who entered as freshmen in 1989 declared themselves either "very satisfied" with their four years (more than 60 percent) or "somewhat satisfied" (roughly 30 percent). Only 6–7 percent of either race said that they would be unlikely to enter the same college if they had to make the choice again. Surprisingly, students of all races who dropped out of college were virtually as enthusiastic as those who remained.[17] Apparently, then, relations at these colleges were not sufficiently strained to spoil the undergraduate experience for either blacks or whites.

If black tables existed, they did not prevent social interaction across racial lines. Among the students entering the

26 colleges in 1989, 88 percent of blacks claimed to know at least two white students well, while 55 percent of whites knew at least two black students well. More than 60 percent of whites and more than 70 percent of blacks felt that college had contributed "a great deal" or "a fair amount" to their ability to "work effectively and get along well with people from different races/cultures." Substantial majorities (76 percent of blacks and 55 percent of whites) considered such improvement "very important."[18]

Comparisons between the views of the 1989 freshmen and those of the cohort entering the same colleges in 1976 revealed significant increases in the percentages reporting substantial interracial contact, improved ability to get along with people of other races, and support for the college's policy of admitting a racially diverse class.[19] Such trends suggest that these institutions, at least, have made progress in helping students learn from diversity and appreciate its value.

Other research tends to confirm these findings. Surveys of undergraduates from the late 1980s showed that two-thirds felt that "students of different ethnic origins communicate well with one another," while only one in four perceived "a lot of racial conflict" on their campus.[20] Another large-scale survey revealed that 69 percent of undergraduates had at least one friend of another race, while 62 percent felt a sense of community on their campus.[21] Still another survey at the end of the 1990s involving 8,897 students at 115 four-year institutions found remarkable degrees of racial interaction, with only 16 percent reporting that all their close friends were of the same race.[22] Among minority students, the percentage was even smaller—approximately 5 percent.

There is also some reason to suspect that many reports of racial segregation in colleges are exaggerated. For example, black tables in student dining halls have come to symbolize the racial separation and voluntary segregation that still exist in varying degrees at most colleges. What is often overlooked is that many other groups—football players, student newspaper editors, drama majors, and the like—also sit together often. Unlike these affinity groups, however, black students stand out and their tables are instantly noticed. Moreover, meals take up only part of the day, and undergraduates can find plenty of other opportunities to mix with students of other races. As large-scale surveys repeatedly show, substantial majorities of black undergraduates claim to have close acquaintances of another race.*

Interestingly, students themselves may have an inflated sense of racial balkanization. One survey of undergraduates at UCLA, for example, found 93 percent agreeing that "students on campus are predominantly clustered by race/ ethnicity," although 72 percent of the white students claimed to have at least one minority friend and more than 60 percent had friendship groups in which at least a quarter of the members were from other races. Even students who claimed to have diverse friendship groups *in which no single race*

---

*See, for example, William G. Bowen and Derek Bok, *The Shape of the River: Long-Term Consequences of Considering Race in College and University Admissions* (1998), p. 233. (Eighty-eight percent of black students at 26 selective colleges and universities claimed to know at least two white students well.) See also Anthony L. Antonio, "The Role of Interracial Interaction in the Development of Leadership Skills and Cultural Knowledge and Understanding," 42 *Research in Higher Education* (2001), pp. 593, 604. Antonio observes that "compared with white students, students of color are much more likely to engage in many forms of interracial interaction on predominantly white campuses" (p. 612). While this result is mostly attributable to the fact that it is much easier for minorities to meet whites than the reverse on predominantly white campuses, it does suggest that few minorities are quite willing to have continuing social contact with students of other races.

made up a majority were almost unanimous (94 percent) in thinking that their campus was predominantly segregated by race or ethnicity.[23] Such findings suggest that appearances can be deceiving and that even those who live and work on a campus can exaggerate the degree of racial separation.

While much research suggests that progress has occurred in college efforts to promote racial tolerance and understanding, contrary evidence is not difficult to find. In a 1997 survey, 56 percent of student affairs officials reported that undergraduates of different races do not often socialize together on their campus.[24] Racial incidents continue to occur at colleges across the country, and many deans admit that conflicts among their students often have racial overtones. The most careful assessment of racial violence and harassment reported in 1990 that 20 percent of black students experience some form of racial violence or harassment during an academic year (although reliable estimates of this kind are extremely hard to make and should be looked upon with great caution).[25]

In the end, the fairest verdict must be a mixed one. While race relations have improved on many campuses, many others still experience significant tensions.[26] Even colleges that have done much to improve racial tolerance and understanding through their policies on diversity find that total success still eludes their grasp. Although there is more racial mixing and interracial friendship than most critics acknowledge, few colleges can yet boast honestly that their students consider race relations ideal. Even on outwardly harmonious campuses, underlying tensions and misunderstandings often persist, albeit in muted form. Most surveys reveal that undergraduates do not blame the faculty or the administration for any frictions that remain but consider students primarily responsible. However, they disagree sharply about which students are at fault. Blacks tend to feel that whites are chiefly to blame; whites typically believe that the reverse is true. Similar differences also exist between the perceptions of black and white students on other issues involving race relations in America.[27]

What can campus leaders do to overcome the continuing tensions? Although students seem to want to learn about diversity in college and are less satisfied with colleges that do not afford them this opportunity, merely increasing the number of minority students will accomplish little or nothing. In fact, one large-scale study found that expanding minority enrollments, without doing more, *decreases* white students' sense of community. The same study discovered that simply adding to the number of minority faculty also has negative effects on white students' satisfaction with college and sense of community.[28] To encourage understanding and tolerance, then, colleges must do more than merely augment the minority presence on campus.

An important first step is to emphasize to students that diversity is an important value for the institution. Simply making this point in college literature and speeches to students can improve attitudes toward race relations for students of all races. Without reinforcing actions, however, such pronouncements will eventually lose their credibility with undergraduates, who are always quick to recognize hypocrisy and sham in all their forms.

As mentioned earlier, most institutions have chosen to proceed in the way that comes naturally to a university—through courses on cultural diversity and by workshops to increase racial awareness and understanding. Almost all colleges have courses (even majors) in Afro-American studies and the history and status of other minority groups, and classes of this kind frequently include substantial numbers of white students. Many colleges offer workshops on race relations in which discussion leaders try to have participants come to understand the feelings and perspectives of students of other races. In this sense, diversity classes can be viewed as a particular form of moral education in which instructors try to extend the empathy that almost all entering students have toward those nearest and most similar to them to include groups that are more distant and dissimilar. By most accounts, these experiences have an effect. A number of studies have found that students who complete such courses and workshops gain more in racial tolerance and understanding than classmates who have not had such instruction, even after controlling for prior differences in background and attitude between the two groups.[29]

At the same time, efforts of this kind carry significant risks. If courses and workshops are voluntary, they tend to "preach to the choir" by attracting mostly undergraduates who are already interested in other cultures. If the college tries instead to make the courses and workshops mandatory, it runs the risk of making blacks feel uncomfortable at being singled out for special attention and white students feel unjustly suspected of bigotry and intolerance. The best-intentioned programs can leave participants fearing that it is not really safe to express their true feelings. Even well-designed efforts to honor different cultures can overemphasize divisions in society and cause students to feel marginalized if they do not strongly identify with any ethnic group.[30] These dangers do not counsel against offering programs of this kind; the need for tolerance and understanding is too great and the evidence of positive effects too strong. Still, the risks involved are surely great enough to call for careful planning and continued vigilance to keep the classes and programs from falling into the hands of doctrinaire instructors who will almost always leave students feeling resentful and unfairly manipulated.

Courses and workshops are not the only way of improving racial understanding. Those who study methods of combating prejudice and invidious stereotyping generally support the prescription first laid down by Gordon Allport in 1954.[31] According to Allport, promoting sustained contact between members of different groups is the best way of increasing tolerance and understanding. To be effective, however, contact should occur under certain conditions. Participants need to occupy a similar status; daily encounters among unequals will not necessarily breed mutual respect. Contact will also be more productive if it is face to face rather than accomplished through the medium of books or television. The interaction will likewise be more fruitful if carried on through cooperation to achieve a common goal rather than through competition. Finally, mixing potentially prejudiced groups seems to have much better results if it occurs with the visible approval and encouragement of those in positions of authority.*

Campus life is full of opportunities to enjoy the kinds of sustained contact between blacks and whites that satisfy Allport's conditions. Participation in football and other team sports provides an excellent way for members of different races to work together toward a desired goal. Community service programs can serve the same purpose. So can working in student government, singing in a glee club, producing a play, and engaging in numerous other extracurricular pursuits.

On the other hand, college activities can produce the opposite result if they pit different races against one another.

---

*Thomas F. Pettigrew later added another condition: that the contact be such as to offer opportunities for friendships to develop across group lines; "Intergroup Contact Theory," 49 *Annual Review of Psychology* (1998), p. 65.

Intense competition for grades may have this effect, especially if members of the minority group consistently perform less well than members of the majority. Campus politics may intensify prejudice if students form political parties defined by race. Fraternities and sororities can have the same result if they admit only members of a single race. (Indeed several studies have found that fraternities and sororities—presumably those with restricted memberships—tend to increase racial prejudice among their members.)[32]

College authorities have an important role to play in fostering the kinds of contact that promote tolerance while discouraging activities and organizations that separate members of different races and promote competition rather than cooperation among them. Officials can also try to encourage informal interracial discussions about all kinds of subjects, including the issues and problems that tend to divide and create misunderstanding and hostility.[33] Multiracial residence halls, where informal give-and-take occurs spontaneously and often, offer an ideal setting for fruitful interchange of this kind.

Paradoxically, racial incidents present uniquely valuable opportunities for dialogue. Such tense occasions attract wide attention and concern, making it possible to draw students into candid discussions of racial problems who would otherwise be unwilling to participate. An administration that has prepared residence hall staff to respond effectively and has already enlisted student leaders to play an active role in promoting racial understanding can capitalize on these "teachable moments" to produce much valuable introspection and conversation about racial differences.*

---

*More generally, as Ernest T. Pascarella, Marcia Edison, Amaury Nora, Linda S. Hagedorn, and Patrick T. Terenzini have concluded, based on extensive survey data, "the more students interact with diverse peers and the greater the extent to which such interactions focus on controversial or

Few people would quarrel with the basic message just conveyed. Almost everyone favors efforts to promote a healthy interaction among the races so that students can discover common ground through cooperative endeavor and discuss their differences with candor and civility. Yet advice of this kind is sometimes easier to accept in principle than to implement in real life. For example, despite the agreement on the need for racial interaction, the consensus can quickly evaporate when black students insist on living together in a separate dormitory or socializing by themselves in a Third World center.

The reasons for such demands are understandable. Blacks tend to feel more at ease with members of their own race and want relief from the daily aggravations and tensions they often experience on predominantly white campuses. They naturally seek opportunities to enjoy their own food and music instead of always having to adapt to the dominant white culture. Such considerations have persuaded many observers to accept a degree of separation. As Sharon Gmelch declares, "To expect students of color not to want to group together on the basis of common background and interests would be to hold colleges up to an unrealistically high standard of racial and ethnic integration."[34]

If racial tensions are sufficiently widespread, establishing safe havens where minority students can socialize by themselves may seem the best available choice. Still, when a college agrees to practices that keep different races apart, it suffers at least a partial defeat in the effort to reap the benefits of diversity. It also dilutes the message it sends to students

value-laden issues that may engender a change in perspective or opinion, the greater one's development of openness to diversity and challenge"; "Influences on Students' Openness to Diversity and Challenge in the First Year of College," pp. 174, 188.

about the importance of learning to live and work together harmoniously.

Fortunately it is far from clear on every campus that refusing to open a Third World center will set "an unrealistically high standard." At one university that has consistently opposed such centers, an interviewer talked with hundreds of undergraduates and found the opposite reaction:

> A solid majority of the nonwhite students, and nearly all the white students, report an evolution in their feelings about making it too easy for individuals to withdraw into the confines of a physical space where everyone else looks like them. Many seniors comment that if they had withdrawn to a Third World center they would have missed many learning opportunities. . . . A second reason students recommend a policy of inclusion is that they believe such a policy sends a message. It sets a tone . . . for everyone and an attitude toward life on campus. The tone is that it is quite natural for students from different backgrounds to learn from each other.[35]

This does not mean that minority students should have to conform 24 hours a day to the prevailing white culture. On the contrary, an important part of the effort to help students learn from diversity is to promote opportunities for members of every race to share their heritage and culture with interested classmates. When black students seek to form a gospel singing group, or eat "soul food" in the dining halls, there is every reason to help them do so. It is only when they exclude students of other races that acquiescence by the college threatens to send the wrong message and obscure the very lessons that officials should be trying to convey.

Overall, despite many bumps in the road and many differences among colleges, the progress in relations between blacks and whites is encouraging. Notwithstanding the continuing attacks on race-based admissions practices in courts and statewide referenda, most colleges have maintained their efforts to recruit diverse classes. The percentage of blacks earning B.A. degrees is higher than it has ever been (far higher than it was several decades ago), and minority students on many campuses seem to be feeling more comfortable and welcome.[36] This record compares favorably with the unhappy experience of America's public schools, which are more segregated today than they were in the early 1970s.[37] On most campuses, majorities of students from all races affirm the value of a diverse student body and feel that their undergraduate experience has increased their understanding of other races and their ability to live and work in a multiracial environment. If colleges persevere, it is not too much to hope that historians will one day look upon their efforts as one of the great successes of American higher education.

MEN AND WOMEN

Although Oberlin College became coed as early as 1837, women only began to enter previously male colleges in significant numbers after the Civil War. The earliest arrivals were pioneers in a strange land, often looked upon suspiciously as interlopers in a masculine preserve.[38] Most of them lived by themselves in rooming houses and had little contact with their male classmates. Such social life as they enjoyed tended to be with one another or with faculty members and their families. The majority were serious, hardworking students who came to college to prepare for an academic or professional career. Most of them eventually gained employment, chiefly as teachers. Finding a place in the professions, however, proved very difficult. By 1910, women made up only 6 percent of America's physicians and only 1 percent of the nation's lawyers.[39] They had virtually no presence in the executive ranks of American business.

College presidents initially disagreed on whether women should go to college at all. Many leaders from private institutions expressed concern over the burdens advanced study would place on women's frail constitutions and delicate brains, while spokesmen for the newer public universities tended to welcome the prospect of coeducation with greater enthusiasm. In his inaugural address, President Charles W. Eliot of Harvard observed that "the world knows nothing about the natural mental capacities of the female sex. Only after generations of civil freedom and social equality will it be possible to obtain the data necessary for an adequate discussion of women's natural tendencies, tastes, and capabilities."[40] On the contrary, declared John Bascom, later president of the University of Wisconsin, "the young lady is quicker, more enthusiastic. . . . Her lively memory and imagination and perception would enter like yeast into the heavy, torpid mass, . . . arouse the sluggish young men to a better use of their powers. And cause a little light to find its way into their spirits."[41]

In the end, Eliot and his followers lost the argument decisively. The number of women entering college grew rapidly. In 1900, 71 percent of them were already enrolled in coed institutions, and approximately half of all colleges admitted both men and women. By the mid-1950s, more than 90 percent of college women attended coed institutions, and only 13 percent of all colleges remained single-sex.[42]

Once the female presence on campus was well established, universities started building women's dormitories to convince anxious parents that their daughters would be safe at college. By the 1920s, as the number of women continued to rise, many arrived with more than intellectual purposes in mind. Social life grew more important, sororities gained prominence, and finding a mate became an absorbing preoccupation. The results were striking, contrasting sharply with the experience of earlier generations of college women. In 1900, at a time when more than 90 percent of American women were marrying, fewer than 50 percent of the women graduating from college ever exchanged marriage vows.[43] After 1920, the proportion of women with B.A.s who eventually wed steadily rose, approximating that of the entire female population by midcentury.

As social contact between the sexes increased, universities imposed parietal rules to regulate the relationship. Women were not allowed to stay out beyond a certain hour, and strict limits were imposed on men entering women's dormitories and bedrooms. Though often circumvented, these restrictions signaled a determination on the part of college authorities to permit socializing while discouraging promiscuity. For the next several decades, most men and women in college came to know one another well only through their romantic involvements. Although undergraduates could make casual acquaintances of the opposite sex through classes, extracurricular organizations, and student government, close friendships between the sexes were relatively rare.

The role of women on campus, and their relationships with men, changed dramatically during the 1960s. After World War II, many women had foregone employment to embrace domesticity. Marriage and children took precedence over a professional career. The share of Ph.D.s earned by women fell sharply from levels achieved in the early decades of the century. The percentage of women in medical school abruptly dropped from 12 percent in 1949 to 5 percent by the mid-1950s, and similar trends occurred in law schools.[44] By the late 1960s, however, with the rise of feminism and the advent of the women's liberation movement, the trend turned quickly in the opposite direction. As women poured into graduate schools—especially in law, medicine, and business—professions felt increasing pressure to take down any remaining gender barriers. Congress speeded the process through laws guaranteeing equal access to universities and outlawing discrimination in employment.

Almost simultaneously, a sexual revolution was gaining momentum, spurred by successful efforts to win abortion rights and the development of oral contraceptives. Once the threat of unwanted pregnancy had receded, pressure mounted to relax and even abolish the parietal rules that restricted contact between men and women. Colleges began experimenting with housing men and women in the same residence halls. As students expressed enthusiasm over these new living arrangements, and early research seemed to show no adverse effects on study habits or social behavior, "coed dorms" quickly became the norm.[45] In 1969–70, 77 percent of undergraduates still lived in single-sex dorms, 19 percent resided in dorms with men and women occupying alternate floors, and barely 3 percent lived in alternate rooms on the same floor. By 1989–90, only 10 percent remained in single-sex dorms, 40 percent lived in coed dorms with men and women on alternate floors, and 50 percent were housed in residences where men and women lived on the same floor.[46]

These changes had a marked effect on relations between the sexes.* Across the table in dormitory dining halls and in bull sessions in one another's rooms, men and women began

---

*Many of the findings reported in the next few paragraphs relate only to women, because the author found much more research on the behavior and reactions of women on coed campuses than about men.

to form close friendships of a kind that had previously been uncommon. By century's end, when college seniors were asked to name their five best friends, it was rare to find respondents listing only members of their own sex.

At the same time, with women and men living in such close proximity and alcohol readily accessible, casual sex also became more common. In a recent poll, 91 percent of students reported that "hooking up"—an ambiguous term that may or may not include sexual intercourse but is typically free of genuine affection or desire for a continuing relationship—was very common or fairly common on their campuses. Of the women surveyed, 40 percent acknowledged having "hooked up" themselves.[47]

The social roles of women and men have also undergone a marked change. In earlier decades, males would almost always initiate relationships by asking women to go on dates or "go steady" or engage in sexual intercourse. Today women are much more likely than they once were to take the lead. Moreover the frequency of the traditional date—in which a man asks a woman to go to a movie or a party or a dance at his expense—has declined sharply (though it has by no means disappeared). Women and men are much more likely to go places in informal groups, with all participants paying for themselves. Whatever its merits, this practice has at least helped remove some of the anxiety students previously shared over not being asked for dates or, in the case of men, being turned down.

In the current campus environment, the role of women on campus and the nature of their relationships with men resist easy generalizations. More women today are undoubtedly planning on professional school and a career, and the average age at which they marry has consequently increased substantially. Yet campuses exist where romance still trumps everything else, much as it did in the 1940s and 1950s. As Dorothy Holland and Margaret Eisenhart discovered in interviewing women at two Southern colleges, "Gender relations dominated student culture and activities. . . . Even women who came to [the university] with other interests and intentions found themselves surrounded by a peer culture that encouraged them toward romance. . . . Everybody had to deal with the peer culture and being discussed, evaluated, and ranked in terms of attractiveness to men."[48]

Although it is sometimes said that dating has disappeared from college campuses, recent surveys show that half of all senior women claim to have had at least six dates in the course of their undergraduate careers. Similarly, whereas attitudes toward sex have undoubtedly become more permissive, with many more students thinking that premarital sex is perfectly acceptable, approximately one-third of senior women still report that they have never had intercourse.[49] By most informed accounts, moreover, just as in the case of racial segregation on campus, students believe that there is much more sexual activity at their colleges than would appear to be the case on the basis of reports from undergraduates about their own behavior.

With relations between the sexes becoming so varied and with many norms and tacit understandings having disappeared, undergraduates today find it harder than their forebears did to know what behavior is expected and acceptable. Who is supposed to ask whom for a date? Who makes romantic overtures? What kind of sex life should a student have now that the range of possibilities has expanded to include everything from a chaste, old-fashioned relationship to the most casual, emotionless sex on first meeting?

Although much is now uncertain and confusing in relationships between men and women, two positive results have occurred. First of all, the advent of coed dormitories—whatever their other pros and cons—has greatly increased opportunities for men and women to discuss, argue, and explore ideas together. True friendships between the sexes have become a commonplace, not an exception. These relationships have produced greater understanding, more relaxed and easy interaction, and less stereotyping. As Ernest Pascarella and Patrick Terenzini note, "research indicates that the equality of men and women—socially, educationally, occupationally, and within the family—becomes more accepted by students of both sexes during the college years."[50] The gains during college are approximately the same for both sexes, although, not surprisingly, women begin and end their college careers with more liberal views on this subject than their male classmates.

A second positive result of contemporary college life is that overwhelming majorities of students on most residential campuses are satisfied with their social and living arrangements. An impressive 86 percent of undergraduate women agreed in a recent national survey that "co-ed dorms are a good thing." An even larger proportion—88 percent—declared that they were pleased with the social life on their campuses.[51] Cynics will retort that coed dorms and easy sex naturally meet with wide approval. Yet anyone who talks with undergraduates knows that support for their living conditions rests on much more solid foundations and much deeper and more rewarding human relationships than casual sex.

As for the "hooking up" that occurs in coed dorms, opinions will vary sharply. Many adults look askance at such behavior, feeling that it cheapens the most intimate relationship between a man and a woman while producing much confusion and self-recrimination on the part of inexperienced young people. Others regard such behavior as a part of growing up, while pointing out that, in an American culture saturated with images of explicit sex, casual intercourse often begins long before young people come to college.

Whatever one's opinions on this controversial subject, one conclusion will command general agreement. Students should not have sex forced upon them against their will. It is extremely difficult to measure the extent of unwanted sex in college, since definitions vary widely and the findings rest on self-reports of questionable validity. According to several careful studies, however, 15–30 percent of college women claim to have experienced rape or attempted rape at least once.[52] In more than 80 percent of these incidents the perpetrator was reportedly known to the victim, and in almost 60 percent of the cases the act in question occurred on a date.*

As any caring parent would affirm, colleges should take vigorous steps to overcome this problem, whatever its incidence may be. But finding effective remedies is far from easy. Proper disciplinary procedures and appropriate penalties are plainly necessary, but proving acquaintance rape or attempted rape is often impossible, since the man and woman involved are usually the only witnesses and their memory is frequently clouded by drinking. Because alcohol seems to be involved in such a high percentage of these incidents, efforts to discourage its use are an obvious solution, at least in theory. In practice, however, controlling alcohol has proved extremely difficult, especially when so many social activities take place away from the college.

---

*Since this chapter has to do with relationships between male and female undergraduates, I do not take up the issue of sexual overtures by faculty members toward their students.

Institutions have also tried to "harden the campus" by improving lighting, installing emergency telephones, and providing escort services for women after dark. Unfortunately, although such measures may cut down on robberies and assaults, they do little to curb unwanted sex, which typically involves acquaintances, not strangers, and usually occurs in settings such as parked cars, dormitory rooms, and fraternities rather than in dark, secluded areas on campus. Another popular response is to stress protective measures ranging from self-defense and assertiveness training to warnings not to walk alone on campus, drink immoderately, or enter fraternities unescorted. While these measures may reduce unwanted sex, they seem to place the responsibility entirely on women and can even interfere significantly with a woman's right to enjoy a normal campus life.

For all their deficiencies, most of the measures just described deserve a place in a comprehensive program to reduce sexual assaults. But a full response to the problem is hardly complete without some serious effort to change the male culture that seems so often implicated in cases of rape or attempted rape. Research suggests that a disproportionate percentage of sexual assaults involve men from particular fraternities, athletic teams, or all-male residences which often breed attitudes that having coercive sex is "macho," that men and women are in a competition in which the object is for the male to "score," and that women who say no really mean yes.[53] Changing such attitudes—through education or by organizing countervailing peer networks—could be a helpful means of getting at the root of the problem. A few colleges have already taken steps to form organizations of male students for this purpose.[54]

Fortunately there is evidence that attitudes toward unwanted sex among all students tend to improve, albeit modestly, during college.[55] Even so, experience suggests that altering behavior will be difficult. Many researchers believe that the stereotypes and beliefs involved are firmly in place long before students come to college. No one seems to know for sure how to go about eradicating them. As yet, few attempts to do so have been identified and described, and even fewer have been carefully evaluated. Among the handful of assessments made, some successes have been reported, but several others have found that the program in question either failed to cause even a temporary change in male attitudes or did not produce any lasting effect.[56]

Amid these difficulties, a few propositions seem reasonably clear. Campus officials who respond to reports of unwanted sex by trying to ignore the issue—and there are some who do—are making a mistake. The problem is too serious, and probably too widespread, to brush aside in this fashion. Officials who do make conscientious efforts to respond seem wise in taking a variety of steps, from imposing strict penalties to educating students about the problem and encouraging women to take sensible preventive measures.* Because alcohol is so often implicated in unwanted sex (and various other misadventures), programs to limit drinking are definitely worthwhile even if they are only partially effective. Eventually, through a process of trial and error, colleges may

---

*As with efforts to discourage racial intolerance, programs to reduce unwanted sex can get out of hand. At one Ivy League university, for example, women created an uproar by posting pictures throughout the campus of a male student previously found to have engaged in unwanted physical contact; see Sarah Crichton, Debra Rosenberg, Stanley Holmes, Martha Brant, Donna Foote, and Nina Biddle, "Sexual Correctness: Has It Gone Too Far?," *Newsweek* (October 25, 1993), p. 52. At another college, authorities introduced a code of conduct requiring men to obtain explicit permission from their partners for each stage of sexual contact from kissing through intercourse.

arrive at better strategies than they currently possess to cope with this vexing problem.

TOWARD A COMPREHENSIVE PROGRAM OF INTERPERSONAL RELATIONS

Efforts to promote understanding among blacks and whites and men and women are not the only ways to improve the interpersonal capabilities of students. A full agenda could include many other items as well: developing the skills of collaboration, persuasion, and negotiation; expanding capacities for leadership; improving the ability to listen perceptively and acquire greater insight into the feelings and motivations of others. In earlier times, colleges rarely paid attention to this agenda but simply threw students together in living units and extracurricular activities, leaving them to learn for themselves how to get along with one another. The growth of diversity programs, however, coupled with the progress of researchers in exploring other aspects of human relations, invites the question whether colleges should recognize the development of interpersonal skills as a major aim of undergraduate education, to be consciously pursued through a mixture of formal coursework and extracurricular experiences.*

*Up to now, the impact of college on interpersonal competence has been hard to interpret. According to George D. Kuh, the percentage of seniors reporting that they have made "very much" or "quite a bit" of progress in interpersonal relations during college has varied from 75 to 79 percent from 1969 to 1997; "How Are We Doing? Tracking the Quality of the Undergraduate Experience," 22 *Journal of Higher Education* (1999), p. 99. But most studies based on standardized tests of interpersonal competence report little or no gain; Ernest T. Pascarella and Patrick T. Terenzini, *How College Affects Students*, Vol. 2, p. 225. Overall, in the words of Pascarella and Terenzini, "the evidence on the net effects of college on student abil-

This issue will surely arouse strong feelings on either side. On the one hand, traditionalists will argue that the study of human relations, at least in terms as broad as this chapter suggests, has not reached sufficient maturity to warrant an important place in the curriculum. Courses on topics such as leadership, cooperation, and sensitivity to others arguably lack a substantial base of empirically tested observations. At best, such subjects are little more than a kind of skill training akin to learning the rules of etiquette or the methods for running a productive meeting—useful things to know but hardly the stuff of serious undergraduate teaching. At worst, such training can degenerate into attempts to teach students how to manipulate others for personal advantage.

On the other hand, proponents will point out that interpersonal competence is vitally important to many students. Success in life often requires it. Employers increasingly demand it. The nation needs it if America is to maintain a cohesive society and an effective democracy with a population increasingly splintered by racial, religious, and ideological differences. Happiness itself comes in no small measure from having fulfilling personal relationships. In short, the subject is simply too important to be ignored during such a formative time in students' lives.

As for the claim that courses in interpersonal relations consist of teaching "mere" skills or, worse yet, the black arts of manipulation, much the same could be said of classes on writing. Yet composition has long been a compulsory course in most American colleges. Besides, the study of interpersonal relations has certainly progressed beyond a mixture

---

ities to interact in mature ways with their peers and others is mixed, methodologically weak, and thus inconclusive"; *How College Affects Students*, p. 234.

of self-evident banalities and unsubstantiated theories. Most important aspects of the subject rest on substantial bodies of research and appear in regular courses offered by psychology departments and professional schools.

The differences of opinion over interpersonal competence must be seen as part of a more pervasive tension, mentioned in Chapter 2. On the one hand, most liberal arts professors are chiefly interested in conveying knowledge and understanding, the more profound and the more empirically verifiable the better. On the other hand, most students (and the organizations that employ them) are increasingly preoccupied by a need for skills—not just critical thinking and writing skills but oral communication, listening, quantitative reasoning, and, now, interpersonal competence.

There is nothing intrinsically wrong with this tension; universities are always involved in reconciling the views of the professoriate with the demands of the larger society. But tensions of this kind can be resolved in better and worse ways. One way is to recognize the needs of the outside world and somehow reconcile them with the views and capabilities of the faculty in a manner that respects the legitimate claims of both sides. The other is to provide for coursework on skills but put it in the hands of graduate students or part-time instructors, so as to leave the regular faculty uninvolved. The latter alternative leads to the problems encountered in teaching basic writing, oral communication, and foreign languages. More and more of the education important to undergraduates will be relegated to instructors who are not selected with the care accorded to faculty appointments nor given the training, the supervision, and the compensation to ensure high standards of quality.

The ultimate fate of efforts to teach interpersonal skills has yet to be determined. In all probability, the issue will eventually be resolved on most campuses not by a decisive faculty vote but by the gradual accumulation of separate courses and extracurricular programs that address particular facets of the problem. Illustrations of this process have cropped up repeatedly in these pages through references to such initiatives as mandatory classes on diversity, courses on oral communication, programs of gender studies, experiments in group learning, sessions for incoming freshmen on racial awareness or sexual relations, and coed dormitories. Eventually a wide variety of activities will exist on almost every campus having to do in one way or another with helping individuals learn to live and work together more fruitfully. The question for America's colleges, then, will not be whether to pay serious attention to interpersonal relations. Rather the choice will be whether colleges continue to address the subject in a piecemeal, uncoordinated fashion or whether they acknowledge it as an important aim of college and try to weave its disparate elements into an effective, integrated whole.

9 | PREPARING FOR A
GLOBAL SOCIETY

The world outside the United States received surprisingly little attention from America's colleges prior to World War II. As late as 1940, fewer than two-tenths of 1 percent of the nation's 150,000 professors were specialists in international subjects, and students from abroad were few and far between on American campuses. All that changed after 1945. The Cold War helped to keep the United States from drifting into isolationism as it had following World War I. Scholars and scientists quickly became important sources of ideas and expertise to support the nation's international policies. Government agencies and major foundations actively encouraged universities to train additional specialists in foreign affairs and conduct more research on global issues. Language study flourished, international relations courses multiplied, and area centers sprung up to foster interdisciplinary work on every major region of the world. Through these efforts, America became the acknowledged leader in internationalizing higher education. By 1980, more than 20 universities *each* employed more professors in international subjects than the 200 or so that had existed in the entire United States only 40 years before.[1]

Unfortunately, the growth of international research and expertise in American universities has not been matched by increasing global sophistication on the part of students coming to college. Studies have repeatedly shown that young people in the United States have less knowledge of world affairs than their counterparts in most other industrialized nations. For example, in a test prepared by a panel of experts to determine students' knowledge of international affairs, freshmen at American colleges answered only 42 percent of the questions correctly, and scores improved from freshman to senior year by only 10 percent.[2] Another test administered in 1986 by the National Geographic Society found that Americans aged 18–24 had less knowledge of geography and related international matters than their counterparts in all eight of the other countries tested. The United States also enjoyed the dubious distinction of being one of only two countries in which young adults were less informed about world affairs than their fellow citizens from older age groups. Worse yet, young Americans performed less well than a comparable group of the same age that had taken a similar test 40 years before.[3]

Clearly colleges have a responsibility to try to remove such ignorance and prepare their students adequately for lives increasingly affected by events beyond our borders. America has become the principal actor in an increasingly interdependent world, and government officials, business executives, and professionals of many kinds must be prepared to work effectively in and with foreign countries and cultures. In this global environment, what do today's undergraduates need to learn? What should colleges do to prepare them for the worldwide challenges that lie ahead?

Four objectives seem especially important to guide universities in this task.

First, the federal government and private organizations with extensive international interests will require the services of increasing numbers of specialists who are fluent in foreign languages and highly knowledgeable about particular countries, regions, and international problems. These experts may have to acquire much of their specialized learning in graduate school. But colleges can help them develop an interest in obtaining such knowledge and give them an intellectual foundation on which to build through subsequent study.

Second, all undergraduates need to learn something about international relations, global problems, and America's role in the world in order to be well enough informed to meet their obligations as citizens. International issues are often vital to the nation, and America's policies are shaped, at least in general ways, by public opinion. It is important, therefore, that colleges prepare their students to know enough to arrive at reasonably informed, thoughtful views on world affairs.

Third, more and more college graduates will find themselves traveling abroad and making decisions as executives and professionals on matters affected by people and events beyond our borders. Colleges must help their students gain enough sensitivity to other societies to understand foreign cultures and function effectively in an increasingly cosmopolitan environment.

Fourth, college graduates should know enough about other nations and cultures to give them a better understanding of their own country and the complex of customs, values, and institutions they have come to take for granted. It is difficult for anyone to fully comprehend and evaluate our distinctive form of government, our institutions and policies, or our attitudes toward freedom, equality, individual responsibility, and other important values without some awareness of the practices and beliefs in other societies and the reasons behind the similarities and differences. Colleges are uniquely situated to provide this comparative perspective.

It is easier to describe the goals of an international studies program than to figure out how to accomplish them. Each of the many nations in the world has its own history, language, culture, and political system. No one knows which countries will assume critical importance in the lives of today's undergraduates. Who could have predicted 50 years ago that the United States would find itself preoccupied with Bosnia, Afghanistan, and Iraq? Who could have known that China would become a major market for American business or that radical Islam would pose a major threat? In the face of such imponderables, how can colleges possibly prepare their students to comprehend the multitude of countries, cultures, and global problems that may eventually affect their lives and careers?

Martha Nussbaum illustrates the problem by offering the following account of what a mythical young college graduate called Anna ought to know to be prepared for an assignment by her corporate employer to open a Beijing office:

> She needs to know how Chinese people think about work (and not to assume there is just one way); she needs to know how cooperative networks are formed, and what misunderstandings might arise in interactions between Chinese and American workers. Knowledge of recent Chinese history is important, since the disruptions of the Cultural Revolution still shape workers' attitudes. Anna also needs to consider her response to the recent policy of urging women to return to the home, and to associated practices of laying off women first. This means she should know something about Chinese gender relations, both in the Confucian tradition and more recently. She should probably know something about academic women's studies in the United States, which have influenced the women's studies movement in Chinese universities. She certainly needs a more general view of human

rights, and about to what extent it is either legitimate or wise to criticize another nation's way of life. In the future, Anna may find herself dealing with problems of anti-African racism, and with recent government attempts to exclude immigrants who test positive for the human immunodeficiency virus. Doing this well will require her to know something about the history of Chinese attitudes about race and sexuality. It will also mean being able to keep her bearings even when she knows that the society around her will not accept her view.[4]

Even a cursory reading of the rest of Nussbaum's book reveals that the preceding summary, daunting as it is, is only a partial list of the subjects Anna ought to know. She will also need to understand the Chinese language, be conversant with the country's literature, and have some acquaintance with its religion and philosophy. She will surely have to know something about the way the Chinese government works and how the Communist regime behaves toward business. This is a formidable list of needs. How to satisfy them is a difficult problem, the more so since Anna could not have known in college that she would find herself in Beijing and may, in any event, be relocated in a couple of years to Budapest, Bangalore, or Buenos Aires.

Faced with this challenge, Nussbaum scatters proposals for required courses throughout her book. "All students should gain some understanding of the major world religions." "It seems sensible for students to be required to study in some depth one non-Western culture." "Given the history of our nation, it is imperative for all citizens to understand the achievements and sufferings of its African-American people." We must acquaint all students "with some fundamentals about the histories and cultures of many different groups." "All students should also master a foreign language, to a level of proficiency that makes possible the reading of newspapers and simple literary texts, and the understanding of radio and television broadcasts."[5]

How to fit all these requirements into a curriculum and still leave room to fulfill the other important goals of a liberal education is a problem Nussbaum never addresses.[6] Even so, if her prescription seems too ambitious to be practical, at least she offers a plan. Most educators do not even do that. More than 80 percent of university presidents (and more than 70 percent of all chief executives of four-year colleges agree that internationalizing undergraduate education is "very important."[7] However, after asking some 40 or so presidents how to provide a suitable international education, Richard Lambert and a team of investigators reported that "we did not discover, nor could we offer, any completely satisfactory answer."[8]

OPPORTUNITIES FOR GLOBAL EDUCATION

Although blueprints for internationalizing undergraduate education may be in short supply, one can at least identify the principal opportunities that most American colleges provide for gaining greater understanding of the world. One obvious example is the wide array of courses on other countries and cultures available in subjects and departments ranging from political science and anthropology to literature and the arts. Another is the chance to learn a foreign language. Still another is the possibility that exists in most colleges to go abroad to work or study. Finally, the presence of foreign students on American campuses gives opportunities for American undergraduates to gain a greater understanding of other cultures, values, and perspectives. Each of these ingredients has something important to offer in preparing students to live more cosmopolitan lives.

Coursework. Although most college presidents give a high priority to "internationalizing" their institution, barely half of American four-year colleges require even a single international course (other than foreign language classes), and more than 60 percent of those that do demand only one course. No more than 10 percent of four-year colleges require as many as three international courses.[9] Overall, according to Richard Lambert, undergraduates in the late 1980s completed on average approximately 2.5 international courses during their college careers. (Students at liberal arts colleges took an average of 4.4 courses.) Half of these offerings were in literature or history with another 10–15 percent in the arts, while only 10–15 percent of the courses were in political science and less than 5 percent were in economics.[10]

More recent data on the total number of international courses students take are not available, but there is little reason to believe that the figures have shifted dramatically. The American Council on Education issued a report in 2003 which found that almost half of the undergraduates in four-year colleges had taken no international courses during the preceding year, while fewer than one-third had taken as many as two courses.[11]

Only a small minority of students appear to take any coursework that would prepare them as citizens to understand America's role in the world and the global problems that confront it. Findings from the Department of Education suggest that fewer than 10 percent of undergraduates ever take a class in international relations while only 5 percent or less take courses in foreign policy, international trade and finance, or comparative government.[12]

Much larger numbers of students take classes in literature, history, and foreign languages that could conceivably help them to understand other cultures and cultural perspectives. Nevertheless, the data do not show how many of these courses are specifically designed to teach students how to understand another society or appreciate cultural differences in values, customs, public policies, and the like. The best guess one can make is that the vast majority of offerings, say, in French literature or European history, are taught from the standpoint of the instructor's discipline and that insights into contemporary cultures are largely incidental to the main purposes of the course.

In fairness, one should add that most undergraduates are now required to take a course on diversity and multiculturalism. Such offerings take many forms, and only a minority of them are devoted to foreign cultures. Still, roughly one-third of all four-year colleges require a course "that primarily feature[s] perspectives, issues or events from countries or areas other than Canada, Australia, or Western Europe."[13] Moreover, even classes having to do with the experience of women or minority groups in the United States try to teach students to appreciate values, life experiences, and attitudes different from their own. Presumably such courses seek to encourage qualities of tolerance, empathy, and sensitivity to other perspectives that enter into the appreciation of any foreign culture.

All in all, the preparation given to students both as citizens in a country deeply affected by world events and as professionals likely to be engaged with foreign cultures seems haphazard at best. Courses do exist in most colleges that could help to meet these needs if students only chose to enroll. But opportunities are one thing and taking advantage of them quite another. Although the data leave much to be desired, it is a safe bet that a majority of undergraduates complete their four years with very little preparation either as citizens or as professionals for the international challenges that are likely to confront them.

The possibilities for would-be specialists in international affairs are considerably brighter. As of 1990, more than three-quarters of all universities and 44 percent of four-year colleges offered a major in at least one international subject. More than one-quarter of all colleges and more than a third of universities offered majors in international relations, while a small but growing fraction of undergraduate business programs include an international business concentration.[14] In addition, most research universities offer a wealth of courses not only in international politics and economics but in the history, sociology, and culture of different regions of the world. True, not every college provides these opportunities, so that some students who decide to pursue an international career may have to transfer to find a college that can give them the foundation of knowledge they seek. Even so, this burden is hardly insurmountable. Besides, it would be hopelessly uneconomical for every college to try to provide the full array of courses and faculty needed to give a suitable preparation for the small minority of students seeking to specialize in some aspect of international studies.

Foreign Languages. Amid all the talk about globalization and the growing interdependence of nations, more than 80 percent of college faculty members agree (either "strongly" or "somewhat") that language courses should be required of all students. Surprisingly, however, fewer colleges require language study for at least some students (73 percent) than was true in 1966 (89 percent), while the share of total college course enrollments devoted to language learning dropped from 16 percent in the 1960s to 8 percent in the late 1970s and has not risen since. Where language courses are mandatory, requirements tend to be quite modest; fewer than 20 percent of four-year colleges demand more than two years of study.[15] Among all undergraduates, a majority never move beyond elementary courses, while fewer than 15 percent are enrolled in advanced classes.

As currently organized and practiced, language teaching has much in common with English composition. Like composition, it is usually located in literature departments, and its goals are a matter of dispute. Some teachers stress proficiency in speaking; others seek competence in reading; still others call for understanding other cultures as revealed through their languages.[16] Those who look upon language learning as a skill and stress its practical uses remain at odds with those who regard it as an entrée to foreign literatures. Meanwhile, the variety of teaching methods exceeds even the number of different approaches to teaching composition, although too little research has yet been done to determine which techniques are most effective.*

*See, for example, Alice O'Maggio, *Teaching Language in Context* (1986). Behaviorism (with its love of drill and positive reinforcement), Chomskyite linguistics, and cognitive psychology have all given rise to separate schools of thought on the subject. Various groups have argued, and still argue, for their own distinctive approach: total immersion in the language, careful sequencing of material from the known to the unknown, speaking English in class, not allowing English to be spoken, emphasizing grammar, not emphasizing grammar, total physical response (beginning with listening and calling on physical movement to facilitate understanding), role playing, listening to music to promote understanding, and more. Although no one knows which of these methods are most effective, differences in course objectives and in the learning styles and preconceptions of different students probably call for a variety of approaches in any event.

Embedded in literature departments, language teaching suffers from many of the same problems that have afflicted writing programs. Since many literature professors look upon language learning as a simple skill that is easy to teach, instruction in Ph.D.-granting institutions is usually delegated to inexperienced graduate students.[17] Although language departments increasingly offer some form of preparation for these teaching assistants, such training is not universal and is often superficial, especially for those teaching languages other than French, German, and Spanish. Only rarely are instructors prepared enough to adjust their teaching to meet differing student needs or to take advantage of new pedagogical methods and technologies that might increase interest and enhance learning.

The weaknesses of language programs have been cited repeatedly by experienced practitioners. After surveying enrollments in language courses nationwide, Richard Lambert has concluded that "many students stick with language learning for so brief a time that any hope of providing even a minimum level of communicative competence is slim."[18] According to Wilga Rivers, long-time professor of foreign languages at Harvard, while competency in language speaking is more creative than imitative, "many language teachers continue to teach as though imitation, repetition, and reconstruction and transformation of models were the be-all and end-all of language learning."[19] Little research has been done on the effects of language teaching, and even the evidence on whether formal instruction has *any* effect on language acquisition is skimpy and weak at best.[20] Under these conditions, it is not surprising that only 8.1 percent of the thousands of college seniors surveyed by Alexander Astin felt that their foreign language skills had grown "much stronger" over the course of their undergraduate careers.[21]

Education Abroad. Programs of foreign study offer another way of learning to understand and adapt to other cultures. Although such programs have existed for a long time, their number has grown substantially in the past few decades. Eighty-five percent of our colleges now provide them, and the total number of undergraduates receiving credit for such study exceeded 160,000 in 2001–2.[22] Experience of this kind can benefit undergraduates in multiple ways.[23] Their ability to speak and understand a foreign language is likely to improve, especially if their stay abroad lasts for a semester or more and they live with a foreign family or are otherwise forced to use the native language frequently. In all probability, a stay of substantial length in active contact with foreign nationals will also yield many of the fruits of a well-taught course on another culture: a loss of parochialism, a greater realism about other societies, and an abiding sense of their complexity and the hazards of easy generalization. There is evidence that education abroad can produce significant attitudinal changes as well: greater interest in world affairs, greater commitment to peace and international cooperation, and greater appreciation of the differing views and customs encountered in other nations.[24] Beyond these benefits, several studies suggest that living in a different culture helps many students gain self-confidence, independence, and an ability to function in complex environments.[25]

In its current form, however, overseas education (or service work abroad) achieves far less than it might in increasing the global understanding of undergraduates. Although the numbers participating in such programs are increasing, they still reach only 12 percent of all full-time, four-year college students.[26] For part-time students, who now make up roughly one-quarter of the four-year college population, going abroad is generally impossible, since most have jobs they cannot afford to leave. Even for those who do participate, overseas programs are often too brief to bring substantial results. Rather than spending the "junior year abroad" that was so common in the 1950s, more than 70 percent of American undergraduates currently studying in foreign countries are enrolled in programs of six months or less. Most of them choose countries reasonably similar to the United States. Britain is the leading choice, followed by France, Spain, Italy, and Germany. Fewer than one-fifth of all undergraduates studying overseas go to non-Western nations where the cultural differences are greatest and the impact on parochial attitudes is likely to be most profound.[27]

Whatever the country chosen, opportunities to study abroad often fail to give students a deep engagement with a different culture. Like other pieces in the mosaic of international studies, such programs are seldom closely coordinated with other parts of the curriculum that might prepare participants to make the most of their overseas experience. More than one-third of the undergraduates who go abroad have never studied the language of their host country, and barely 20 percent of those who do have prior training have progressed beyond the beginner's level.[28] Most have never studied the history, politics, or culture of the country they are visiting. With such skimpy preparation, only a minority of enterprising students truly immerse themselves in the local society. Fewer than 10 percent are enrolled as regular students in a foreign university with many of the rest ending up in courses specially designed for Americans. All in all, therefore, most overseas study programs fall far short of their full potential in teaching students about other cultures and societies.[29]

International Students. The final contribution to internationalizing undergraduate education is supplied by the growing number of foreign students on campus. By now, close to half a million of these students are enrolled in American universities, more than 15 times the number only 50 years ago. Since undergraduates learn so much from one another, the presence of many young people from different countries could be a valuable resource in opening minds to other values, traditions, and perspectives.

As in the case of overseas study, however, the potential benefits of enrolling international students have not been fully realized on many campuses. To begin with, undergraduates from other countries, though large in numbers, still account for less than 3 percent of the total student body. Moreover they are not especially representative of the countries from which they come. Most are well-to-do, since two-thirds report that they receive no outside financial support.[30] Very small proportions come from the poorest countries. Furthermore, they are rarely sought out, as American students are, for their intellectual abilities or special talents. With relatively few exceptions, the only international students that colleges seriously recruit are children of wealthy parents (who, it is hoped, will eventually reward the college with a generous gift) and talented athletes capable of playing at the varsity level.

Although many international students enter into undergraduate life, not all manage to do so. Some are less than fluent, making easy social intercourse difficult. Others live off campus or in special residential units. Many socialize mainly among themselves, so that only those who are outgoing and gregarious have close contact with their American classmates. Thus far, few colleges have succeeded fully in overcoming these tendencies.[31]

Fortunately, the presence of students from abroad is augmented by the increasing numbers of undergraduates with fathers and mothers who have come to America from other countries. Most of these students are fully integrated into campus life. Most of them know a good deal about the cultures of their parents; many speak another language at home and have made special efforts to learn about the history and traditions of the countries from which their families came. While they may not equal international students in the depth and immediacy of their knowledge of other cultures, they nonetheless have much to contribute to broadening the perspectives of their classmates.

Looking for Results. It is hard to gauge how much college students gain over their four years in knowledge and understanding of the world outside America. The data are sparse and rather dated. The only comprehensive study of the subject was a test given by the Educational Testing Service in 1979 to three thousand undergraduates at 185 colleges. On an extensive multiple-choice exam graded from 0 to 100, the typical freshman scored only 41.9 percent. The average score of seniors improved, but only to 50.5 percent, a result the authors of the test termed "a smaller difference than one would expect of students who have had four years of higher education."[32] The other scrap of available evidence is the report already mentioned from Alexander Astin, revealing that only 8 percent of college seniors believed that their foreign language proficiency improved substantially in college.[33] Findings such as these are too fragmentary to be more than suggestive. However, taken together with the other findings previously discussed—on the courses students take, the extent of education abroad, and the amount of contact with international students—the overall impression is that most colleges do a modest job at best to prepare their students for the international challenges that await them.

BUILDING BETTER PROGRAMS

How then can colleges shape and strengthen the opportunities currently available to equip students for a more global, interdependent world? With so many countries, so many languages, and so many problems, the question has no easy answer. Specialists call for more of everything—more international courses, more education abroad, more language training, more foreign students. Still lacking on most campuses, however, is a thoughtful, comprehensive plan to combine these opportunities into well-integrated programs that can be fitted in with all the other legitimate aims of a rounded undergraduate education. What follows is only a preliminary sketch of the possibilities and problems college officials face in trying to achieve this goal.

Coursework. In considering college's role in preparing citizens, Chapter 7 described the need for a course that would acquaint undergraduates with the policies the United States has pursued in dealing with other nations, the institutional framework for addressing international problems, and the challenges posed by some of the more important global issues, such as those involving national security, human rights, international trade, and the environment. No offering of this kind can possibly anticipate all the questions that America will confront during the lifetime of the students. Still, a well-constructed course can at least awaken interest in foreign affairs, provide some familiarity with the kinds of considerations that enter into foreign policy, and explore the methods and procedures with which the United States and other nations try to resolve common problems. If nothing else, such courses can provide a framework for evaluating subsequent accounts of emerging issues and problems of an international nature.

In addition to taking courses on foreign policy and international relations, students need preparation in how to understand other countries and cultures. Here the practical problems seem especially formidable. Within the limited space available in the curriculum, students cannot hope to learn about even a small number of other nations in more than an extremely superficial way. Whatever the countries studied, they are unlikely to be the ones that will touch students' lives most directly after they graduate.

Martha Nussbaum makes some helpful suggestions for coping with this problem.[34] No course, or handful of courses, she admits, can give students all the information and insight they need to understand even the most important foreign countries and cultures. What *is* possible, Nussbaum argues, is to explore one country in such a way as to make students aware of the common misconceptions and parochialisms that many people have on first approaching another society and culture. Even a single course can teach students that values, habits, and attitudes many Americans take for granted are not widely shared and that people in other nations, though similar in some ways, are not "just like us" in every respect. Such a course can also reveal the differences between our institutions and our culture and those of other societies and why values and customs we consider fundamental are not universally accepted. A well-taught class can likewise temper the tendency of some undergraduates to romanticize other cultures, while helping others to recognize that Americans are not necessarily more virtuous or well intentioned or successful than people from other nations in addressing similar social problems. Above all, such courses can help students understand that other countries and cultures are far more complicated than one might think, that most sweeping generalizations oversimplify reality, and that prominent foreign statesmen and intellectuals are not always accurate in describing their own societies.

Ideally a college should go further and introduce foreign and comparative material into a number of courses in fields ranging from literature to economics and political science. Apart from reinforcing the international courses already described, comparative perspectives would enrich the study of our own society. It is hard to fully appreciate the strengths and weaknesses of our political system without comparing it with parliamentary democracies or multiparty states. It is equally difficult to grasp American culture without contrasting it with other cultures or to evaluate our health care system and our policies for dealing with other social problems without comparing them with their counterparts in Europe, Canada, and Japan. Unfortunately experience shows that introducing new material through the curriculum is a goal more often prescribed than achieved. Success is likely only if college officials are prepared to press the point repeatedly and offer time off and modest sums of money to help professors undertake the considerable effort of revising their courses appropriately. Although most colleges have not yet taken these steps, a substantial minority do arrange workshops and offer funding for faculty members seeking to introduce comparative material into their classes.[35]

Foreign Languages. No issue in the field of international education has received more attention than the appropriate role of language learning in the undergraduate curriculum. A threshold issue is the much-debated question of whether or not to require all students to study at least one foreign language. Proponents emphasize the growing likelihood that college graduates will eventually find themselves needing to speak another tongue. That is the justification most often mentioned by those outside the university. Within the academy, foreign language professionals are less inclined to stress such practical considerations, preferring subtler arguments that appeal more to the scholarly community. Some point out that studying foreign languages is an excellent way to overcome ethnocentrism and promote interest in other cultures.[36] Others observe that such study can help bring about a deeper understanding of one's own language.

Those who oppose requirements, however, have strong arguments of their own. Forcing unwilling undergraduates to learn a foreign language can be unpleasant for instructors and unproductive for the students. It is not altogether obvious that the need for language competence justifies such burdens. Despite increasing globalization, not everyone will have to speak and read a foreign language. Some will travel very little. Even professionals who do go abroad frequently may be able to get by without knowing the language now that English is increasingly becoming the lingua franca for the worldwide business, legal, and scientific communities.

An even more persuasive argument against requirements is that undergraduates seldom know where they will be in later life, let alone what foreign languages they will need. As a result, college graduates who will eventually use another language are likely to find that the one they want is not the one they studied. Even if they are fortunate enough to need the very language they have learned, they will rarely have gained enough fluency as undergraduates to allow them to function easily in a foreign culture. The Foreign Service estimates that 240 classroom hours are required to enable their officials merely to conduct a basic conversation about a familiar subject in one of the "easy" languages.[37] Non-Western languages require twice as much time. (Bear in mind that Foreign Service officers are intelligent, highly motivated, and taught under optimum conditions.) These 240 hours are the equivalent of more than five three-hour-per-week semester courses, a total well beyond what most colleges require and most undergraduates take. As a practical matter, it is highly unlikely that many colleges will agree to increase their requirements to the recommended level.

The remaining reasons for requiring languages are equally unconvincing. There have been very few attempts to test the effect of foreign languages in overcoming ethnocentrism, and the only major study that exists found no significant relationship.[38] Conceivably, a foreign language course could convey something useful about another culture; certainly experienced language instructors often speak of trying to build cultural awareness into their teaching.[39] Still, it seems unlikely that language classes can do as much to foster such awareness as a course specifically designed for the purpose.[40] Few of the graduate students and adjunct instructors who currently staff language courses are trained to teach about foreign cultures, and the time they can devote to the subject will be limited in a course designed primarily to help students learn to speak and read effectively. Under these conditions, efforts to convey cultural understanding may amount to little more than dubious generalizations of the kind mentioned approvingly in one well-known text: "In examining the role of fast food restaurants in American society, students begin to see how much Americans tend to value convenience, efficiency, and cleanliness."*

---

*Alice O'Maggio, *Teaching Language in Context* (1986), p. 397. Much the same can be said about the role of language courses in helping students understand more about English. Although the study of French or German may give students insights about the structure and properties of their own language, this claim has not been tested rigorously. Without such evidence, one can hardly assume that learning another tongue will

Despite the objections to making students study foreign languages, such a step may be warranted under certain circumstances. In one college, for example, Richard Light discovered that undergraduates rated language courses more highly than any other group of courses in the curriculum except for classes in literature taught in the appropriate foreign language. A stunning 94 percent of the alumni urged as much language training as possible, while 97 percent were in favor of maintaining a requirement.[41]

With such a strong vote of confidence from students and alumni, compulsory language training may be justified. The same cannot be said under prevailing conditions on most campuses. Often it is unclear whether the requirement exists to teach undergraduates to function effectively in another country or to serve the interests of the literature departments in supporting their graduate students. In either case, the usual result is a dreary compromise that requires enough study to interfere with students' freedom without demanding enough to make them reasonably proficient in the language of their choice.

Whether or not colleges *require* language study, they should certainly *encourage* students to become competent in another tongue. Although most undergraduates take less than two years of language study, surprising numbers of entering freshmen bring some linguistic ability with them. More than 90 percent have studied a foreign language in high school; more than 40 percent claim to be able to read a novel or a textbook in another language; more than two-thirds even think that they can carry on informal conversation in a lan-

---

do as much as a course specifically designed to analyze the English language, especially since most foreign language instructors will have had little training in linguistics, psycholinguistics, or philology.

guage other than their own.[42] While these claims may be exaggerated, colleges could help students acquire a basic proficiency in a reasonable length of time by inducing more of them to build on their existing skills. Oddly, however, such sequencing does not seem to occur with any frequency, since fewer than 20 percent of the undergraduates who have taken language classes have enrolled in advanced courses.[43]

Aside from formal instruction for undergraduates of varying levels of ability, colleges can, and often do, encourage language learning in other ways. They can organize language tables in dormitories to encourage students to practice conversational skills. They can establish smaller living units emphasizing another culture with foreign language speakers as resident advisors. They can make serious language study a prerequisite for enrolling in attractive programs for study or internships abroad. For more advanced students, sections of courses on foreign literatures and cultures can be conducted in the native language.

None of these measures is likely to succeed, however, unless colleges take steps to ensure that their instruction is of high quality. This goal will be hard to reach if colleges rely primarily on graduate students and part-time adjunct instructors, especially if they are inadequately trained and told by senior faculty members not to take their teaching too seriously.[44] As in the case of composition, colleges will rarely succeed in teaching foreign languages well unless they devote the money and effort to recruit a talented and experienced cadre of instructors, provide them with proper training, compensate them adequately, and monitor their performance to make sure that high standards are maintained.

Education Abroad. Foreign study can supplement language learning and other international courses and thereby claim an important place in an overall strategy to help students become more cosmopolitan. But colleges will have to do much more if they are to capitalize on the possibilities. At present, the United States lags behind Europe in the numbers of students studying in other countries and in the extent to which they are integrated into the normal life of the host university. Programs in American colleges tend to be too short, too isolated from the surrounding society, and too often situated in cultures similar to our own. For greater effectiveness, students need to remain abroad for at least a semester. Before embarking on such study, undergraduates should be strongly encouraged to reach a minimum level of proficiency in the language of the country involved. In addition, they should either have to take a course or be asked to complete some form of orientation, with appropriate readings, about the country they will visit, so that they arrive with a rudimentary understanding of its history, political system, and culture. Finally, programs of education abroad should be designed to put participants in as much contact with the local society as their level of preparation permits. If they cannot take regular classes in a foreign university, they should at least live with foreign families and take some of their coursework in the language of the country.

International Students. Students from abroad can likewise contribute something to the international understanding of American undergraduates, especially if colleges make serious efforts to recruit more representative applicants and offer them the financial aid they will need in order to enroll. The most pressing challenge on many campuses is to integrate these students into the life of the college once they arrive on campus. All kinds of initiatives are possible for accomplishing this purpose, from encouraging Muslim students to participate in panel discussions on Middle East attitudes toward the United States to asking students from France to preside over French language tables for interested classmates. Many American colleges have programs that assign undergraduate volunteers to foreign students in order to learn one another's language or help introduce the newcomers to campus social life.[45] Probably the most effective strategy is simply to have international students reside with American classmates in undergraduate living units. This may be a hollow suggestion for the many colleges that house no more than a small fraction of their undergraduates. Even so, in the case of international students, as with all forms of diversity, the best way for undergraduates to learn from one another is not through taking classes but in the dorm room discussions, mealtime conversations, and other group activities that occur spontaneously in a student residence.

PROSPECTS FOR PROGRESS

Global understanding (for want of a better term) is a relatively new arrival among the goals of undergraduate education. Its meaning is still imperfectly understood, with no consensus that adequately defines the body of skills, attitudes, and knowledge needed to help students understand and negotiate a more interdependent world.[46] At best, educators have identified a set of educational experiences that would appear to be relevant and useful. How to put them together in the most effective, mutually reinforcing way remains obscure. It is much like knowing some of the ingredients for baking a cake but not what the finished cake would look like nor even what amounts and proportions of the ingredients to use.

Scholars who have thought most carefully about the problem emphasize the need to acquire what they commonly call "intercultural competence." Their reasons are highly practical. Undergraduates cannot possibly amass all the information they would need to know about even the most important foreign cultures with which they might come in contact. As a result, colleges find themselves in much the same position as law schools late in the nineteenth century, when it became impossible to teach students all the laws of all the states in which they might eventually practice. What law faculties did, following much initial resistance, was to shift from lecturing about existing legal rules and procedures to teaching students how to reason about legal problems after looking up the applicable rules and procedures for themselves. In much the same way, professors need to concentrate on teaching students how to explore other cultures on their own rather than showering them with facts about the history, institutions, and culture of particular foreign countries.

Of course, professors will still need to convey a certain amount of information about another country or culture. But such knowledge is less an end in itself than an illustrative body of material with which to develop attitudes and competencies that will help in understanding any foreign culture—attitudes such as openmindedness, tolerance, and respect for other perspectives and points of view, and competencies such as the ability to listen attentively, to be sensitive to other values and perspectives, to recognize differences and similarities, and to reason comparatively. Pursuing the legal analogy a step further, instructors in these courses must be chiefly concerned with teaching students to "think interculturally" much as law teachers devote themselves primarily to helping students to "think like a lawyer."

The difficulty with this objective is not just that "thinking interculturally" is as yet imperfectly understood. It is also a skill (as the term *intercultural competence* implies), and many Arts and Sciences professors are reluctant to teach skills. Given the opportunity, they will often choose to "cover" a body of knowledge and concepts rather than help their students to develop a competence, whether it be writing with clarity and style, thinking critically, or understanding another society. Thus courses on other cultures frequently turn into a series of detailed lectures on a foreign country, leaving students with much information about its history, institutions, and problems but with little capacity for understanding and adjusting to the different societies they will encounter in their later lives.

Another problem in helping students become more cosmopolitan has to do with the way colleges are organized rather than the way their professors teach. As previously described, successful international programs normally include several ingredients. By themselves, however, none of the component parts can accomplish much. Language learning in college rarely leads to proficiency if it is not coupled with overseas study or reinforced by advanced courses in literature and area studies taught in the appropriate foreign language. Courses on other cultures will ideally need to combine perspectives from several disciplines; moreover their impact will be greater and longer lasting if they lead to a period of overseas study, which in turn will be enriched by prior coursework on the country in question. Undergraduates who have studied overseas will benefit when they return if they reach out to foreign students from the country they visited and explore ideas and impressions derived from their time abroad. In all these ways, coordination becomes essential if the several ingredients are to combine to form a successful whole.

The needed integration requires the cooperation of several separate units of the university: the relevant Arts and Sciences departments, the international student office, the overseas study program, and the foreign language teachers scattered through the several literature departments. At present, unfortunately, effective collaboration among these units is the exception rather than the rule. As Richard Lambert points out, "what students are offered on a [typical] campus is a cafeteria of individual courses to choose from, with a menu that reflects the cumulative effect of hundreds of disaggregated decisions by departments as to whom they want to hire, or the decisions of individual faculty members [on what they want to teach]."[47]

Remedying this problem will be difficult. The structure and traditions of the American university do not lend themselves to close cooperation as well as those of European universities, which are more accustomed to receiving central direction from the state. Faculty departments in the United States are usually quite independent and resist outside pressure in making educational decisions. Other important actors, such as the international student office, are detached from any department and often lie entirely outside the faculty of Arts and Sciences. The units that need to work together are often unequal in status, a disparity that can further inhibit cooperation in subtle ways.

Such problems are hardly unique to international education. On the contrary, most faculties cling to a set of practices and understandings that resist efforts to achieve effective cooperation of any sort. The principle of academic freedom, originally conceived to safeguard a scholar's right to express unpopular ideas, has been stretched to protect individual professors from having to join any collaborative effort to improve the quality of teaching and learning. In turn, through a form of senatorial courtesy, departments enjoy almost complete freedom to decide for themselves how to construct their concentrations or whether to engage in interdisciplinary ventures proposed by deans or other departments.

One can understand why individual professors and departments wish to protect themselves from outside interference. Yet the prerogatives created to ensure such protection have unfortunate effects on the quality of undergraduate education. They undermine the teaching of composition by hampering attempts to develop programs of "writing across the curriculum." They inhibit efforts to secure closer cooperation between vocational departments and liberal arts faculties. They block collective action to keep concentrations from undermining other important aims of undergraduate education, such as developing moral reasoning, improving writing skills, or preparing citizens. And, just as clearly, they have blunted attempts on many campuses to build a properly integrated program to prepare students for a more cosmopolitan, interdependent world.

Under such difficult conditions, it is wise to proceed cautiously. Despite the vast scope of international studies, only two courses seem essential enough at present to be prescribed for all students: a basic course on America's role in the world to help equip undergraduates to be reasonably informed citizens and a course on how to understand another culture that prepares them for lives characterized by increasing contact with other societies. Beyond these two courses, colleges can try to introduce more comparative material into existing classes and encourage students to take advantage of a broad array of other opportunities—learning foreign languages, studying abroad, taking courses on a variety of international subjects. In addition, campus authorities can continue to create a more cosmopolitan environment by enrolling more foreign students, establishing residential units (or theme houses) built around other cultures, arranging forums and speeches on international issues, and providing countless other events and programs of an international nature. In time, the Internet may open even greater possibilities by allowing American undergraduates to join with students overseas in courses and seminars to discuss a wide variety of subjects, ranging from literature and culture to politics, economics, and environmental problems.

A last important step that is often neglected by college authorities is to work at developing better ways of measuring the extent to which their campuses are becoming internationalized. Current measures tend to focus on inputs—how many international courses are offered, how many undergraduates study abroad, how many international students are enrolled, and so forth. While answers to these questions may be better than nothing, they tell very little about how well the college has prepared undergraduates to live in a more interdependent world. It may be impossible for now to measure "intercultural competence" directly. But important ingredients, such as what percentage of undergraduates are proficient foreign language readers and speakers or how much they know about international affairs, can surely be assessed. Moreover, work can at least go forward to try to develop more comprehensive measures of intercultural competence. Without better ways of evaluating results, colleges will surely make much slower progress toward the goal of providing an effective international education.

In view of all the difficulties involved, it would be folly to expect dramatic improvements anytime soon. Developing successful introductory courses on understanding America's role in the world and approaching other cultures would be a big step forward. Beyond that, progress will probably have to consist of slow, incremental growth in the number of professors putting comparative material into their courses, the number of foreign students becoming integrated into campus life, and the number of American undergraduates choosing to take international courses, go abroad to study, or take a foreign language. Some campuses will achieve enough coordination among these several initiatives to bring the whole somewhat closer to the sum of its parts. Others may increase not merely the number of students taking language courses but the number achieving meaningful competence in another language, not simply the total of undergraduates enrolled in overseas programs but the total studying abroad with enough linguistic ability, enough knowledge of the host country, and enough immersion in the foreign culture to make the experience potentially transformative. Individually such forward steps may seem small. Collectively and over time, they can result in substantial progress toward giving students a more thorough international education.

It is impossible to predict how much improvement will occur or how soon. One hopeful sign, however, is that all the campus constituencies seem firmly agreed that progress needs to occur. Large majorities of students believe that it is important for their careers to understand other cultures and know more about international issues and events. Even larger majorities believe that international students enrich the learning of everyone. Well over half of professors and students alike agree ("strongly" or "somewhat") that all undergraduates should be required to take international courses, that all should have an opportunity for education abroad, and that all members of the faculty have a responsibility to help students be more aware of foreign affairs and foreign cultures.[48] With such widespread support, continued progress, however incremental and slow, seems all but certain to occur.

10 | ACQUIRING BROADER INTERESTS

"College has breathed new life into my mind and given me new views of things, a perception of new truths and of new aspects of the old ones."[1] These words, spoken by Helen Keller in 1904 on the eve of her graduation from Radcliffe College, epitomize what educators everywhere hope their undergraduate programs can achieve. Students receive many opportunities to breathe new life into their minds and acquire new views of things. A concentration in history, literature, or astronomy may set the stage for a lifelong engagement with the subject. The opportunity to choose electives allows undergraduates to explore latent interests in music, anthropology, or other intriguing subjects, while the chance many colleges give to take such courses pass-fail permits students to experiment without risk to their grade point averages. Outside the classroom, extracurricular activities provide yet another feast of potential interests to pursue in later life. Student orchestras, choral singers, dramatic societies, dance groups, campus newspapers, literary magazines, community service programs, political clubs—the list goes on and on. Commuter schools are likely to have fewer opportunities than residential colleges, and even the latter could provide better facilities and more coaching for some of their programs (say, in community service or the arts) by diverting part of the vast sums lavished on intercollegiate athletics. Still, the wealth of extracurricular pursuits is a distinctive feature of the American college and one of its glories too. Many lifelong interests are nurtured through these activities, and many lasting memories as well.

Amid these opportunities, the general education program represents the principal *curricular* means for expanding intellectual horizons and taking students beyond a narrow specialization to become more broadly cultivated. To be sure, general education is not only about providing breadth. In recent years, faculties have come to invest this segment of the curriculum with responsibility for many other aims of undergraduate education—improving moral reasoning, increasing racial tolerance, even teaching students to write well or speak a foreign language.* For the sake of clarity, however, the discussion that follows only concerns the attempts colleges make through general education to awaken intellectual interests and help undergraduates comprehend the world and their place in it with a greater breadth of understanding than they could achieve by concentrating on a single discipline or special field of study.

How to provide the necessary breadth has prompted a long and inconclusive debate. The discussion has focused primarily on four different schools of thought. The first of these calls for a careful study of the Great Books, the finest works of intellect and imagination produced by humankind. The second offers an introduction to a variety of important subjects and fields of human experience by having students take a series of survey courses on broad topics such as West-

---

*The new goals, with their accompanying requirements, have usually been added without increasing the space allotted in the curriculum to general education; D. Kent Johnson, James L. Ratcliff, and Jerry G. Gaff, "A Decade of Change in General Education," 125 *New Directions in Higher Education* (2004), pp. 9, 20. Hence the process of adding new goals threatens to reduce the space available for providing breadth to the point of seriously interfering with the original aims of general education.

ern civilization or science, values, and technology. A third, and newer, approach would organize the general education curriculum around the principal methods of thought by which human beings have tried to understand themselves and the world in which they live. The fourth and last method seeks to ensure a suitable breadth of study by simply requiring all students to choose a stipulated number of courses from each of several large categories of the curriculum, such as science, social science, and the humanities.

All four models have their supporters. The intensity with which each is promoted, however, varies inversely with the extent of its use. The most passionate advocates are those who support the Great Books—an approach that has never in a hundred years taken root in more than a tiny fraction of the nation's colleges. The least vocal group (indeed, one rarely hears their voice at all) consists of those favoring a simple distribution requirement, the option chosen in one guise or another by an overwhelming majority of all American colleges.

DISTRIBUTION REQUIREMENTS

Distribution requirements are the easiest model to describe and administer. In their simplest form, they merely call upon students to complete a certain number of courses or credit hours in each of three major areas—the sciences, the social sciences, and the humanities. Variations of this model also exist which create more narrowly defined categories that students must sample—for example, by dividing the sciences into biological and physical or the humanities into literature and the arts.

One attraction of simple distribution requirements is that students tend to prefer them to more prescriptive models. Most undergraduates will initially favor any system that gives them greater freedom to choose their own courses. By maximizing choice, supporters claim, distribution systems will also bring other educational benefits. Students will gravitate to subjects that seem especially interesting or to courses taught by professors with a reputation for first-rate teaching. The greater the choice the greater the chance that undergraduates fulfilling their distribution requirements will look forward to their courses instead of regarding them as unwanted intrusions that keep them from classes they would rather take. This rationale echoes the arguments made by champions of the elective curriculum more than a century ago.[2] Just as proponents of student choice insisted then, allowing undergraduates to choose their courses offers the greatest chance of arousing their interest and hence of drawing forth their best efforts.

Another argument for emphasizing choice stresses the fact that different students develop their mental abilities in different ways. For example, some students gain most in cognitive skills by taking music courses, others by learning economics, still others by studying mathematics.[3] As a result, efforts to develop students' minds by prescribing the same courses for everyone are likely to be disappointing. The wiser policy, arguably, is to give undergraduates the freedom to educate themselves in the manner best suited to their peculiar intellectual makeup.

These arguments have some initial appeal. For example, it is undoubtedly true that different students learn best in different kinds of courses. The obvious problem, however, is that students will seldom know in advance what courses will help them the most to advance intellectually. As a result, giving them greater freedom to choose will not necessarily lead them to enroll in courses that will help them progress more rapidly.

Experience also suggests that students pick their courses for various reasons besides a desire to increase their mental powers or satisfy intellectual interests. They may take an easy class in order to leave more time for other pursuits, or choose one that lets them be with friends or allows them to study something they think (often wrongly) will help them get a job or gain admission to professional school. Recall that in the heyday of free electives, a century or so ago, only a minority of students used their freedom to pursue genuine intellectual interests in a serious way. The majority responded by electing easier introductory courses that left them ample time to enjoy extracurricular activities and fulfill their social ambitions.[4] Today it is more likely that students will choose the bulk of their courses for vocational reasons to prepare themselves as well as they can for the careers they hope to pursue.

Despite these risks, a few colleges—notably, Brown, Amherst, and Smith—have expanded student choice even further by doing away with all general education requirements so that undergraduates have complete freedom to acquire intellectual breadth in any way they choose. According to reports at Brown, students have not used their freedom to narrow their programs of study; very large majorities have continued to take courses from all three of the major areas of knowledge—science, social science, and humanities.[5]

A closer look at the Brown experience, however, reveals the special set of conditions that allows such expanded choice to work successfully. The most important prerequisite is an intensive system of faculty advising that helps students make enlightened decisions.[6] Almost as important is a highly select student body filled with undergraduates who are intelligent, intellectually curious, and enrolled in college for a broad liberal education rather than vocational training. Finally, Brown allows students to take any number of courses on a pass-fail basis so that they will not resist exploring subjects in new and different fields out of fear of lowering their grade point averages.

These are not conditions that can be widely replicated. Good advising with conscientious faculty participation is a goal that has eluded most colleges, especially those with large undergraduate enrollments. Students dedicated to the liberal arts are a small minority. More than 60 percent of all seniors in four-year colleges have majored in vocational programs and regard getting a job as the principal reason for attending college.

Yet another drawback for many simple distribution systems is that few of the offerings from which students choose are designed for the specific purpose of furthering the goals of general education. Instead they have been created with different aims in mind. Some are introductory courses for students planning to major in a department; others are staple items in an established discipline; still others simply reflect the current interests of the professors teaching them. Of course, some of the courses may turn out to be ideally suited for awakening lasting interest in a new field of knowledge or for acquainting students with intellectual works of enduring significance. But such an outcome is more or less accidental, creating risks that distribution programs will force students to choose among courses that do not further the aims of general education at all.

This problem is particularly likely to arise in the case of science. Awakening an interest in chemistry or biology or geology among ambitious business majors or aspiring novelists is a daunting challenge at best. It requires an imaginative choice of subject matter and considerable flair in presenting it to students. What many distribution plans provide, however, is nothing of the kind but merely a choice among the standard introductory courses for each branch of science. Such offerings are normally constructed for an entirely different purpose—to build a foundation for students intending to major in the field and perhaps go on to obtain a Ph.D. Most of the readings impart large quantities of basic information, material essential for those planning further work in the discipline but precisely the stuff that other students will soon forget.

Sheila Tobias has studied these basic courses in detail in an effort to discover why many able students come to college with an interest in science only to drift away and major in other fields.[7] She finds that the standard introductory courses are an important contributing cause. Some students are turned off by the large size and competitive intensity of the classes; others by indifferent instruction and an emphasis on cookbook problem-solving rather than gaining a real understanding of the underlying concepts. While some students are discouraged by the difficulty of the material, many others find the work to be shallow and intellectually unrewarding. If introductory courses have this effect on students with an initial bent for science, one can imagine their impact on undergraduates who have no interest in the subject but enroll simply to fulfill a requirement.

All in all, simple distribution schemes seem likely to succeed only where faculty are willing to spend considerable time advising students, where undergraduates are highly motivated to secure a well-rounded education, and where special courses are provided (especially in science) that are specifically designed to awaken curiosity and create enthusiasm in young people whose principal interests lie in other areas of the curriculum. These conditions probably exist in relatively few colleges. Where they are not present, the drawbacks to a simple distribution requirement seem so apparent that one must ask why the approach has survived at all, let alone become the dominant means of ensuring the desired breadth of study. The most likely explanation is that distribution requirements have something to offer every constituency. Students can achieve some semblance of breadth with minimal restraints on their freedom to choose from the vast array of courses in the catalogue. The faculty is not called upon to create new courses or to teach any subjects they do not wish to teach. College officials can provide a general education program without incurring any new costs. In this way, presidents and deans can talk eloquently to their alumni about broadening young minds while the faculty are not distracted from their research and budget officers do not have to scrounge for extra resources.

There is doubtless something to be said for simultaneously pleasing students, avoiding problems of implementation, and saving money. But such benefits should never be allowed to outweigh substantial educational considerations. For most colleges with simple distribution requirements, the price does seem too high. Administrative advantages have been purchased at the cost of diluting the legitimate aims of general education and fostering an impression that undergraduate education is little more than a vast smorgasbord amounting to "an admission of intellectual defeat," in the words of Daniel Bell, "a mishmash of courses that are only superficially connected."[8]

THE GREAT BOOKS

The polar opposite of a distribution requirement is the Great Books curriculum. In its true form, such a general education program will consist entirely or mainly of a study of original texts from a variety of fields. Advocates such as Robert Hutchins and William Bennett, who argue passionately for this approach, believe that it will not only kindle intellectual interests but accomplish much more besides.[9] By immersing themselves in the finest books that civilization has produced, students will come to grips with fundamental questions of human existence, social organization, and the natural and physical environment.[10] Better yet, they will explore these subjects through the works of the greatest intellects that ever lived. Such an experience offers the education that enthusiasts consider best calculated to increase students' self-knowledge, elevate their tastes, enhance their powers of reasoning, deepen their insight into recurring social issues and moral dilemmas, and build a continuing interest in many fields of human inquiry and experience.

As if these advantages weren't enough, proponents point to still another benefit. Unlike a distribution requirement, the Great Books curriculum ensures that all undergraduates will have studied the same substantial list of readings and grappled with the same set of fundamental questions. Moreover, most advocates of this approach believe in teaching, not by lecturing to a passive audience, but by engaging students in active argument about the texts. Stimulated by these encounters and armed with a common set of readings, students will naturally carry their discussions beyond the classroom into their dining halls and dormitory rooms. In this way, a requirement to study the Great Books leads to a deeper, more intense intellectual experience than undergraduates can have in a series of courses taught primarily by lecture. Better yet, such study may create a common core of learning within an increasingly diverse student body and thus provide a counterweight to the divisive tendencies of race, religion, and class.

Unfortunately the Great Books approach brings formidable problems along with its considerable benefits. To begin with, the faculty are very likely to oppose this model because of the burdens it entails. To make the most of the chosen books and the ideas they convey, students need opportunities to argue and discuss and test their ideas against the greater knowledge and experience of the teacher. Thus a Great Books course does not lend itself to large lectures; it calls for courses divided into many small sections of students, each with its own capable instructor. Therein lies the problem. Faculty members are not recruited with an eye to teaching Great Books, and few of them have the training or experience to do so. Because they must fulfill other responsibilities in the university, such as conducting graduate training, staffing concentrations, and carrying on research, their knowledge and skills normally lie elsewhere. Hence they will often resist teaching a Great Books course. Even Columbia's esteemed Humanities requirement has had to employ a number of adjunct teachers, and that is but a single course.[11] Mounting a full-blown Great Books program is a much vaster enterprise that will either force many members of the faculty to offer courses they do not wish to give and are not qualified to teach or compel the college to assemble a large cadre of graduate students and part-time instructors to staff the many small sections. Neither alternative promises to yield high-quality teaching or appeal very much to the professors who ultimately control the curriculum.

Faculty resistance may be less of a problem for colleges that have no graduate programs and employ few professors with strong research interests. Still, mounting such a program will require many additional courses and thus be too costly for many of these institutions. Moreover, even if the faculty can be persuaded to go along, few of them are likely to have the training or the aptitude to teach the Great Books well. Other objections could also arise. Students may protest that the list of Great Books contains few if any women authors and throws too little light on non-Western cultures. Worse yet, prospective students rarely like heavily prescribed curricula, especially when they are laden with required texts of ancient vintage having little apparent connection to today's world. As a result, colleges contemplating a Great Books program run the risk of attracting fewer applicants. Since most colleges without research-oriented faculties have a chronic problem recruiting enough students to keep the budget balanced, the prospect of adopting a program that could turn away applicants is particularly unappetizing.

Proponents may reply that a Great Books curriculum will have no difficulty attracting students, provided the courses are well taught. Evidence for this conclusion, however, is not easy to find. The best-known pure Great Books curriculum currently in existence is at St. Johns College, but, even though it has only a handful of competitors, St. Johns attracts relatively few applicants and most of those accepted do not enroll.[12] The likelihood that any large number of colleges could adopt such a program and still have enough students to fill their classes seems remote.

On balance, therefore, the practical disadvantages of a full-blown Great Books approach will usually outweigh the benefits. That is doubtless the reason why so few colleges have elected to take this route. A much more common practice is to include one or two courses on the history of ideas or the development of literature utilizing a list of great texts. In this way, a college can reap some of the benefits of the Great Books approach, using subjects in which the method works to best advantage and the problems of implementation are not insuperable.

SURVEY COURSES

Like Great Books programs, the prospect of a rich array of survey courses carries much initial appeal. More than any of the other alternatives, the survey model holds the promise of imparting the breadth of learning students need in order to call themselves educated. Under this banner, faculties can create a battery of sweeping courses covering the growth of Western civilization, a glimpse of other major cultures and civilizations, an introduction to the great periods of Western art and music, the evolution and functioning of democratic institutions and political processes, the development of modern science, the operation of a free and competitive economy, and the nature of the human mind and personality. In the hands of great lecturers, such courses offer the prospect of a panoramic view of human achievement and an impressive foundation for later experience and learning.

That, at least, is the hope. In reality, this approach, like its competitors, is not without difficulties. The principal problem is that survey courses of this kind can easily become superficial. There is so much to include that instructors will rarely be able to probe a subject in depth but instead will impart large quantities of facts and information, quickly learned and quickly forgotten. In the end, a general education program built on survey courses may give a comforting sense of covering vast amounts of ground but leave a lasting residue of knowledge that is actually quite meager.

Efforts to teach the survey courses can also cause serious problems. Either a college must create a large number of small or medium-size classes for each required course in order to cover the entire student body, or it must offer each survey in the form of a set of lectures by a single professor. The former model will be extremely hard to staff, since most faculty members do not like to teach introductory courses covering vast subjects, and many may not even feel competent to do so. The latter alternative is likely to prove unpalatable for students, since it subjects them to huge, impersonal lectures with multiple discussion sections taught by inexperienced, loosely supervised graduate students. Either way, therefore, the survey alternative promises to encounter serious opposition and yield disappointing results. For this reason, although a faculty may prescribe a survey course or two on subjects such as the growth of Western civilization, it will rarely devote all or even a substantial part of its general education program to courses of this type.

THE MODES-OF-INQUIRY APPROACH

The fourth and last model is the so-called modes-of-inquiry approach.[13] Proponents of this curriculum argue that the volume of knowledge today is far too large and changes much too rapidly to justify a program founded on a single set of books or a fixed body of essential information. Under these conditions, the best approach to take is to have students learn about the principal ways in which scholars and scientists acquire knowledge. For example, courses in history can demonstrate how a historian understands the evolution of a major problem in the contemporary world and how conditions, events, and decisions in the past contributed to its development. Courses in literature, painting, or music may give students a sense of the possibilities and limitations of different art forms and a feeling for how individual talent, artistic tradition, and the surrounding society interact to produce great works. A course in physics may convey a sense of the way science is done by considering how a series of investigators gradually conceived and validated theories leading to important laws and principles governing the world around us.

Those who favor this approach argue that it will lay a foundation that enables students to keep on learning throughout their lives. Information will become outdated and new facts come to light, but the principal methods of intellectual inquiry are likely to remain pretty much the same. By learning these methods, students will know enough about the techniques and terminology of different disciplines to overcome the inhibitions that could otherwise keep them from proceeding on their own to study more advanced material. Becoming truly cultivated and broadly educated is a lifetime's work, not an enterprise achievable in four short undergraduate years, but learning the principal modes of thought is the ideal way to begin. Or so proponents claim.

Such a curriculum also escapes some of the practical problems that beset the other strategies. Unlike a distribution requirement, the modes-of-inquiry approach calls for courses specially designed for the program. Thus it avoids the weakness of the distribution requirement in trying to achieve intellectual breadth by using offerings created for other purposes. At the same time, it is much more flexible than a Great Books program, since a variety of courses can illustrate any given method of scholarship. Thus professors can offer a modes-of-inquiry course without having to teach outside their specialized fields, while students have the freedom to choose from at least a limited menu of courses that will acquaint them with the major ways of apprehending the world.

It is no easy matter, however, to teach students all the principal methods of thought in the limited number of courses allotted to general education. Because of this problem, modes-of-inquiry curricula are often attacked for being too superficial to accomplish much of value. For example, taking a single course that traces the process of inquiry leading to the discovery of nuclear fission may prove interesting, but will it be enough to enable students to continue learning about science on their own or to teach them how to understand other scientific issues that later come to their attention? Conceivably students will become interested enough in the process of scientific discovery to extend their readings to other problems and do so with some comprehension. But we do not know how effectively student interests can be awakened in this way, and no one has yet bothered to find out.

A second criticism of the modes-of-inquiry curriculum is that it emphasizes method over other qualities of a cultivated mind. Presumably it makes *some* difference whether one is introduced to the social sciences by taking basic economics or a course on anthropological investigations of remote South Sea cultures, even though each may provide a competent introduction to a recognized form of social science inquiry. Despite all the controversy over the existence of a canon, surely *some* books are more valuable than others and *some* bodies of knowledge are especially important to an educated person. If a faculty were to choose courses simply by their suitability for demonstrating a particular mode of thought, it could produce a curriculum conveying a hodgepodge of information that omitted many of the greatest works of literature and social thought.

Implementing a modes-of-inquiry strategy can also give rise to practical difficulties. Although the curriculum does not force professors to teach outside their areas of expert knowledge, it does require a substantial number of specially created courses in addition to the regular department offerings. Because the approach demands more work from professors and imposes added costs that may take funds away from other needs, deans and presidents will have to display considerable skill to gain the necessary approval and commitment from the faculty. Once in place, moreover, the new model will need continuous monitoring to ensure that all courses approved for the program actually help to achieve its purposes and that the curriculum does not gradually erode into incoherence. These costs have to be weighed before an institution decides to take this path.

HYBRID MODELS

If any conclusion emerges from examining the principal methods for acquiring breadth, it is that none of them by itself offers an ideal solution. Each alternative has advantages that rival approaches cannot readily duplicate. Each has special disadvantages as well that are serious enough to make its adoption problematic. For this reason, many faculties are reluctant to adopt any of the models wholesale as the chosen way to give their students a broad general education.

The most common response is to create a hybrid curriculum that borrows from several of the traditional models. Many possibilities exist. Faculties wedded to a distribution requirement can provide a larger number of well-defined categories and restrict the choice of courses in each to ones that seem most suited to awakening new intellectual interests and introducing students to an important field of knowledge. A faculty may even go further and add one or more required courses that are deemed to be of particular importance, such as specially designed offerings in fields like the sciences where existing introductory courses seem especially unsuitable for the goals of general education. Faculties partial to Great Books may limit this approach to a few courses, especially in the humanities and social thought, while filling out their program by creating a set of survey courses or giving students a limited choice among offerings from each of several broad fields of study. Colleges favoring a modes-of-inquiry approach may urge professors in the program to include classic texts in their courses or supplement the curriculum with yearlong offerings on literature and the history of ideas built around a study of Great Books.

Faculties that seek a hybrid solution quickly learn that borrowing an attractive feature from another model almost always requires giving up something valuable in return. Since there is no established metric for weighing what is gained against what must be given up, no one can be sure which combination will be best. This problem threatens to cast doubt on all collective efforts to revise the curriculum.

Even if perfection is impossible, however, faculties should still try periodically to review and improve upon their general education programs. Although no one proposal may be demonstrably better than other plausible approaches, each of the leading alternatives may be preferable to the curriculum currently in use. Over time, any system of requirements is likely to erode into incoherence through the gradual accumulation of exceptions and expedient solutions to unanticipated problems. Eventually few members of the faculty remember what the original curriculum was meant to accomplish, and more and more lose interest in the enterprise. At this point, any thoughtfully constructed model will at least be comprehensible to students and faculty and represent an improvement on the status quo. If suitable efforts are made to engage the faculty throughout the process of review, the discussions leading up to the final choice may also elicit new interest from professors in teaching undergraduates. The proper way to evaluate a curriculum review, therefore, should be to ask not whether it has produced the one best curriculum—for no such thing exists—but whether it has arrived at a carefully considered result through a process that has strengthened the faculty's commitment to undergraduate education and united them in a clearer understanding of their common purpose.

LOOKING FOR RESULTS

All curricular efforts to provide a breadth of learning are founded in the belief that reading great texts, or encountering important fields of knowledge, or sampling important modes of thought will benefit students for years to come by cultivating their minds, awakening new interests, and inspiring further study and reflection. It is not at all clear, however, that these aspirations will be realized. Great texts are often hard to read; indifferently taught, they can discourage rather than inspire further study. Survey courses suffer from the rapid memory loss that typically accompanies attempts to bombard students with heavy barrages of information. Reading accounts of how investigators discovered subatomic matter will not necessarily inspire English majors to keep up with scientific developments. Such uncertainties as these call for efforts to discover just what general education does contribute to the intellectual development of undergraduates.

In view of the differences among the several leading models of general education, one might at least suppose that the choice of models would have a significant influence on the intellectual development of undergraduates. If it does, however, the impact has escaped the gaze of investigators. Working with a sample of some 24,000 students, Alexander Astin examined the effects of different forms of general education on a wide range of outcomes. (Of course, none of the outcomes used may have captured exactly what proponents of general education hope to accomplish; after all, who can devise a test to measure lasting interests, wider perspectives, deeper insights?) Still, having reviewed the test scores of his sample of college seniors and asked them to estimate how much progress they had made in developing a long list of intellectual competences, values, and beliefs, Astin concluded that "the varieties of general educational programs currently used in American higher education do not seem to make much difference in any aspect of the student's cognitive or affective development." Only a prescribed curriculum in which all students take the same courses—presumably the Great Books model or something close to it—seemed to have any advantage over the others, and even that result may not be due to the emphasis on Great Books as such but to the reliance on smaller classes and active discussion* that is typical of such programs.[14]

What else have researchers found about the effects of general education and other efforts to broaden the minds of undergraduates? Unfortunately little research has been done on the subject, and most of what exists merely attempts to measure whether interests in literature and the arts increase during the college years. Ernest Pascarella and Patrick Terenzini summarize this work as follows:

---

*As Lee Shulman points out, "one of the 'secrets' of the remarkable impact of the Hutchins [i.e., the University of Chicago Great Books] College was probably the persistent and all-encompassing effort—course after course—of critical dialogue within small seminars as the pedagogical practice of the college"; *Teaching as Community Property: Essays on Higher Education* (2004), p. 25. If this supposition is correct, the long-standing debate over what subjects to study and what texts to read may have merely diverted attention once again from the more important question of how college students should be taught.

The literature is remarkably consistent in indicating increases in students' interests and activities in creative writing, reading, classical music, art, and other cultural and aesthetic experiences and activities. In some cases, the changes involve a growth in students' cultural and aesthetic appreciation; in others, the changes are behavioral (for example, attending concerts or art shows, writing poetry). In all cases, the changes are toward a greater valuing of cultural and aesthetic experiences and activities.[15]

More recently, George Kuh has surveyed seniors from a broad sample of colleges by asking them how their cultural interests have evolved during college. His data confirm that interests do develop but that the gains are far from universal. Only 36 percent of the respondents reported substantial increases in understanding and enjoying literature, while only 30 percent recorded such gains in appreciating art, music, or theater. Both percentages have dropped by more than one-third since the 1960s.[16]

Although the changes just described are modest, at least they reflect growing intellectual and aesthetic interests. But do the changes endure over time or, better yet, do they increase and expand with age? On this point, the evidence is slight and not especially encouraging. In their study comparing individuals in 1972 (upon graduation from high school) and in 1986, William Knox, Paul Lindsay, and Mary Kolb found that those who graduated from college had greater involvement than nongraduates in sports clubs and "literary, art, discussion, music or study groups." Only 8 percent of the respondents holding B.A. degrees, however, and 11 percent of those with advanced degrees belonged to cultural groups. Moreover, when the authors introduced the proper controls, they concluded that the differences in participation among adults with varying levels of education were attributable to differences in intelligence and other personal qualities rather than anything the respondents learned as undergraduates.[17]

Pascarella and Terenzini are only slightly more optimistic in summing up the few additional studies that have tried to answer this question:

> While the available evidence is limited, it is at least consistent in suggesting that no recidivism appears to occur (at least not to any significant degree) in graduates' attitudes and values related to cultural and intellectual matters. Neither, however, is there any evidence to suggest that the changes that occur in college are merely the early stages of a lifelong trajectory toward greater and greater cultural and aesthetic appreciation.[18]

More positive findings appear in studies of the long-term effects of college on reading and other intellectual habits of college alumni. For example, investigators have shown that college graduates are more likely than those with only a high school education to have taken continuing education courses (58.2 percent versus 30.7 percent); read a book in the past six months (83 percent versus 57 percent); engaged in some form of creative writing (14 percent versus 4 percent); or read a newspaper or magazine every day (42 percent versus 27 percent).[19] Granted, these results may not be a direct result of going to college but simply a reflection of earning higher incomes and holding jobs that require more intellectual effort and continued reading. Nevertheless, at least one study managed to control for differences in income and occupation and still found that college alumni made 2.5 times as many visits to libraries as high school graduates.[20] Whether this result comes about through general education, however, or from some other aspect of the undergraduate experience remains a mystery.

Since general education programs are intended to have effects that last for many years after graduation, it would be extremely useful to learn more about their long-term results. Investigating this question is admittedly difficult. The enduring results of general education are often too subtle to be captured by objective tests, and suitable comparison groups might be hard to find in any event. But colleges could at least ask seniors whether their required courses in humanities and science increased their understanding of these subjects or inspired further study or reading. Better yet, investigators could ask alumni 10, 20, or even 30 years after graduation how their undergraduate experience has affected their later lives and whether the courses they took (or any other activities in college) helped to awaken interests that have survived and flourished over the intervening years. Surveying graduates may throw at least a bit of light on whether studying the Great Books or completing a modes-of-inquiry curriculum has any effect on the midlife interests and beliefs of alumni. More generally, have graduates who immersed themselves in some extracurricular activity in college pursued a related interest in later life more frequently than classmates who occupied themselves in other ways? Can alumni trace *any* serious intellectual, aesthetic, or avocational interest they possess to experiences they had as undergraduates?

Surveys of this kind are admittedly problematic, for middle-aged alumni may not be entirely sure why their current interests developed as they did, let alone how they originated. In trying to trace the origins of later life interests, it will be hard to disentangle the effects of college from earlier events and experiences. Still, there is something unsatisfying about continuing to prescribe programs of study to convey a breadth of knowledge or cultivate lasting interests without having any idea whether what is being taught will survive for any length of time following graduation. Asking alumni may be an imperfect way of trying to answer such questions, but it is surely better than never trying to answer them at all.[21]

WHAT IS TO BE DONE?

What conclusions can one draw about the quest for breadth after all the words devoted to the subject? For a debate that has gone on so long and commanded so much of the attention paid to undergraduate education, the results are surprisingly meager. The model that calls for the least effort is the one most widely used in colleges across the country. Moreover, unlike other aims discussed in earlier chapters, researchers have not established that any of the methods used to ensure breadth have accomplished much toward attaining their goals.

Meanwhile, the space traditionally provided in the curriculum for achieving breadth has shrunk with the advent of new requirements in subjects such as quantitative literacy, the study of other cultures and races, and moral reasoning. Added competition may eventually come from courses on American government, political philosophy, international relations, and economics if colleges begin to think seriously about their responsibility to prepare students to be active and informed citizens. Though conceived for separate purposes, these newer offerings guarantee that an undergraduate course of study will not be excessively narrow. As a result, they are not only diminishing the space available for distribution requirements and modes-of-inquiry curricula; they are chipping away at the rationale that gave rise to such programs in the first place.

These trends, coupled with the doubts about how much general education has accomplished, may even cause some to question whether such programs ought to be continued. At the least, the newer requirements ensure a reasonable exposure to the social sciences, especially for any college that calls for courses in economics and political science as part of a proper civic education. Abandoning general education, however, could still have serious consequences. There would be no assurance that undergraduates would have any introduction to literature and the arts, any exposure to history, or even a single basic offering in the sciences. True, they would be free to take elective courses in these subjects or even major in a humanistic or scientific discipline. Nevertheless, some students, perhaps many, would graduate from college without ever having explored one or more of these great sources of human knowledge and experience.

The importance of the three fields hardly requires elaboration. Science not only contains many of humankind's great intellectual achievements, it explains much about ourselves, our environment, our way of life, and many of the problems that threaten our well-being and our very existence. History not only helps students understand how the world we know developed; it offers a more complex, contingent view of human affairs and social change that helps to leaven the simpler theories and assumptions often found in disciplines such as political science and economics. Learning to understand and appreciate literature, aside from its intrinsic value, contributes to most other aims of undergraduate education as well. It makes vivid the predicament of others and thus can awaken moral compassion. It offers abundant examples of great writing. It brings an understanding of other human beings and other experiences and perspectives that helps break down crude stereotypes and enhance understanding of differences in gender, race, and culture.

If importance were the only criterion for continuing to impose requirements, there would be no point in arguing further. But this is not the case. Besides agreeing that an aim is important, responsible educators should have good reason to believe that the goal will actually be accomplished to a meaningful degree within the time allotted in the curriculum. It is on this basis that general education programs must be judged and on this basis that they are most vulnerable.

Although specific evidence of long-term effects is still lacking, ordinary experience would lead one to believe that courses do exist that awaken lasting interests in history or science or literature and the arts. Many colleges have professors on their faculty who are reputed to "breathe new life" into their students' minds and give them "new views of things, a perception of new truths and of new aspects of the old ones." Since experiences of this kind are so valuable and because the subject matter is so important, it is worth exposing as many students as possible to such teaching even if the longer-term effects have not yet been verified.

At the same time, making sure that such teachers play a prominent role in general education demands much more than a simple distribution requirement. It requires a determined effort to identify the exceptional professors, persuade them to participate in the program, and give them the support they need to succeed in their mission. It matters less whether the courses that result are built around great texts or modes of thought than whether the instructors have a commitment to the enterprise and a demonstrated capacity to arouse the interest and enthusiasm of their students.

In the hands of gifted teachers, courses in science or history or literature can be among the most memorable of all the classes students take. If colleges cannot find the right professors, however, or will not give them the support they need, it would be better to abandon the quest for breadth entirely than to perpetuate the sham of pretending to accomplish something intellectually valuable by installing an ungainly compromise devised to win approval from a reluctant faculty or by forcing students to rummage for themselves among long lists of courses created for very different purposes. Broadening knowledge and awakening lasting interests are among undergraduate education's noblest aspirations. They are not impossible to achieve. But they require exceptional teaching backed by a much more sustained, determined effort than most colleges have thus far been willing to make.

11 | PREPARING FOR A CAREER

Vocational courses have long been a burr under the saddle of those who teach the liberal arts. According to one survey, 60 percent of Arts and Sciences professors do not even think that preparing for a good job is a particularly important goal for undergraduates.[1] In sharp contrast, almost three-fourths of entering freshmen regard it as the *most* important reason for going to college.[2] One can easily understand why students feel this way. Most of them will spend more time making a living over the next several decades than they will doing anything else. The careers they choose and the success they achieve at work will have a great deal to do with defining who they are, how satisfied they feel about their lives, and how comfortably they will live. No wonder they take their careers so seriously. The puzzle is that so few liberal arts teachers seem to agree.

Why are these professors so cool to the vocational needs of their students? How can they educate young people in so many ways and for so many purposes yet refuse to help prepare them for the work that will shape their future lives so profoundly?

Part of the explanation, surely, is the tendency of much vocational education to offer training without intellectual depth.* However

---

*It should be noted that evidence is mixed on whether the vocational emphasis of a college either helps or hinders the development of cognitive ability (including critical thinking skills); Ernest T. Pascarella and Patrick T. Terenzini, *How College Affects Students*, Vol. 2, pp. 172–73.

worthy their place in the economic order, hotel management, mortuary science, and public relations do not engage the frontiers of thought in the same way as mathematics, physics, or philosophy. Much of what students need to prepare for these callings takes the form of practical skills rather than the kinds of knowledge that are the intellectual's stock in trade. To many liberal arts professors, such competencies should be either learned on the job or taught in some kind of trade school, but surely not studied in a university under the tutelage of scholars.

Another contributing cause is the fear that students will be so concerned about their careers that, once vocational education gains a foothold in the college, it will spread like crabgrass and eventually take over the entire curriculum. Money and commercialization already exert undue influence over university behavior. Making room for vocational training will arguably exacerbate these worrisome trends. Undergraduates are deeply preoccupied with succeeding in their careers, especially in a world they perceive as increasingly competitive and in constant flux. Given the opportunity, they may well neglect other purposes of undergraduate education in their eagerness to take any course that promises to give them a competitive edge in the struggle for success and financial security.

At the same time, the threat posed by vocational courses cannot be removed by simply ignoring their existence. Denying vocational concerns any place in the curriculum will diminish the chance to help undergraduates think about their careers in terms broader than simply making money. Moreover, such opposition is impractical in any event. Since students can choose which college to attend, market pressures force institutions to give them the practical training they desire. University officials who worry about filling the seats in the college cannot afford the fantasy that finding a job is a matter of little consequence. They understand full well the depth of student desire to prepare for a career. As a result, apart from a few score institutions that remain wholly dedicated to the liberal arts, virtually all colleges have established vocational majors, often separated from Arts and Sciences in schools of their own.

The question, then, is not whether to banish all vocational courses but whether to join in giving students a larger view of the professions that goes beyond mere skills training. Unfortunately, in universities with both liberal arts and vocational faculties, cooperation has been conspicuous by its absence. According to one report, "In many colleges and universities, a lamentable chasm separates the liberal arts college and professional departments. Competition for resources is keen, autonomy is jealously guarded, and cross-disciplinary discourse is fraught with difficulty."[3]

Liberal arts faculties have paid a heavy price for their ostrich-like response to the demand for practical courses. Given a choice, students have deserted the traditional disciplines in droves. Today 60 percent of all college seniors are majoring in a vocational program. Whereas substantial majorities once chose a liberal arts concentration, only about one-third do so now.[4] The rest must often make their way through programs that receive little help from Arts and Sciences faculties to ensure that the courses students take outside their vocational majors afford them the full benefit of a first-rate liberal education.

These disadvantages have finally begun to persuade some Arts and Sciences faculties to reexamine their connections with vocational education and think about responding to students' employment concerns in new and creative ways. The challenge is critical, and not just for practical reasons. Successfully met, it could invigorate both the liberal arts and vocational programs while accomplishing much to serve the needs of undergraduates.

CHOOSING A CAREER

Despite faculty resistance to vocational courses, going to college, including a strictly liberal arts college, does much to improve the job prospects of undergraduates. Of all the influences that determine occupational status and earnings, education is the most important—and earning a B.A. gives almost twice the boost of graduating from high school. Just why this is so is not entirely clear. In jobs held by both college graduates and non–college graduates, comparisons do not show that B.A. recipients perform better (after controlling for differences in such characteristics as intelligence and parental education). Still, the economic advantage enjoyed by college graduates seems to rest on more than a mere credential; earnings and vocational status rise for each year of college even if students have never earned a degree. Moreover, the gap in status and earnings between college and high school graduates does not diminish over time, but, if anything, grows larger.[5]

Today's undergraduates need more help than in the past to prepare for a lifetime of work. Employers increasingly expect the individuals they hire to take responsibility for managing their own careers and acquiring the skills they need to move ahead. Meeting this demand is more of a challenge today than it once was. Not only do students have more occupations to consider in choosing a career, but counselors tell them that they should expect to make up to five career shifts in their lifetimes and to change jobs 10–15 times.

Not all undergraduates have to look for work immediately after leaving college. While most still move directly into the labor force, a substantial minority will first enroll in a Ph.D. program or a professional school. Whereas the former must normally graduate with enough skills to find a job, the latter can wait and get their practical training later. Both groups of students, however, are alike in one respect. Both will often need help from some source in deciding what calling to pursue after finishing their undergraduate studies.

Some freshmen enter college without any idea of what they will do when they graduate. These students are especially likely to require a good deal of information over the next four years about their interests and aptitudes, on the one hand, and possible careers, on the other. Without help, many of them will never arrive at a clear decision. Some will drift into law school or enter some other vocation almost accidentally or on impulse, unable to choose what they want to do.

Other freshmen, even if they think they have decided on a vocation, will change their minds during college. One study found that between one-third and two-thirds of all undergraduates fall into this category.[6] Another survey of 30,000 students matriculating at 26 selective colleges in 1976 discovered that fewer than half of those aspiring to medical degrees or Ph.D.s ever achieved their goals.[7] Even students who come with clear vocational plans need to test their ambitions against hard evidence, for many of them harbor unrealistic expectations. Among starting football and basketball players at Division I colleges, for example, almost half expect to play in the NFL or NBA, although less than 2 percent ever receive as much as a tryout and many fewer last a single season. Would-be students of architecture are notorious for aspiring to be the next Frank Gehry or I. M. Pei, despite the fact that only a minority of those who earn architecture degrees will ever have primary responsibility for designing a single private home, let alone a series of great public buildings.

Students have quite similar views about the characteristics that matter in a job and a career.[8] They want work that is interesting, well paid, respected, and worthwhile. They want to serve in an ethical environment where they do not feel pressured to do things they consider wrong and can count on being judged fairly in matters of pay and promotion. They want a career that fits their aptitudes and talents yet challenges them in ways that help them develop further.

Finding the right kind of work is sometimes described as a process of matching occupations with one's interests, aptitudes, and values. This formula, however, makes the process seem too easy, too mechanical. Many young people find their calling in accidental, haphazard ways. A random experience or conversation may spark an interest that eventually leads to a job and a career. Still, colleges can enlarge the variety of experiences from which these pivotal moments arise and can help students gain the knowledge to evaluate the options that occur to them along the way. It is no easy matter for many students to know their interests and values well enough to make a satisfying match. Moreover, as Howard Gardner and his colleagues have found in their massive study of "good work," different occupations, specialties, and employers vary greatly in their ability to provide the stimulation, ethical norms, and opportunities for creative, meaningful work that most students seek.[9] As a result, undergraduates need to know quite a bit if they are to maximize their chances of choosing a satisfying career.

Much of the information students use in making their choice comes naturally without deliberate efforts by the college. By taking a variety of courses and participating in extracurricular activities, undergraduates can learn a great deal about their abilities and interests. To take but one notable example, organic chemistry has a well-deserved reputation for convincing many would-be doctors not to go to medical school. Conversations with classmates and family members are another source of useful information. When college graduates are asked how they heard about the job they ultimately took, the most likely response is that they learned about it from relatives or friends.[10]

Valuable as these sources are, colleges can supplement them in many ways to help students make better choices. Career guidance offices have a wealth of information about different occupations; administer tests to determine a student's interests, aptitudes, and values; and offer group or individual counseling to help clarify choices. At many colleges, alumni from various kinds of jobs come to campus to talk with undergraduates about their work. Placement officers organize "career days" with talks from representatives from various professions; they also arrange internships or summer jobs to give students a taste of actual work in a hospital, business, or law office.[11]

Researchers find that students become progressively clearer and more realistic about their career plans as they move through college.[12] How much of this growth comes from specific career guidance efforts, however, or even how much comes from college rather than simply growing older, remains obscure. Those who go to a career service office seem to appreciate the help and feel they benefit from the advice. Yet relatively few students take advantage of the opportunity. A Gallup poll of college graduates in 1995 found that only 17 percent of respondents remembered ever using such offices.[13]

In an effort to reach more students, at least half of all colleges offer special courses (with or without credit) to teach students how to make more enlightened career choices and search more effectively for jobs. Participants discover how to take an inventory of their aptitudes and interests and how to conduct research into different kinds of careers and employment opportunities. They learn how to prepare resumes and how to conduct themselves in job interviews. Surveys suggest that these courses are not only popular but also very effective in helping students to clarify their preferences and find the positions they want.[14]

With or without professional help, Americans have been quite successful in finding satisfying jobs; more than 80 percent enjoy their current work according to recent polls, and the percentages who are very satisfied are higher in most of the jobs commonly held by college graduates.[15] Even students who are less than thorough or systematic in exploring possible vocations are often adaptable enough to find satisfaction in careers that were clearly chosen with inadequate information.

At the same time, several professions long esteemed by college graduates are experiencing rising levels of discontent. From publishing and journalism to law and medicine, one hears complaints of diminishing autonomy and growing economic pressure to sacrifice professional values to the bottom line.[16] Working hours have increased for college graduates over the past 20–30 years, creating added strains for women trying to combine work and family and for men wanting to share more child-rearing responsibilities.[17] In several institutions popular with college and professional school graduates — for example, law firms, investment banks, and consulting groups — many young professionals must accept a Faustian bargain, working 60–70 hours every week in return for large financial rewards. These occupational strains raise fundamental questions about personal values and priorities, questions that should be considered with care before making career decisions that could have lasting consequences. What better time and place to mull over such problems than college, where students still have opportunities to inform themselves in detail before committing themselves to a job or professional school.

The law offers a good example of a calling in which later difficulties might be avoided with better guidance. The legal profession has long been a magnet for bright students of high ambition and uncertain direction. A substantial percentage of college graduates entering leading law schools claim not to know whether they will ever practice. Large majorities do not think they want to join a large corporate law firm, and as many as one-third hope to work in some form of public interest law. Despite these initial intentions, up to 80–95 percent of recent graduates from leading schools end up joining corporate law firms, while less than 5 percent find positions in a public interest organization.[18]

For students who begin their legal training hoping to fight for social justice, law school can be a sobering experience. While there, they learn a number of hard truths. Jobs fighting for the environment or civil liberties are very scarce. Defending the poor and powerless turns out to pay remarkably little and to consist often of work that many regard as repetitive and dull. As public interest jobs seem less promising (and law school debts continue to mount), most of these idealistic students end by persuading themselves that a large corporate law firm is the best course to pursue, even though many of them find the specialties practiced in these firms, such as corporate law, tax law, and real estate law, both uninteresting and unchallenging.[19]

Idealistic law students also come to realize that the lawyer's job is not so much to promote worthy causes as to represent clients as effectively as possible regardless of one's private opinion of their behavior. There are reasons why lawyers need to suppress their personal beliefs and simply do their utmost to serve their clients. Under our adversary system, it is the judge's job to decide the proper result. Lawyers are thought to serve justice best if they argue for their clients as persuasively as possible. Yet some law students are uncomfortable with such a system, believing that it reduces the lawyer to a "hired gun" whose success depends more on being clever than on being right. These students often graduate either cynical or disillusioned, even though they go with the great majority of their classmates to join an established law firm.[20]

If all these young graduates lived happily ever after, one might conclude that the system works well enough after all. As it happens, many do go on to become partners in their firms and report living satisfying lives. But not everyone is so fortunate. Almost half of the young lawyers leave their firm within three years.[21] Many complain of having too little time for their families and feeling tired and under pressure on most days of the week. Many more are weary of constantly having to compete for advancement with other bright young lawyers or troubled by what they regard as a lack of redeeming social value in their work. Within the profession as a whole, levels of stress, alcoholism, divorce, suicide, and drug abuse are all substantially above the national average.[22]

Law students are not unique. Every calling has its own particular stresses and sacrifices that students need to ponder.

Could colleges keep their students from making unwise decisions by helping them to learn more about these problems in advance? Surely not in every case. Ever since Adam Smith discussed the subject in *The Wealth of Nations,* observers have noted the remarkable tendency of young people to cling to unrealistic expectations about their future careers while considering themselves immune to the occupational risks that strike large numbers of their contemporaries.[23] Even so, much is known about the legal profession (and other callings) that could presumably be of help at least to some students who are considering law school and wondering whether they can find a way "to live greatly in the law," as Oliver Wendell Holmes once put it.[24] A number of books and surveys exist describing different forms of legal practice and the rewards and discontents of each. Other thoughtful essays consider the dilemmas attorneys face in reconciling their obligations to clients with their duties to the court and to their own consciences. Works of fiction offer food for thought about the joys and travails of law practice and the opportunities and obstacles it presents to anyone seeking to live a fulfilling and socially responsible life. Such materials, along with similar works on other professions, could supply readings for demanding courses that could help students test their ambitions more carefully.

Other offerings of a more familiar kind might help less-focused undergraduates narrow their career options to a few that they could explore in greater depth. A course on the professions — tracing their history, their role in American society, and the contemporary challenges they face — would accomplish the purpose reasonably well. No one has described the value of such classes more eloquently than Kenneth Andrews, a Ph.D. in English literature who went on to become a distinguished professor at the Harvard Business

School and a master of one of the residential houses in Harvard College.

Where undergraduate education and professional education have become clearly separated by the baccalaureate degree, it is especially difficult for prospective professionals to become informed about the nature of the profession they are considering, how professional practice differs from other forms of work, what the controlling standards and criteria are, and what the intellectual, material, and social satisfactions might be. One or more courses on the role of the professions in society might prepare students for more intelligent choice, might extend their sensibilities to the moral dilemmas of the profession they are entering, and might acquaint them with the nature of responsible competence and the ways in which it is extended or subverted.[25]

Some courses could inform students of the special challenges of different callings while simultaneously serving other goals of a liberal arts education. For example, moral reasoning courses might focus on issues arising in particular professions and, in so doing, engage students with a variety of compelling ethical problems. In a course on the ethical dilemmas of modern medicine, for example, students could grapple with such questions as euthanasia, abortion, cloning, and genetic engineering, not to mention the difficulties doctors face in deciding how much truth to convey to desperately ill patients or whether to undertake research on drugs produced by companies in which they hold a financial interest. Such classes would not only take up a wide range of practical ethical issues, they could also give valuable insights into the nature of medical practice while sparking an interest in moral reasoning more intense than anything achieved by courses not so intimately tied to the future lives of students in the class.

In short, various courses can be imagined that are not narrowly vocational and would do much to stimulate students to think constructively about their lives and values. Nevertheless they do not fit the conventional academic mode or fall neatly within an existing discipline. Although sociology makes room for those who write about the history, organization, and behavior of professions, such scholars rarely consider it their mission to help undergraduates make more enlightened career decisions. Most professors of moral philosophy are likewise uninterested in the practical ethical dilemmas of lawyers and doctors. Thus classes of the kind just described may join the lengthening list of subjects in which the needs of undergraduates do not match the professional interests of Arts and Sciences professors.

Under these circumstances—as with writing classes, foreign language teaching, and instruction in quantitative reasoning—many colleges will have to look outside the ranks of the regular faculty if they wish to mount the kinds of courses that will help their students most in choosing a career. In large universities, members of professional school faculties may be willing and able to fill the need. In colleges with vocational majors, professors from these departments can be recruited to offer suitable courses for Arts and Sciences students. Liberal arts colleges will sometimes find individual practitioners in the surrounding area with the scholarly interests and abilities to serve the purpose effectively.

Faculties may resist hiring such instructors on the ground that they do not meet normal Arts and Sciences standards. Admittedly there are risks in importing outsiders to teach parts of the undergraduate curriculum. Proper oversight by the regular faculty will be necessary to ensure that such courses satisfy reasonable standards of rigor and intellectual depth. To reject such courses entirely, however, would be a strange result for faculties that allow beginning graduate students, part-time adjunct instructors, and even undergraduates to teach important material in the college, often with little training or supervision. To draw the line at courses on the professions would seem to reflect not so much a legitimate concern for academic standards as an instinctive prejudice against vocational instruction in any form.

VOCATIONAL MAJORS

Most college seniors do not move directly to an advanced degree program after they graduate; they look for work. Since the average length of time people stay in their first job has shrunk dramatically, more and more employers want their employees to "hit the ground running" without having to receive costly training from the company. As a result, undergraduates today are more likely than ever to feel that they must not only choose a career but also prepare themselves for a job while still in college. Spurred by competition for students, university officials have responded by mounting a wide array of vocational majors ranging from traditional staples, such as business and engineering, to such exotic entries as prison administration, sports management, and even video game design.

There has long been disagreement over whether vocational majors are actually better preparation for a career than a liberal arts degree. In most cases, the answer depends on the line of work a student wishes to pursue. Undergraduates who plan to move directly into a highly specialized or technical career had best enroll in vocational programs. No employer looking for an engineer or a hospital technician will be eager to hire someone with a major in English literature. On the other hand, students who expect to take a professional degree in law or medicine will be well advised to follow a liberal arts program in college and leave their vocational training for later. The choice is not so clear, however, for undergraduates who want to find some sort of managerial or supervisory job in business without acquiring an M.B.A. Should such students select a business major or take a traditional liberal arts degree? Since many thousands of undergraduates face this choice every year, the question has considerable practical importance.

A number of researchers have tried to supply an answer.[26] Their work seems to show that vocational majors have an easier time than liberal arts graduates in finding an initial job in business and tend to advance faster and earn more money during their first 10 years of work. After 10 years, the picture becomes more complicated. As time goes on, the technical and practical skills that vocational majors learn in college become less important to continued success. Such abilities as communication skills, human relations, creativity, and "big-picture thinking" matter more. Since liberal arts faculties appear to do a better job than their vocational colleagues in fostering these qualities, graduates with traditional Arts and Sciences majors begin to gain ground. Within the ranks of top management, neither liberal arts nor vocational majors have an advantage.

Studies also show that the nature of one's education has a bearing on *what kind* of position one will occupy in business. Management and engineering majors tend to gravitate toward careers in accounting, production, and finance. Their comparative advantage seems to lie in manufacturing companies. Liberal arts majors are more likely to specialize in marketing, human resources, or public affairs and to move into companies in the service sector.[27]

Future trends are harder to predict. Corporations are becoming more technical and science based, trends that favor business and engineering majors. On the other hand, companies also seem destined to witness faster change, more frequent career shifts, increasingly diverse workforces, and expanding global operations, all of which favor a broad liberal arts education.

In light of these findings, what can one say about the choice between liberal arts and vocational degrees? All in all, though many undergraduates may be excessively concerned with getting a job and earning money, it is hard to fault them for choosing vocational programs. The degrees they earn are essential for many technical jobs and offer advantages in business for at least a decade following graduation. Even in the longer run, there is little indication that students with business degrees will suffer a disadvantage. The practical question, then, is not whether many students are unwisely choosing vocational majors but whether *both* liberal arts *and* vocational programs could do a better job of reconciling the career needs of students with the other goals of a rounded undergraduate education.

How should vocational majors be constructed to respect the other important aims of college? In principle, the guidelines seem fairly clear. Like all majors, vocational programs should not take up so much space in the curriculum that other important educational goals must be sacrificed. Professors should not spend valuable time teaching skills better learned at work, nor ought they to be excessively preoccupied with teaching competencies that may be relevant to a first job but will soon become obsolete. Since critical thinking is as important to almost every occupation as it is to the liberal arts, instructors should try to use active methods of teaching with appropriate feedback. Moreover, because there is more to a calling than making money, vocational concentrations should offer breadth and perspective by including material on the history of the profession, its current role in society, and the recurring moral dilemmas that practitioners face in carrying out their work. Finally, like all majors, vocational programs should include some sort of culminating project that gives students an opportunity to increase their powers of reasoning and analysis by exploring a challenging problem in depth.

How successful are the more prominent occupational majors in meeting these specifications?

Engineering. Engineering is undoubtedly one of the most rigorous and demanding undergraduate programs. Majors must take substantial amounts of math and science to undergird their work in more applied subjects. The courses themselves are generally difficult and time-consuming, with a steady stream of problem sets to solve. The number of courses required also tends to be far greater in engineering than in most other majors. New fields, such as medical robotics, photonics, and nanotechnology, are constantly emerging and creating pressure to add courses to the curriculum.

Most observers would agree that the typical concentration prepares students well to perform technical engineering tasks. The heavy diet of specialized courses exposes them to a wide variety of problems. Along with all the knowledge, the concentration's emphasis on problem-solving does more than most undergraduate programs to help build competence in analysis.

The critical problem in engineering education is that the many requirements of the major leave too little room to pursue other aims of a rounded undergraduate education. This tendency does not seem to matter much to most engineering professors. As Samuel Florman has observed, "Disdain for the liberal arts has become endemic in the engineering community, and the carriers of the disease are too often found among engineering academics."[28] The result is that engineering students take an average of only 9 percent of their courses in the humanities and another 9 percent in the social sciences.[29] Since they rarely receive much guidance about *which* courses to take outside the concentration—and because the heavy demands of the major leave little time for other subjects—many concentrators meet their humanities and social science requirements by flocking to easy courses without much regard for their likely contribution to a rounded education. Of all the well-known college majors, therefore, engineering is surely the narrowest.

There is a price to be paid for focusing so much on vocational skills. By all accounts, the demands of most engineering concentrations interfere with other aims of undergraduate education. In his detailed survey of 24,000 undergraduates, Alexander Astin found that majoring in engineering is negatively associated with a long list of important outcomes, including writing ability, cultural awareness, understanding other races, and foreign language skills. Majors tend to be less satisfied than their classmates with the curriculum, the quality of instruction, and the overall college experience.[30] Norman Nie and Sunshine Hillygus have subsequently added that engineering courses tend to depress political participation after graduation.[31]

In recent years, sources close to the profession have grown more concerned about the narrowness of the standard engineering curriculum. High-level commissions and organizations have issued a series of critical reports. Employers have started to complain that technical mastery is not sufficient for the needs of modern business. Engineers themselves are beginning to recognize that they may be relegated to increasingly limited roles unless they are more broadly educated. In the words of Ernest Smerdon, president of the American Society for Engineering Education, "From Utah to the Ukraine and from Milwaukee to Manila, industry is demanding that our graduates have better teamwork skills, communication abilities, and an understanding of the socioeconomic context in which engineering is practiced."[32] More recently, the National Academy of Engineering has issued a report calling for "engineers who are broadly educated, see themselves as global citizens, can lead in business and public service, as well as in research, development, and design, and are ethical and inclusive of all segments of society."[33] In response to these pressures, the Accreditation Board for Engineering and Technology revised its requirements in 2000 to emphasize a broader set of outcomes, including such basic capabilities as communications skills, ethical sensitivity, ability to collaborate, cultural awareness, and understanding of the sociopolitical environment.[34]

Competencies of this kind are much more closely associated with the liberal arts than with traditional engineering courses. Nevertheless, the engineering curriculum is already too crammed with technical offerings to achieve a broader set of goals merely by directing students to take more classes in the humanities and social sciences. Success will require having liberal arts professors join with their engineering colleagues to integrate work in writing, ethics, and socioeconomic perspectives into existing engineering courses.

It may well be that success in broadening engineering education will only arrive when engineering becomes a graduate program similar to business and law. Even in this event, however, cooperation with the liberal arts faculty will be essential to develop moral reasoning, global awareness, communications skills, and other competencies emphasized by leaders in the profession.[35] Whether Arts and Sciences faculty will agree to collaborate, however, and whether engineering professors will acknowledge the deficiencies in their programs and reach out for help are questions only time can answer. The habits that have inhibited collaboration in the past are deep-seated enough to require basic changes in attitude if engineering faculties and their liberal arts colleagues are ever to build a concentration that will satisfy the needs of employers and achieve the broader aims of a college education.

Education. Education majors offer a sharp contrast to engineering programs.[36] While the latter are noted for their rigor and heavy demands, the former are widely accused of not being rigorous and demanding enough. The typical education major consists of "foundation" courses (including subjects such as developmental psychology or the philosophy and history of education), "methods" courses (covering such matters as pedagogy, curriculum planning, and classroom management), and practice teaching under supervision. All have encountered sharp criticism. Foundation courses are often attacked for being too shallow and too detached from the problems teachers actually encounter in the classroom; methods courses are widely condemned for being too practical; and practice teaching is frequently accused of being poorly supervised and largely disconnected from the rest of the curriculum. Throughout the major, instructors are charged with lecturing too much and providing poor models of teaching for their students.[37]

In one respect, however, the prospects for building a well-rounded program are better in education than in engineering. Education majors have ample time to take liberal arts courses. In fact, undergraduates can major in an Arts and Sciences discipline and still take enough education courses to get accredited in most states. In many states, prospective high school teachers are even required to take the equivalent of a liberal arts major in the subject (e.g., history or English or mathematics) that they intend to teach. Elementary school teachers have no such requirement but still take most of their courses in the liberal arts.

Both Arts and Sciences faculties and education professors have much to gain by cooperating with one another. Education faculties can help their students by working with colleagues from the liberal arts to shape a set of general education requirements for the major that serve the needs of prospective teachers better than the smorgasbord of courses currently available under the distribution programs of most colleges. In addition, education professors can benefit from the help of faculty members in Arts and Sciences departments to infuse more substance into "foundation" courses on subjects such as human development, cognitive science, philosophy of education, and the politics and policy issues of public education.

Arts and Sciences professors likewise have a stake in helping to improve the education concentration. As matters now stand, after controlling for differences in intelligence, socioeconomic status, and the like, researchers find that majoring in education is negatively correlated with critical thinking and problem-solving, general knowledge, openness to diversity, and voting in elections.[38] Every member of the faculty should feel some obligation to help overcome these deficiencies so that education majors, like other students in the college, have a chance to enjoy the fruits of a rounded undergraduate education.

Even from a purely self-interested standpoint, liberal arts professors should want to do their part to make sure that all children have the best possible primary and secondary education. After all, today's public school students will be tomorrow's undergraduates. With this in mind, members of traditional departments, such as English, history, and mathematics, ought to do what they can to ensure that aspiring teachers have a proper foundation to teach these subjects well.

Despite these common interests, the prospects for greater cooperation are not promising. Arts and Sciences professors tend to look down on education departments as havens of superficial learning for students of inferior ability. University officials themselves often seem to share these sentiments. As Jean King observes, teacher education exists in many institutions as "a second-rate subject, tolerated in principle but rarely supported in practice."[39] In more than a few institutions, education programs are deliberately administered as "cash cows" to generate profits for other parts of the university. College officials who count on education schools to help their bottom line will not be quick to sponsor costly reforms. Education faculties naturally respond to such treatment by feeling resentful and defensive. Until these attitudes change, creative collaboration between education departments and their liberal arts colleagues seems destined to remain one of the major unrealized opportunities of the contemporary university.

Business. Business studies, most popular of all concentrations, seek to give students the knowledge and skills they need to function as managers in fields such as accounting, finance, marketing, and human resources. In addition, most business majors include broader courses on such subjects as ethics, corporations and society, and the social responsibilities of business. Unlike engineering, business concentrations need not interfere with other purposes of a broad undergraduate education. The Association to Advance Collegiate Schools of Business (AACSB) requires that at least 40 percent of students' courses be in the liberal arts, and most students take 50 percent or even more.

Despite this accommodation, management studies seem to have an adverse effect on some important aims of a college education. After surveying many thousands of undergraduates, Alexander Astin found that majoring in business is negatively correlated with appreciation of other cultures and interest in promoting racial understanding.[40] Norman Nie and Sunshine Hillygus report that taking business courses leads to lower voting rates and lower political and civic involvement.[41] More work is needed to discover the reasons for these results. Whatever the cause, the findings are distressing, since they not only run counter to the aims of undergraduate education but also contradict what most companies claim to want in the students they hire.

Employers find additional grounds for criticizing business majors. The most common complaints include poor oral and writing abilities, lack of ethical sensitivity, weak human relations and leadership skills, inadequate powers of analysis and critical thinking, and insufficient global awareness.[42] Conscious of these concerns, the AACSB announced new accreditation standards in 2003 calling for more emphasis on communication and analytic skills, multicultural awareness, and ethical sensitivity.[43]

Once again, therefore, conditions seem ripe for closer cooperation between a professional school faculty and its liberal arts counterpart. All the added skills and abilities identified by the AACSB are linked more closely to the liberal arts than to specialized courses in business. Thus both faculties have common interests and complementary strengths. Liberal arts faculties have a special understanding of competencies such as communication, cultural awareness, and ethics by virtue of their long experience in teaching many of these subjects and considering their use in a variety of contexts. Management professors bring a more concrete understanding of how the competencies connect with the practical needs of business organizations.

These converging interests may still not suffice to bring the two faculties together. Liberal arts professors may condemn their business colleagues for being too practical, while management faculty reject Arts and Sciences professors for being too abstract. It would be a pity if such differences prevented serious cooperation. Both the liberal arts and business education will be diminished if the two faculties cannot overcome their traditional separation and learn to collaborate effectively.

LIBERAL ARTS MAJORS

Many undergraduates who plan to move directly to a job and know what sort of job they want still seek a liberal arts degree. What, if anything, should colleges do to prepare these students for their careers? This issue rarely arises in debates about liberal education. While participants often question whether vocational programs are consistent with a suitably rounded education, they seldom inquire whether liberal arts programs are sufficiently respectful of undergraduates' desire for a successful, satisfying career. More's the pity. A well-crafted college curriculum, even if it offers no vocational majors, can do much to help students find jobs and fare well in their chosen careers.

The most important step that Arts and Sciences faculties can take is simply to do a better job of achieving the traditional goals of liberal education. As previously noted, when business leaders describe what they most need from the young managers and engineers they employ, they regularly stress not only strong communications skills and an ability to think critically and solve problems, but also a capacity to collaborate with others and work with diverse populations, a sensitivity to ethical problems, a strong self-discipline, and — for increasing numbers of companies — an appreciation of global issues and an ability to understand foreign cultures.[44] These are all important aims of a liberal education and are accepted by almost every college faculty. As previous chapters have pointed out, however, many students graduate having made only modest progress in acquiring these capabilities. That is why employers who complain about the college graduates they hire grumble not only about the lack of sufficient technical and vocational skills but also about deficiencies in speaking, writing, and other competencies long associated with a traditional college education.

A very different complaint from employers is that many of the young B.A. recipients they hire are lacking in self-discipline. According to their superiors, they often have difficulty being on time, working hard enough to do each job well, or listening carefully and following instructions. In view of these concerns, it is worth asking whether faculties themselves are not partially to blame by permitting a certain laxity to become entrenched on many campuses. Colleges have allowed widespread grade inflation and shown increased tolerance of late or incomplete work. As George Kuh points out after surveying hundreds of colleges, "There seems to be a breakdown of shared responsibility for learning —on the part of faculty members who allow students to get by with far less than maximal effort, and on the part of students who are not taking full advantage of the resources institutions provide."[45] If undergraduates can receive high marks for sloppy work, routinely get extensions for assignments not completed on time, and escape being penalized for various forms of minor misconduct, it is hardly a surprise that employers find them lacking in self-discipline. Doing something to remedy this problem is not a crass concession to commercial interests but a useful reform that serves the interests of faculties and students as well as employers.

A much more controversial step would be to allow undergraduates to take a small number of elective courses in practical vocational subjects, such as accounting, marketing, or finance. Arguably even two or three courses of this kind would help undergraduates decide what kind of business career to pursue and improve their prospects for employment. Recognizing these advantages, a number of colleges have already begun to provide this opportunity, but some liberal arts faculties still resist, fearing that any vocational courses they provide will become a beachhead for undermining the entire liberal arts curriculum and subverting the larger purposes it serves.

Barring all vocational courses makes little difference in colleges where almost all seniors go on to graduate or professional school. The consequences are more serious, however, for the majority of colleges in which most liberal arts students go directly into the workforce. Some companies have begun paying business schools to give a summer "crash course" in the basics of management for the new liberal arts graduates they have hired.[46] While this step may solve the problem for some undergraduates, it does nothing for seniors seeking employment in companies that cannot or will not sponsor a program of this kind. Without any exposure to the skills and knowledge of the business world, such students could easily find themselves at a disadvantage in competing for jobs when they graduate.

At present, most business majors take at least half their courses in the liberal arts. In contrast, liberal arts majors have traditionally taken an average of less than 2 percent of their total courses in business.[47] In effect, therefore, many undergraduates are choosing between a curriculum entirely devoted to the liberal arts and a vocational program that reserves half the curriculum for the liberal arts and half for courses specifically related to a career. It is not at all clear that such a choice is helpful for students or even in the best interest of Arts and Sciences faculties. A mere two or three elective courses in business or some other practical pursuit could help many undergraduates prepare for work without interfering significantly with the broader values of a liberal education. By encouraging such courses, faculties might even attract some undergraduates who would prefer a liberal arts curriculum but fear the consequences when they have to look for a job.

THE CRITICAL CHALLENGE

Efforts to prepare students for a career are pulled in different directions by the two most powerful forces shaping American undergraduate education: the views of the faculty, on the one hand, and, on the other, the market pressures that students exert through their power to choose which institutions to attend. A few colleges have enough prestige that their faculties are not much bound by student opinion, leaving them reasonably free to build their educational programs according to their own ideas of what is appropriate. At most colleges, however, faculties must pay close heed to what prospective students want in order to attract enough applicants to fill their classrooms with undergraduates of adequate ability and promise.

Unfortunately neither faculty nor students can be counted upon to make fully appropriate choices about the role of vocation in a rounded undergraduate education. Arts and Sciences professors tend to attach too little importance to student career needs. Undergraduates, and the vocational faculties that prepare them for work, often neglect educational goals that serve the larger community, such as moral sensitivity and civic responsibility, and take too narrow a view of the competencies needed to succeed in a career. Achieving an ideal balance, then, requires a collaborative effort on the part of everyone involved.

Most universities have not yet managed to reconcile these two conflicting tendencies. Liberal arts programs seldom take adequate account of the crucial importance of students' careers—careers that will inevitably affect what kind of persons they become, how well they balance the claims of work and family, and what opportunities they have to serve others besides themselves. Vocational faculties, either by choice or because they have been rebuffed by their liberal arts colleagues, do not collaborate enough with Arts and Sciences faculties to prepare their students well for purposes other than performing the tasks demanded by their jobs.

The pressure to respond appropriately to vocational needs will not diminish in the foreseeable future. Liberal arts professors are unlikely to find their students becoming less preoccupied with their careers. The growing numbers of older and part-time students and the continuing high priority freshmen place on making money promise to keep vocational concerns at the forefront of their minds. At the same time, vocational faculties do not merely encounter pressure to pay more attention to specific practical skills; instead they are being urged to do a better job of developing precisely the competencies and qualities of mind traditionally associated with a liberal education.

The evolving priorities of employers make it easier for vocational programs and Arts and Sciences departments to collaborate, since the needs they serve increasingly overlap. Both faculties have good reason to cooperate. Without the help of liberal arts colleagues, vocational programs are likely to fall far short both in meeting the needs of employers and in preparing students for a rich, fulfilling life outside of work. Without paying greater attention to the career needs of their students, Arts and Sciences faculties seem destined to go on serving a minority of undergraduates while leaving the rest to vocational programs that deny them the full benefits of a rounded college education. Only if both faculties recognize the cost of going their separate ways will they achieve the full potential of both the liberal arts and vocational education in serving all the needs of their students.

12 | IMPROVING THE QUALITY OF UNDERGRADUATE EDUCATION

It may seem surprising that a former college president would write an entire book on the weaknesses of American undergraduate education. After all, public schools are supposed to be the problem child of our educational system. America's universities are generally acknowledged to be preeminent in the world. No fewer than 17 of the 20 leading universities on this planet (and 35 of the top 50) are located in the United States, according to a recent international survey.[1] A whopping 93 percent of Americans agree that "colleges and universities are among the most valuable resources to the U.S."[2] Students compete furiously to gain admission to the leading colleges, and large majorities of all alumni in this country pronounce themselves satisfied with the teaching they received and with their overall undergraduate experience.[3]

While these results deserve our respect, they are not as impressive as they seem, at least as far as colleges are concerned. International rankings reflect a university's research reputation rather than the quality of its teaching, and they are based at least as much on graduate and professional schools as on undergraduate education. The satisfaction felt by students and alumni is not entirely reassuring either. American undergraduates undoubtedly enjoy college and think they benefit from it. But students are not infallible judges of their own learning, nor do they become so after they graduate. They can certainly recognize poor teaching, but, having experienced only their own college, they lack the comparative perspective to know whether they are receiving the best instruction — or even close to the best — that universities are capable of providing.

When one moves from opinion polls to direct evidence of student learning in college, the reasons for concern grow clearer. Most studies do show evidence of growth, but almost all the findings leave ample room for improvement.[4] Even among the selective colleges that are ranked so highly and attract so many applicants, fewer than half of the recent graduates believe that college contributed "a great deal" to their competence in analytic and writing skills or in acquiring knowledge of their major fields of study.[5] Tests of cognitive ability show considerable gains during college, but the vast majority of graduating students are still naïve relativists who "do not show the ability to defensibly critique their own judgments" in analyzing the kinds of unstructured problems commonly encountered in real life.[6] Surveys of student progress in other important dimensions, including writing, numeracy, and foreign language proficiency, indicate that only a minority of undergraduates improve substantially, while some actually regress.[7]

College curricula also have notable weaknesses, despite the periodic reviews by countless faculties across the country. Much time is wasted in the halfhearted pursuit of unrealistic goals — required foreign language courses that do not lead to proficiency, introductory writing classes taught by untrained graduate students with little reinforcement from other courses in the curriculum, basic science courses never designed for the nonscientists who are forced to take them. Additional hours are spent fulfilling concentration requirements that have expanded beyond the purpose that led to concentrations in the first place. Meanwhile majorities of students graduate without receiving instruction in quantitative methods or moral reasoning or in the subjects needed to prepare them as knowledgeable citizens in a democracy or as perceptive actors in a world in which their country will be increasingly influenced by other countries and cultures.

There are few outward signs of serious distress over these conditions. After decades of preeminence in the world, American universities are showing signs of becoming self-satisfied. While pockets of innovation exist throughout American higher education, most professors teach as they traditionally have, confident that the ways that have worked well enough in the past will continue to serve in the future. Though trained in research themselves, they continue to ignore the accumulating body of experimental work suggesting that forms of teaching that engage students actively in the learning process do significantly better than conventional methods in achieving goals, such as critical thinking and problem-solving, that faculties everywhere hold dear.

Now is hardly the time for such complacency. Our society is growing ever more complex, requiring greater skill and knowledge from its public servants, its professionals, its executives, and its citizens. Our college graduates face increasing competition from ambitious, intelligent young people overseas, eager to claim whatever skilled work can be digitized and outsourced to distant places around the globe. Sensing the opportunities, governments in other advanced and developing countries are beginning to pay more attention to improving their universities. In such an environment, the moment has surely come for America's colleges to take a more candid look at their weaknesses and think more boldly about setting higher educational standards for themselves.

WHY COLLEGES UNDERPERFORM

Why do colleges seem so reluctant to make major changes in the way they conduct their educational programs? The reason is not that they are indifferent to the welfare of their students, and critics are wrong to suggest the contrary. Most college presidents and deans genuinely care about undergraduates and want to see them educated well. The great majority of professors enjoy their teaching, like their students, and devote much time to their classroom responsibilities. Yet enjoying teaching and caring about students do not necessarily bring a willingness to reexamine familiar practices and search for new methods that could serve the purpose better. Indeed, the opposite is often true, at least for professors whose classes are going reasonably well. And competition from bright young people in Bangalore and Beijing is unlikely to change matters, at least for the foreseeable future. So long as professors continue to teach conscientiously in their accustomed way and colleges keep up with the competition in facilities, tuition, and financial aid, no one need fear any immediate consequences for failing to do their best to lift the quality of teaching and learning to the highest attainable level.

The lack of compelling pressure to improve undergraduate education helps to explain the manner in which most faculties carry out their shared responsibility for the enterprise—their casual treatment of its purposes, their neglect of basic courses that develop important skills, their reluctance even to discuss issues of pedagogy, their ignorance of research on student learning, and their unwillingness to pay attention to much of what goes on outside the classroom. These patterns of behavior in turn have their roots in the way in which research universities train prospective faculty members. Most other forms of professional education make some effort to impart the skills that students need for all the important tasks they will perform—or at least all the skills that can effectively be taught. Ph.D. programs are the conspicuous exception. Preoccupied with research and suspicious of anything "vocational," Arts and Sciences departments have never made a serious effort to prepare Ph.D. candidates as teachers, even though most of their graduate students over the course of their careers will be primarily interested in their teaching and will spend more time at it than they devote to scholarship.[8] In the eyes of most faculty members in research universities, teaching is an art that is either too simple to require formal preparation, too personal to be taught to others, or too innate to be conveyed to anyone lacking the necessary gift.* Lacking formal preparation, gradu-

---

*Granted, Ph.D. students do have opportunities to develop pedagogic skills by serving as teaching fellows leading discussions in weekly sections of large lecture courses. In recent decades, some universities have even created centers that hold seminars about teaching for Ph.D. candidates and offer videotaping to help fledgling instructors watch themselves in action under the tutelage of a helpful coach. It is noteworthy, however, that these centers have rarely been started by academic departments; instead they generally owe their existence to college administrators who are well aware of the chronic complaints of undergraduates about the uneven quality of instruction offered by teaching fellows. Use of the centers is typically optional, availed of only by teaching fellows who care to participate. Moreover, valuable as they are, many of these centers are chiefly concerned with helping graduate students improve in the use of traditional ways of teaching. They seldom question existing forms of instruction in any fundamental way or train graduate students in the use of new methods that may be more effective in improving critical thinking or achieving other aims of undergraduate education. Nor do they acquaint students with the research on learning by cognitive psychologists or even teach them how to construct a proper exam, assess their own teaching, or evaluate the success of innovative methods of instruction.

ate students have learned to teach by modeling themselves after the professors they admire who have taught them. This tradition introduces a profoundly conservative bias into faculty behavior that acts as an anchor to deter major changes in established forms of instruction and educational practice.

Once Ph.D.s begin their academic careers, they find that the development of appropriate teaching methods is rarely treated as a subject for collective deliberation but instead is typically left to the discretion of individual professors. Most of the latter do adapt their courses regularly, abandoning outmoded material and lectures that have not seemed to work well while incorporating new knowledge when it comes to their attention. Since faculty members normally keep abreast of published work in their fields, the *content* of their courses tends to be reasonably up to date. The same cannot be said of their teaching *methods*. Professors seldom receive clear evidence of how much students are learning. Classes themselves offer few clues, especially in large classes taught by lectures to a passive audience. Course evaluations offer some insight, but they usually focus on whether the instructor was clear, knowledgeable, and accessible to students while saying little about how much students think they learned.* Papers and exams are not terribly informative either and, in any event, are often read by teaching fellows, not by faculty members themselves.

Despite the lack of reliable feedback to show them how much their students are learning, some professors do try new techniques. Across the country, one can find instructors ex-

---

*According to one survey, only 40 percent of college instructors even use student evaluations in planning or revising their courses; Joan S. Stark and Lisa R. Latucca, *Shaping the College Curriculum: Academic Plans in Action* (1997), p. 121.

perimenting with collaborative learning, experiential learning, service learning, problem-based learning, learning communities, and other promising initiatives. But these innovators remain a minority. Safely insulated from reliable evidence of how their students are progressing, most faculty members have happily succumbed to the Lake Wobegone effect. As surveys have confirmed, close to 90 percent of college professors consider their teaching "above average."[9]

Beyond individual teachers lies a deeper reluctance on the part of academic leaders and their faculties as a whole to undertake a continuous, systematic effort to improve the quality of education. In this respect, universities are badly out of step with the times. Most successful organizations today, regardless of the work they do, are trying hard to become effective "learning organizations" that engage in an ongoing process of improvement by constantly evaluating their performance, identifying problems, trying various remedies, measuring their success, discarding those that do not work, and incorporating those that do. In theory, universities should be leaders in such efforts, since they have pioneered in developing methods for evaluating other institutions in the society. In fact, however, they leave a lot to be desired when it comes to working systematically to improve their own performance.

It is true that after much external prodding many colleges have begun to assess how their students are progressing toward various educational goals. Nevertheless fewer than one-third of all colleges nationwide conduct comprehensive evaluations to determine whether they are achieving the purposes of their general education program. Higher proportions try to assess student progress toward certain individual goals, such as competence in writing or critical thinking. Still, as one recent review pointed out, "just because an institution assessed student learning outcomes relative to a general education goal [does] not mean that the assessment information was used in [planning the curriculum]."[10] Nor is there much indication that these evaluations affect how professors teach their courses or how departments develop their concentrations. Still less evident are campuswide efforts to combine assessments with an ongoing process for identifying problems, finding innovative ways to address them, and testing the new methods to see whether they work. In short, faculties seem inclined to use research and experimentation to understand and improve every institution, process, and human activity except their own.

Illustrations of this tendency abound. For example, convincing evidence exists that various groups of students consistently perform well below the levels one would expect from their SAT scores and high school grades. Most black and Latino students fall into this category.[11] So do most recruited athletes in the revenue-producing sports.[12] Careful analysis would doubtless reveal other groups that also tend to underperform. The success achieved by a handful of colleges with minority students suggests that the problem of underperformance can be overcome. But efforts of this kind are very rare. On most campuses, no systematic attempt is even made to determine which students are underperforming or how they might be helped to do better, despite the claim in countless college catalogues that the institution is committed to "helping all our students develop to their full potential."*

---

*It is true that most colleges have ways of giving special assistance to students who are in danger of flunking out. But helping at-risk students is not the same as overcoming underperformance. Many students who perform well below their potential are not in danger of flunking out. Moreover the reasons for underperformance are not necessarily the same as those encountered in the typical student who is failing courses.

There is also resistance to using research on student progress to raise questions about existing teaching methods. The reluctance to engage in such self-scrutiny was aptly illustrated by an episode at one East Coast university a decade or more ago. A curious official managed to insert a new question into the student evaluation forms asking members of each general education class how much the course had helped to improve their ability to think critically and analyze problems. The question was hardly unreasonable, since the faculty had declared in adopting the curriculum that its chief purpose was to teach undergraduates to think critically. As it happened, however, although students had good things to say about most of their professors, in less than 10 percent of the courses did they report that their thinking skills had improved appreciably. At this point, with such a huge majority of students indicating that the general education curriculum was failing to achieve its principal objective, one would have thought that the faculty and administration would rouse themselves to review the problem thoroughly. In fact, nothing of the kind occurred. Instead the troublesome question was dropped from the evaluation forms and did not appear again.

In this environment, new courses and new knowledge regularly find their way into the curriculum, but teaching methods change very slowly. Meanwhile persistent learning problems remain undetected and unresolved. It is therefore not surprising that, in sharp contrast to many human endeavors in which performance and quality clearly improve over time, no one knows whether college students are writing better or thinking more rigorously or making greater progress toward other educational goals than they were 50 years ago.

These observations help to answer a question posed at the end of Chapter 1: Are universities at fault because they cannot show that the quality of teaching and learning in America's colleges has actually improved over the past half-century (despite vast increases in faculty size, library holdings, facilities, and other material resources)? Admittedly the answer is not self-evident. Undergraduate education is not the only enterprise in which no one knows whether improvement has taken place. The same can be said of poetry or architecture or popular music. In most of these activities, however, the quality of the activity is all but impossible to measure or compare with that in earlier periods. Hence there is no effective way to determine whether progress has occurred, or even to engage in a process of enlightened trial and error in which proficiency gradually improves through constant experimentation and evaluation. Individuals may attempt new methods and progress according to their own personal standards of quality, but others are bound to disagree on whether any real improvement has occurred.

In the case of undergraduate education, some forms of learning are also hard or even impossible to measure, such as achieving self-knowledge or acquiring a philosophy of life. Yet many other important competencies do lend themselves to rough but usable assessments. Student writing, quantitative reasoning, foreign language proficiency, and critical thinking and analysis are all pertinent examples. Using available measures, colleges can discover important skills that are not being mastered, subjects students do not truly understand, entire groups of undergraduates that are performing well below their apparent capabilities. With these problems identified, faculties can experiment with new methods of teaching and gradually develop more effective ways of improving student learning that can be described and used successfully by others. It is the failure of most college faculties to make serious efforts of this kind that merits disappointment over the way undergraduate education has evolved.

IS SOMETHING WRONG WITH CONTINUOUS EVALUATION AND EXPERIMENTATION?

Critics will offer a string of objections to rebut this conclusion. Some will point out that research on teaching and learning is rarely rigorous enough to meet the exacting scholarly standards to which every self-respecting university should aspire. There is doubtless some truth to this charge. As a practical matter, it is often impossible to assemble perfectly matched control groups or to perform double-blind experiments in which neither of the two groups compared knows which one is receiving the innovative method. Disagreements will also arise in deciding how to measure proficiency in writing, critical thinking, and other educational goals. Even so, to let such problems discredit institutional research would allow the best to be the enemy of the good. The proper test for universities to apply is not whether their assessments meet the most rigorous scholarly standards but whether they can provide more reliable information than the hunches, random experiences, and personal opinions that currently guide most faculty decisions about educational issues. By this standard, there are surely many important forms of intellectual development that can be described and measured well enough to conduct useful studies to evaluate existing educational programs and assess new methods of instruction.* If faculties are willing to examine their stu-

---

*One can easily construct a list of simple questions that seem quite susceptible to assessment. To mention but a few: How much active discussion goes on in each undergraduate course? Do the exams in current use

dents and record the results on official transcripts, it is hard for them to argue that they are incapable of devising methods of assessment reliable enough to evaluate the effects of their teaching on student learning.

Other skeptics will dismiss investigations of this kind, claiming that the results often conflict with one another and rarely reveal large, unambiguous gains from using one method of teaching rather than another. Even if these assertions are true, however, the conclusion hardly follows. Research results do differ, either because the students involved varied from one study to the next, or because the research methods were faulty, or because the measures that different investigators used to determine student progress were not the same. Yet the proper response is surely not to ignore research but to conduct investigations on one's own campus, taking care to construct them as carefully as possible. Similarly the fact that research on new methods of teaching rarely shows dramatic gains is hardly a valid reason for abandoning the effort. An accumulation of small improvements over time

---

test critical thinking or only the recall of information? Do students feel that their courses have improved their powers of analysis and critical thinking? What proportion of students who complete the college's foreign language requirement can conduct a conversation or understand a television broadcast in the language they have studied? How much writing do students do during their four years, and how does the writing of seniors in different concentrations compare with their writing as freshmen? How do seniors compare with freshmen in their ability to use quantitative skills to solve practical problems? Do new initiatives in promoting civic responsibility lead to increased voting (and other forms of civic engagement) several years after graduation? Does group learning improve student performance on exams, especially exams requiring problem-solving? Which categories of students tend to perform below their academic potential (based on prior grades and test scores), and, if efforts are made to address underperformance, are they successful?

will eventually yield impressive results. That is the way most progress in learning occurs, and it would be folly to give up the quest merely because it may not produce a single new technique that will transform undergraduate teaching.

Finally professors may fear that, once a process of assessment takes hold, colleges will become preoccupied with those forms of learning that can be measured and neglect the subtler yet equally important educational goals that do not lend themselves to testing and evaluation. This worry might be understandable in contemplating assessments imposed by government officials. It is much less persuasive in the case of studies undertaken by the institution itself. It would surely be unfortunate if colleges had so little confidence in their own judgment that they allowed their concern over goals that cannot be measured to block serious efforts to improve those forms of learning that are susceptible to evaluation.*

---

*Some concerned professors may also object that a process of enlightened trial and error, such as the one described herein, will be unfair to students since it subjects them to experiments that could prove unsuccessful. Others may argue to the contrary that, if an instructor truly believes that a new way of teaching will be better than the conventional approach, it is unfair to try out the innovation on only one group of students while leaving the others to make do with less effective methods of instruction. Neither of these arguments is convincing. Education is inherently uncertain in its effects, and teachers continuously try out new subject matter, new readings, and new ways of organizing their courses (even though their methods of instruction rarely change or receive careful evaluation). Hence students are often exposed to innovations of one kind or another, some of which work well and others not. It would be disastrous to abandon this process on grounds of fairness. Over time, all students will benefit from an active process of enlightened trial and error. If they are occasionally subjected to an unsuccessful experiment, they will doubtless be the beneficiaries of others. To halt this process would simply invite stagnation and condemn all students to the continued use of teaching methods that are less effective than they should be.

POSSIBILITIES FOR REFORM

What are the prospects for turning colleges into effective learning organizations? Not good, unfortunately. The weaknesses of undergraduate education may be real, but they serve important faculty interests. Like most human beings, professors do not relish having their work evaluated by others, especially when the evaluators ask potentially awkward questions, such as whether their students are actually making progress toward widely accepted goals. Nor do instructors who are used to lecturing welcome research on new pedagogies that may put pressure on them to change the way they teach. Departments, too, have special interests to protect. They have a natural inclination to resist any effort by outsiders to influence the content of their concentration, even if there are indications that it is undermining other important aims of undergraduate education. They may permit their majors to fill more space in the curriculum than is truly necessary, because such a policy lets them spend more time teaching the courses closest to their professional interests. They allow writing courses and language instruction to remain substandard at many colleges, because professors in the sponsoring departments not only refuse to teach these classes themselves but also find it advantageous to use them to finance a larger cadre of graduate students.

In theory, presidents and deans are supposed to counteract self-interested behavior to make sure that the legitimate needs of students are properly addressed. In practice, however, academic leaders often fail to fulfill this responsibility. Ultimate power over instruction and curriculum rests with the faculty. While leaders have considerable leverage and influence of their own, they are often reluctant to employ these assets for fear of arousing opposition from the faculty that could attract unfavorable publicity, worry potential donors, and even threaten their jobs. After all, success in increasing student learning is seldom rewarded, and its benefits are usually hard to demonstrate, far more so than success in lifting the SAT scores of the entering class or in raising the money to build new laboratories or libraries.

The point of these remarks is not to berate professors or their academic leaders, most of whom are serious, dedicated people. But they are also human and hence are no quicker than anyone else to alter practices that serve important personal and professional interests if there are no compelling reasons to do so. Until Ph.D. programs include a serious preparation for teaching and convey a deeper understanding of the complexities of student learning, faculties will not only have little inclination to change their ways, they will not even perceive much need to do so. Without more prodding and encouragement than they are currently receiving, presidents and deans are also unlikely to challenge the status quo. In the present environment, then, it would be myopic simply to wait in the hope that reform will emerge spontaneously from within.

In the past, forces beyond the university have sometimes helped to bring about educational change. But it is hard today to discern any source of outside pressure powerful enough to do so. Some 15 years ago, Allan Bloom, Dinesh D'Souza, William Bennett, and other writers attracted wide attention with their criticisms of higher education. By and large, however, they chose to direct the public conversation to topics such as political correctness, affirmative action, and the neglect of the Great Books rather than the kinds of issues treated in this study. Now that these debates have subsided, interest has shifted to concerns over college costs, accessibility, and graduation rates. Issues involving the quality of teaching and learning remain off the radar screen for most of the interested public.

In the business world, competition often forces companies to improve as new competitors continually enter the field with innovative methods that increase efficiency and improve quality. In higher education, however, new universities rarely appear, and those that do are generally too frail to offer serious competition. Recently several for-profit universities in the United States have emerged and attracted students, but they too are unlikely to bring about much constructive change. Although they may encourage some innovation, say, in the use of the Internet for distance learning, their greatest influence will almost certainly be to intensify the pressures on struggling colleges to sacrifice liberal education for practical programs of vocational training.

Students are another conceivable force for change. Like consumers, they can exert pressure on colleges by the choices they make about which institutions to attend. Since the competition to attract talented undergraduates is always intense, one might have thought that their preferences would generate a powerful stimulus for educational reform. As previously pointed out, however, prospective students have no real way of knowing which college or program will help them learn and develop best. Competition in attracting applicants may cause colleges to make certain innovations, such as introducing honors programs or foreign study opportunities, that seem particularly popular with undergraduates. On the whole, however, there is little sign that students are clamoring for the kinds of reforms recommended in these pages. If they are looking for anything, it is likely to be something that helps them find a job or reduce their college debts, not better courses in civic education, moral reasoning, or foreign cultures. What competition for students usually brings about are new vocational programs, merit scholarships, and tuition discounts rather than the kinds of changes suggested in this volume.

Among the external agents of reform, state governments are making the most visible efforts to induce colleges to improve. Facing mounting appropriations for higher education and anxious to reap the benefits of a well-trained workforce, state officials have started to ask whether they are getting adequate value for the money they give to colleges and universities. Dissatisfied with the answers they are receiving from campus leaders, they have begun creating measures of their own and adjusting a portion of their budget allocations in accordance with the results. By now, more than 40 states have imposed some sort of program to measure the performance of public colleges and universities.[13]

Though well intended, these efforts to impose accountability have not proved notably effective. For one thing, the standards have typically been devised without input from faculty representatives, thus greatly reducing their chances of having any effect on what goes on in college classrooms. For another, the measures used are generally too crude to be helpful. Some of them track outcomes that are largely beyond the college's control, such as how many graduates remain in the state or how many are employed (and at what average salary) a year after graduation. Other indicators look at how well students perform on standardized tests in their senior year, but the tests are often crude and the results usually tell more about how intelligent students were when they entered college than about what they learned during their four years there.

Officials may eventually correct some of these defects. Past experience, however, suggests an even greater risk that states will put undue emphasis on standardized test scores that do not accurately measure what a good liberal education should be trying to accomplish and cause college authorities to concentrate on excelling in the tests at the expense of other, more important educational goals. It is also doubtful whether officials will ever devise a single set of measures that can reliably assess and compare the effectiveness of the highly diverse set of institutions, educational programs, and student populations that make up a typical state higher education system. Even if they did, budget allocations are a clumsy weapon for reforming undergraduate education. Awarding added funds to the leadership of a successful college may do nothing to motivate the professors who are primarily responsible for the quality of the education offered. Conversely, taking money from the least successful schools may simply deprive them of resources they need to improve their performance.

All in all, there is little prospect that state governments will succeed in imposing effective performance measures from the outside, let alone force improvements in learning by penalties and rewards. Probably the best one can expect from performance budgeting is that it will convey a sense of official dissatisfaction that will cause campus officials to pay more attention to undergraduate education. But even that may not focus much effort on the practices most in need of reform.

A very different source of outside pressure has emerged in recent decades through the rise to prominence of national college rankings, such as those published annually by *U.S. News and World Report*. Most campus officials are sensitive to these ratings and want to move up in the pecking order, hoping to attract better students and more donations. As a result, if the rankings had anything to do with the quality of education, they might force universities to work harder at improving teaching and learning.

Unfortunately nothing of the kind occurs, since the ratings are based on matters that are largely unrelated to the quality of education. The principal factors used to rank colleges include the quality of the student body (measured by SAT scores) and the reputation of the faculty in the eyes of administrators at other institutions. The faculty's reputation has far more to do with research than with education, since few people outside a campus have any idea how effectively its professors teach, let alone how much its students learn. The quality of the student body may appear to be more relevant, since one might think that the ablest applicants would gravitate to colleges offering a better education and that students would learn more at institutions where they were surrounded by brighter classmates. In fact, however, neither assumption may be true. Since applicants have no real way of comparing the quality of education at the colleges they are considering, they tend to choose on other grounds, such as the amount of financial aid available or the average SAT scores of their prospective classmates. As for the effect of brighter students on learning, most studies find that undergraduates at schools with high average SATs do not make significantly greater progress toward critical thinking and other measurable goals than students at schools with lower test scores (after controlling for differences in intelligence).[14]

Doubts about the relevance of college ratings have been confirmed by recent research on how closely they correlate with the use of teaching methods and other forms of active student engagement that researchers consider optimal for learning. These studies show little or no relationship between the ranking of colleges and the extent to which they utilize the recommended practices.[15] If anything, then, the U.S. News ratings, far from improving undergraduate education, help to shift attention away from serious efforts to enhance student learning toward wasteful attempts to climb in the rankings by using scarce resources to fund merit scholarships or lure faculty members with glittering research reputations from other institutions.*

A more promising private initiative to improve undergraduate education is the National Survey of Student Engagement (NSSE). Founded just a few years ago with support from the Pew Foundation, NSSE conducts a survey of all interested colleges and their students to determine the prevalence of active forms of teaching and student engagement on each campus.[16] For example, students are asked how often they speak in class, talk with a professor, write a paper, make an oral presentation, participate in group learning, or engage in community service. They also indicate how often they are called upon to exercise higher-order thinking skills and how frequently they receive prompt feedback on their coursework. All the practices surveyed have been linked by researchers to improved learning of one kind or another. Once college officials receive the results, they will presumably do what they can to encourage greater use of the

---

*Higher education organizations, such as the Association of American Colleges and Universities, have made a more helpful contribution to the quality of education by publishing short monographs summarizing relevant research about teaching. Although these essays are useful, no one can be sure how much impact they have had on the policies and practices of colleges. There is little indication that the publications have penetrated very far into curriculum reviews at large research universities. They have had more influence in some comprehensive universities and smaller liberal arts colleges, where faculties, deans, and presidents often seem more intent on trying to improve the quality of teaching and learning. Whatever their impact, they surely render a valuable service by culling the fruits of research from a host of professional journals and explaining their relevance to the kinds of issues that colleges might consider in reviewing their educational programs.

recommended methods, using the findings as ammunition to persuade their faculties to cooperate.

Valuable as they are, however, the NSSE surveys can only accomplish so much. Although participation has been increasing, only 529 institutions signed up in 2005, roughly 25 percent of America's four-year colleges. Significantly, almost none of the most prominent research universities or liberal arts colleges have seen fit to participate, a result that helps confirm the impression that institutions at the top of the *U.S. News* rankings are rarely leaders in seeking innovative efforts to improve student learning on their campuses.

NSSE's influence is also limited by the fact that its findings are confidential, so that applicants cannot see the results before deciding which college to attend. Thus faculties may use the surveys to make constructive changes, but the pressure of competition and publicity will not force them to do so. Moreover, the survey covers only a list of specific educational practices. Those it includes can improve student learning, but nothing in the survey will prompt colleges to pay more attention to neglected subjects, such as moral reasoning and civic responsibility, or to examine whether their current language requirements and freshman writing programs are worth preserving, or to experiment with new approaches not included in the NSSE list of recommended practices. In sum, what NSSE provides is clearly worthwhile, but it is far from a complete remedy for all that ails our colleges.

GETTING TO THE NEXT LEVEL

The various external pressures just described do not seem capable of breaking through the crust of inertia and complacency that keeps most colleges from challenging accustomed methods of teaching to become genuine learning organizations. Some other energizing force will be needed for this purpose. But who could possibly perform this function and how might they go about doing so?

Could government agencies and private entities do more to encourage constructive reform? As previously mentioned, state officials are not likely to accomplish much by trying to measure outcomes and adjust budget appropriations based on the results. Most faculties will be reluctant to cooperate actively with such a program. In fact, they may well resist for fear that the results will be used (and misused) to distort their teaching by bringing penalties and adverse publicity to institutions that fail to satisfy an inappropriate set of standards.

A better role for government officials (and accrediting agencies) would be to examine what colleges are doing to assess their own performance and how they make use of what they find to attempt improvements. For example, does the institution participate in NSSE, and, if so, how vigorously does it act on the results? What steps does it take to examine its own teaching programs, identify significant weaknesses, and experiment with new methods? What efforts does it make to identify promising innovations in other institutions? Are there serious programs to train new teachers? Does the college make effective use of teaching evaluations and, if so, how well are they constructed? How much account is taken of teaching in making faculty appointments and promotions? Are funds regularly made available to faculty for trying and assessing new methods of instruction?

It is much easier to arrive at answers to these questions than to rate a college using standardized tests that purport to measure the results of educational programs. If state agencies and accreditors began to concentrate on each institution's processes for self-scrutiny and reform, college officials and their faculties would have to pay more attention to developing the procedures most likely to bring about educational progress. Would-be reformers would be emboldened to seek improvements in teaching and learning and feel less inhibited from embarking on what otherwise could strike them as a lonely and thankless task.

Government agencies and foundations could give further impetus for change by funding exemplary efforts by colleges to install a systematic process for evaluating educational programs, identifying problems, and experimenting with potential improvements. In the past, outside sources have periodically supported particular innovations, such as new uses of the Internet or computer-assisted learning. The Department of Education's Fund for the Improvement of Post-Secondary Education has undertaken this task, as have several large foundations. Helpful as such assistance can be, however, it is very different from what is proposed here. Instead of financing specific innovations, public agencies and foundations would contribute to the creation of a continuing *process* to improve the quality of undergraduate teaching and learning. The amount of outside support required for any single institution should not be large, nor need the funding be permanent. Most colleges can easily sustain such a process by themselves once it is up and running. But initial support from governments and foundations, along with funding to develop better measures for assessing progress, would help to legitimate the effort and overcome the inertia that so often discourages initiatives of this kind. In this way, funders would give greater prominence to such reforms and encourage other colleges to consider launching programs of their own.

Another useful step that foundations and funding agencies could take would be to support promising efforts to develop better ways of measuring and analyzing the progress colleges are making toward important learning objectives, such as improved critical thinking, moral and quantitative reasoning, writing, oral communication, and intercultural competence. Some of the existing measures are less exact than one might wish in measuring results. Others reflect continuing disagreement over the nature of the goal to be assessed. Such difficulties hamper the use of evaluation and strengthen the hand of those who resist reform. By helping to improve these measures and techniques of analysis, funders could encourage greater use of assessment, increase its effectiveness, and enhance its credibility in the eyes of the faculty.

Finally boards of trustees could give an added boost to reform by making a point of inquiring regularly into efforts by their colleges to become more of a learning organization. Admittedly, such inquiries would represent a new departure. Successful boards have done useful work by making wise decisions about the hiring and firing of college presidents, providing needed oversight of investment and business matters (in which most presidents have little experience), and aiding mightily in raising money. But rarely have trustees played any significant part in the educational process.

There are reasons, of course, for keeping boards out of educational issues. Most college trustees are business executives or lawyers with no special knowledge of academic matters. Moreover education, like art and architecture, is a subject on which many inexperienced observers feel entitled to express views, views strongly held but often quite wrong. To faculty members, then, and even presidents, the prospect of having a board look at any part of the educational process may well seem threatening.

Yet self-restraint also has its costs. Who else is capable of altering the current system of incentives and rewards to hold deans and presidents accountable for the quality of their educational leadership? No faculty ever forced its leaders out for failing to act vigorously enough to improve the prevailing methods of education. On the contrary, faculties are more likely to resist any determined effort to examine their work and question familiar ways of teaching and learning. Students cannot tell whether current practices are less effective than they might be. Alumni are too far removed to know what needs to be done. As a result, if trustees ignore the subject, there may be no one to press academic leaders to attend to those aspects of the educational program that are in greatest need of reform.

Fortunately the risks of unwise intervention are fairly low, so long as trustees do not try to dictate what courses should be taught and what instructional methods employed but merely ask for reports on the procedures used to evaluate academic programs and encourage innovation. It is surely within the prerogatives of the board to take an interest in these activities and to urge the president to work with the faculty to develop a process designed to ensure continuing improvement in the quality of education. To perform this function well while retaining the confidence of the faculty, boards might take care, if they have not done so already, to include in their number several experienced educators who can participate in the oversight, or, failing that, to recruit a team of educators from other universities to conduct an independent review.

The potential gains from such intervention would be considerable. Involvement by trustees would ensure that evaluation and reform were kept prominent among the priorities of presidents and deans. The latter would in turn receive a powerful mandate to press ahead with programs of assessment and innovation against the silent forces of inertia and indifference that so often stifle efforts of this kind. In this way, prospects for reform would no longer rest entirely on the shoulders of presidents and deans and be at risk of being forever put aside in favor of less controversial ventures.*

Although foundations and trustees can provide an important impetus for reform, and back it stoutly when it occurs, they cannot guarantee change by their own efforts. They can urge a process of self-scrutiny and innovation and give it greater legitimacy, but they cannot bring it about themselves. Real improvement requires the initiative and skills of academic leaders—presidents, provosts, and deans—who understand what needs to be done and appeal successfully to the sense of professional responsibility that most faculties share for the education of their students.

Academic leaders are often inhibited by doubts about whether they have enough influence over educational matters to make a difference. Such a response, however, underestimates the impact that resourceful leadership can have on a university. Although professors must agree to any curricular reform, presidents and deans have more leverage than they may think by virtue of their power to speak out and command attention, their role in raising money and allocating resources,

---

*Trustees could also ask whether faculty and administration have made serious efforts to define the purposes of undergraduate education. In particular, they could inquire whether their college has any programs in place to prepare students for active citizenship and to contribute to their moral development. Granted, it would be unwise for trustees to pass judgment on the quality of the courses and educational methods used to achieve these purposes. But the purposes themselves seem well within the legitimate purview of a governing board. After all, trustees are supposed to act as a mediating agent between the interests of the institution and the needs of the surrounding society. Reviewing the purposes of a college to determine whether they address important social needs would seem a perfect illustration of this mediating function.

and their ability to marshal information that will persuade faculty members to take their proposals seriously.

Perhaps the greatest influence that presidents can exert is to articulate a vision—a clear set of values, educational priorities, and directions—for their universities. In this respect, presidents occupy a unique position, since they have the best vantage point from which to see the institution whole and choose a path for its future. It is unfortunate if they squander this opportunity by simply striving to move their institutions a few notches higher in the conventional college rankings. By doing so, they send a message to their faculties and trustees that success consists in raising the average SAT scores of students and increasing the research "output" of the faculty. The predictable result is to weaken the prospects for educational reform by directing scarce resources and energy into activities that have little or no relation to student learning.

Instead presidents could call upon their colleges to undertake an ongoing process of evaluation, experimentation, and reform. Such a strategy has several advantages. Presidents who want to make a difference in the quality of education have a much better chance of doing so by using this method than by trying to influence curricular debates directly. When deciding which courses to require and how to structure a concentration, faculties will seldom prefer a president's judgment to their own. In contrast, efforts to evaluate the effectiveness of educational programs and experiment with innovative teaching methods are much less likely to be viewed as exclusive prerogatives of the faculty, and presidents will have an easier time enlisting the cooperation of interested professors.

In contemplating such an effort, academic leaders can also take encouragement from the fact that every institution has an equal opportunity to succeed. In fact, leaders of less affluent, less prestigious colleges have significant advantages over their counterparts at institutions in the upper echelons of the *U.S. News and World Report* rankings. The costs involved are not large enough to inhibit them. They need not worry that any self-study that exposes educational weaknesses will appear in the pages of the *New York Times*. Their departments are usually less independent and more disposed to collaborate. Their faculties are more likely to be chiefly interested in teaching and willing to find the time to try new educational ideas and experiment with novel pedagogies. Their professors are not so accustomed to handing the teaching of important courses to graduate students. These advantages can easily offset the greater visibility and superior resources of higher-profile institutions, which may help to explain why so many of the most interesting teaching innovations do not begin in the best-known universities but in colleges with less prominent reputations.

How can academic leaders move forward to implement their vision? What concrete steps can they take to launch a more systematic process of evaluation, innovation, and reform? They can begin modestly by offering released time and seed money to faculty members wishing to try a promising new way of teaching. They can identify experienced professors who are willing to help colleagues seeking to change their teaching style to a more problem-oriented, discussion-based format. They can evaluate faculty experiments to enhance student learning and publicize the results of those that prove successful.

By investing slightly more money, leaders can try to change undergraduate education in other important ways. They can insist on hiring better-qualified, full-time teachers to improve undergraduate writing and foreign language programs. With official encouragement and a bit of funding, they can expand community service programs and link them more closely to the curriculum. By raising somewhat larger sums, they can create teaching centers to help graduate students and interested faculty members discover how to use active methods of learning in their classes.

In every institution, moreover, academic leaders can place their agenda before the faculty and see that it is discussed. They can bolster the chances of achieving results by backing their proposals with research that offers persuasive evidence of problems that deserve attention. Empirical studies can counter skepticism about the value of moral reasoning and civic education by demonstrating how moral awareness and citizen participation can increase through well-planned educational interventions. Careful research can make a powerful case for change by showing faculty members that the quality of student writing in particular departments declines during college, or that certain methods of instruction produce greater gains in critical thinking than others, or that conventional ways of teaching do not produce as strong a performance on exams as group study or self-paced learning.

Such evidence is especially useful when it comes from research conducted in the college itself. Outside studies can identify problems with established practices and suggest new ways to improve student learning, but there is always a possibility that the results were affected by differences in the student bodies involved or by special characteristics of the colleges they attended. Thus few outside studies can equal investigations performed on one's own campus in their power to persuade faculty members that the findings are relevant to *their* college and *their* students. Professors who blithely ignore competent research about student learning when it is buried in obscure academic journals cannot avoid it so easily once a president or a dean has given them telling evidence about their own institution.

Fortunately research of this kind is not financially burdensome. It does not cost much to test students' proficiency in writing, reasoning, or foreign languages and to measure their gains during the college years, nor is it expensive to compare the results in one section of a course using innovative teaching methods with those in another section taught in conventional ways. Almost any college can afford to mount a reasonable program of this kind.

Enterprising leaders can take further steps to bring about change by revising appointments procedures to pay closer attention to the quality of instruction. At present, almost all universities purport to base promotions on a review of the candidate's teaching and research. In practice, however, whereas a candidate's research is analyzed in detail with the help of comments secured from professors outside the university, appraisals of teaching tend to be much more cursory. Typically they are based primarily, if not entirely, on student evaluations. While such assessments are more reliable than many of their detractors acknowledge, they normally focus almost entirely on a few aspects of an instructor's behavior: Was she prepared, accessible to students, interested in her subject? Were her lectures clear and well organized? Were the readings relevant and reasonable in length? Rarely are students asked about how much they learned. As an earlier example in this chapter made clear, students can convey a very different impression of a class when they are asked not only whether the instructor was prepared, enthusiastic, and accessible, but also whether the course helped them to write more competently or analyze problems more effectively. By including such questions, student evaluations will not only give a more complete picture of a candidate's teaching, they will also identify weaknesses in the undergraduate program and create an agenda for reform.

College leaders can strengthen appointments procedures even further by supplementing student evaluations with more probing evidence about teaching. For example, candidates can be urged to submit a statement about each course they teach, explaining the goals they are trying to achieve and the methods and strategies they are using to accomplish their ends. They can be asked to describe any innovations they have introduced for teaching and assessing students together with evidence of the results achieved. Reviewers can then make much more meaningful judgments by examining course syllabi, instructional methods, and means of grading and evaluating students to see how well designed they are to carry out the candidate's aims.*

Presidents and deans of research universities could act more boldly by urging revisions in their Ph.D. programs to include better preparation for teaching. There is persuasive empirical evidence to show that such preparation can significantly improve student learning.† The content involved

---

*A major reason why teaching is not rewarded as highly as research is that evidence of teaching is much harder to find outside a professor's own institution than evidence of published research. With a little imagination, however, universities could do much more to create better evidence (e.g., by making videotapes of actual classes or constructing more probing student evaluations). Collecting such evidence in "teaching portfolios" would not only help other institutions make more informed, balanced hiring choices but also motivate junior faculty, graduate student instructors, and others anticipating a job search to work harder at their teaching.

†Summarizing a variety of empirical studies, Ernest Pascarella and Patrick Terenzini conclude that greater teaching skills "have consistently been linked with increased student achievement. . . . Most important, these characteristics are teachable. . . . Institutions that wish to increase their instructional effectiveness can do so if the will is there and if institutional

need not consist merely of practical training in pedagogy but could include readings and discussion on the history and purposes of the curriculum, the state of research on teaching methods and student learning, and the implications of this research for organizing courses, choosing instructional strategies, and assessing student work.

Deans and presidents seeking to make this change are admittedly venturing into treacherous waters. Ultimately decisions about the content of Ph.D. training must rest with the faculty, and it is likely that many leaders who call for major reforms will meet initial resistance and even firm rebuffs from this quarter. Nevertheless, if they are determined enough, they have important resources at their disposal. For example, they can express their reluctance to continue paying for graduate teaching assistants who do not first undergo substantial preparation. If faculty members protest, they will have to openly defend the proposition that there is nothing wrong with having undergraduates taught by untrained, inexperienced instructors. In such a debate, it is unlikely that enterprising presidents and deans will emerge with nothing to show for their efforts.

Over a longer term, the outlook for reforming graduate education is even more hopeful. Most professors are thoughtful, conscientious people. They will not defend an untenable position indefinitely once the issue has been raised. If challenged to explain why they are not preparing their graduate students adequately for the work which will occupy most of their time during their academic careers, some faculties, at least, are likely to reconsider their current programs. After all, it is no easy matter to insist publicly that

---

and faculty value systems are conducive to that goal"; *How College Affects Students*, p. 652.

teaching is a simple process that graduate students should be able to pick up by themselves. Nor will many professors feel comfortable arguing that research has nothing useful to say about teaching. As investigators continue to enlarge our knowledge of how students learn and as new technologies increase the pedagogic choices that instructors need to make, the case for serious preparation will grow more compelling. Eventually some faculties will agree to make reforms, and others will soon feel pressed to follow suit.

One should not be too pessimistic, then, about the prospects for enlisting faculty support for a more searching, continuous process of self-scrutiny and reform. Already there are signs of growing receptivity. Although a majority of the faculty may be content with the status quo, many individual professors are engaging in small-scale classroom assessment and research to examine their own teaching methods and try out new techniques for stimulating learning. Many are coming together on their own campuses to discuss their common pedagogic interests. As Mary Huber of the Carnegie Foundation has observed in a recent essay on faculty forums of this kind, "What has been surprising to us is not only how *many* forums there are right now for this exchange but how *surprised* people seem to be to find this out."[17] Through discussions of this kind, more faculty members are becoming acquainted with research on teaching and learning and are beginning to think about its application to their own courses. Quietly but steadily, the ground is being prepared for an eventual shift in American colleges away from a teacher-oriented system featuring lectures delivered to passive audiences to a more learner-centered process in which students become more actively involved in their own education and professors adapt their teaching in accordance with more complex understandings of human learning.

Although the professors engaged in this process may still make up only a small minority, they are invaluable allies for any serious effort at reform. Even in the most research-oriented universities, clusters of committed teachers can be found to form a nucleus around which to build support. Neither presidents nor deans may have the authority to order the faculty to change its methods of teaching or revise the curriculum. They do have power to point the way, to document existing weaknesses, and to offer the recognition, rewards, and resources that will encourage interested professors and attract more of their colleagues to a campuswide process of renewal and improvement. Above all, they have the opportunity to persuade members of their faculties that research and experimentation to improve student learning can be as challenging and absorbing as many traditional forms of scholarship and scientific investigation. With encouragement and prodding, careful research, and modest support for innovation, leaders in every college can aspire to create a culture of honest self-appraisal, continuing experimentation, and constant improvement. They could hardly ask for a better opportunity to make a lasting contribution to their institutions and their students.

AFTERWORD TO THE PAPERBACK EDITION

Barely a month after this book was first published, a most unusual fate befell me. On a sunny February afternoon in Sarasota, Florida, as I sat working on a new project, the telephone rang and I suddenly learned, to my surprise, that Lawrence Summers would be leaving the Harvard presidency and that the senior governing board wanted me to take his place for a year while it searched for a permanent successor. Under the circumstances, I could hardly refuse. Thereafter, however, as I thought more about this startling turn of events, I remembered that the Faculty of Arts and Sciences was in the midst of its first comprehensive review of undergraduate education in thirty years, and that by all accounts, the effort was bogging down. Apparently, then, having just written on what to do in theory to improve undergraduate education, I would now have a chance to try to put my ideas into practice.

When I returned to Cambridge three weeks later for a few days packed with meetings, I found a campus in palpable disarray. Many undergraduates and alumni were upset by the decision to abandon a president who was trying to move the University in exciting new directions. The senior governing board was widely accused of giving in to a mob of dissident professors who had turned on their president rather than accept reform. For much of the public, the Faculty of Arts and Sciences had become the chief villain for causing Mr. Summers' departure by twice voting no-confidence in his administration. Some people felt that the Faculty, emboldened by its success in driving out **345** the president, was now intent on expanding its power over the direction of the University.

However one might characterize the events of the preceding months, this last point struck me as highly implausible. I could not imagine that the Faculty was actually plotting to expand its power. Such a course would only mean more of everything professors disliked—more meetings, more arguing, more time-consuming debates. After two years of turmoil and crisis, what the Faculty surely desired was not to run the University but to get back to what its members liked best—their books, their laboratories, their lectures. My initial meetings quickly confirmed this impression, as faculty members made abundantly clear their desire to do whatever they could to be helpful.

My immediate problem was to develop a plan for what I might try to accomplish during my brief return to office. Ordinarily, I would simply be a caretaker, healing wounds, reassuring alumni, and keeping things going until a new president could take over. But these were no ordinary times.

I soon became convinced that the review of undergraduate education was indeed in difficulty. True, the Faculty had taken some positive steps—a totally revamped advising system in particular. But the heart of the review—an effort to create a new general education program—had proceeded through a series of committees to emerge with a proposal that all students be required to take any three courses in the humanities, any three in the social sciences, and three more in the sciences. This outcome seemed to excite no one and left many faculty members frustrated and disappointed. Many of the most active participants felt that the Faculty had now grown weary of the review and that if something were not done soon, the entire reform effort would simply run out of steam.

In these circumstances, I concluded that the only viable course was to press ahead and try to accomplish as much as we could. Several respected professors had approached me privately and told me that the Faculty felt wounded by the criticism of its role in President Summers' departure and very much hoped that something could be done to restore the public's confidence. Clearly, writing op-ed pieces would not suffice. Confidence would not be won by words but only by actions from the Faculty that commanded respect. Serious educational reform would serve that purpose well. On the other hand, to abandon the review, or even to postpone it for a year hoping that a new president would revive the process, could easily make matters worse by confirming suspicions that the Faculty was ungovernable and set on resisting change.

It was also clear that the undergraduate program was in need of repair. Although record numbers of applicants were still seeking admission to Harvard College, surveys showed that our undergraduates looked less favorably on the quality of their education than their counterparts at many other private colleges and universities. I concluded that Harvard could not afford to wait and risk having the entire review collapse. Undergraduate education had to be a major priority for my brief term of office.

Examining the efforts at curriculum reform over the preceding three years, I found the situation much like the one described in chapter 2. In all the committee reports I read, I found no discussion of the purposes that undergraduate education ought to serve. Attention seemed focused primarily on what courses should be required to satisfy the needs of general education with little analysis of what the needs were or how to meet them. Although a committee on pedagogy had been formed and had produced a report with some useful suggestions, none of its proposals seemed to have been discussed by the Faculty or to have attracted any attention. The documents I read did not mention the role of the extra-curriculum or discuss in any detail the purposes of the concentrations. Nor could I find any evidence of attention paid to the vast body of research about undergraduate education, let alone any careful internal studies to determine how much our students were learning.

On the basis of this record, what could be done to reorganize the review and persuade a weary Faculty to recommit itself to the effort? My own position was delicate. By custom, at least at Harvard, the president's role in curriculum reform was very limited. However much I might have written on undergraduate education, I could not intervene directly. In private conversation, or even in talking with a committee, I could speak frankly. But any effort to express my views in a Faculty meeting or to publicly challenge a committee report would be met with immediate disapproval. Constructing the curriculum was the Faculty's prerogative. The president's role was somewhat akin to playing a pinball machine. One could nudge the machine gently in an effort to improve the score, but any firmer push could easily cause the scoreboard to flash the dread word "Tilt," whereupon the game would immediately come to a halt.

One thing the president *could* do, however, was to form committees, give them a charge, and try to persuade the right professors to serve as members. I decided to make full use of this prerogative. A meeting with the existing Committee on General Education convinced me that there was much division of opinion within the group and little real enthusiasm for its simple course distribution proposal. Its usefulness, moreover, was clearly at an end. Accordingly, with the help of the outgoing dean, I created a new task force to start again and write a fresh report over the summer. To my great satisfaction, all of the faculty members we asked to serve accepted.

Of course, there was more to reforming undergraduate education than creating a new general education curriculum. More important than course requirements was what went on in each individual course. Fortunately, Theda Skocpol, dean of the Graduate School and a distinguished professor of great energy and resourcefulness, offered to form another task force to recommend ways of strengthening teaching in the College. A few months later, we established a third committee to address the special problem of improving undergraduate science education under the able leadership of the provost, Steve Hyman, along with Richard Losick, an outstanding scientist and dedicated teacher.

I also used another prerogative of my office by commissioning several studies to assess how much our students were learning. As I indicated in chapter 12, a college cannot develop a sustained effort to improve the quality of education without trying to determine the current extent of student learning in order to identify weaknesses and assess future progress. A small but very capable office of institutional research, created since my first term as president, seemed ideally suited to meet this need. The first evaluation we decided to undertake was a study comparing the critical thinking of freshmen and seniors to discover how much progress students made over the course of their four undergraduate years. The second was a similar study to evaluate improvement in the quality of student writing.

The General Education Task Force worked hard all summer and produced a preliminary report soon after classes resumed in the fall. Elegantly written, the draft contained much of value. It carefully defined the several purposes of the proposed program—a mix of developing essential skills, such as writing, analytic thinking, using empirical evidence, and moral reasoning; preparing students for citizenship both of the United States and of an increasingly interconnected world; and fostering lasting interests in important fields of intellectual endeavor, notably science and literature. Students would be required to take courses to achieve each of these goals, and criteria were provided to determine which courses could qualify. Beyond recommending these course requirements, the Task Force urged participating professors to utilize more active, discussion-based forms of teaching and proposed that the Faculty explore new ways of linking courses to community service and other activities outside the classroom. Finally, the report offered an approach that would supply both a unifying theme and a method for achieving its objectives. Pursuant to the overarching aim of preparing students for a full life, the Task Force specified that several of the new goals could be best achieved by linking subject matter to contemporary problems of importance to many students. For example, a general education course in science might demonstrate the relevance of the technical material to environmental issues as a way of showing nonscientists how maintaining a continuing interest in scientific developments could help them understand problems they cared about deeply.

After distributing its preliminary report, the Task Force began a series of informal discussions with individual departments, department chairs, the Faculty Council, and other interested groups. These meetings were apparently "spirited," to say the least. Some members of the Task Force emerged from them shaken by the vehemence of the criticism as well as by the misapprehensions they encountered concerning what the preliminary report actually said. Still, the members kept doggedly at their work, listened carefully to their critics, and produced an amended report that took account of objections that seemed both sensible and widely shared.

Following this round of meetings, the Faculty as a whole began a preliminary discussion of the report. The first meeting produced a confusing, disjointed debate in which individual members spoke in favor of various alternative curricular models ranging from a simple distribution requirement to a continuation, with a bit of tweaking, of the current Core Curriculum, now almost thirty years old and heartily disliked by many students. If they continued, discussions of this sort could easily end in frustration and disappointment. Since there is no one perfect curriculum but several reasonably coherent models, the Faculty might split into different camps and eventually have to settle for a formless alternative that everyone could stomach but no one truly liked.

Undismayed, the Task Force listened, took note of several sensible concerns about their report, and produced yet another amended version in an effort to satisfy the critics. By the time the second meeting took place a month later, the Faculty had apparently come to the conclusion that the general philosophy and structure of the amended report offered a sufficiently suitable framework that it would be best to argue about the specifics of the plan rather than spend further time debating alternative models. After a lengthy, mainly positive discussion, the dean announced that when the Task Force had completed the final revisions to its work, he would appoint a committee of the Faculty Council to translate the report into legislative language suitable for debate and final approval in the spring.

In due course, the Council produced a set of legislative proposals for the Faculty to consider, and the final series of debates began. Rather than discuss large questions of educational philosophy and method, the Faculty chose to edit the proposed legislation line-by-line. As one would expect, discussing individual sentences in meetings of two hundred or more professors proved to be a very cumbersome process. Hours were consumed debating questions of wording that could have been resolved informally in committee. As one meeting followed another, I grew increasingly worried that we would reach the end of the semester without completing the review, thus essentially wasting a year of hard work. Eventually, after scheduling several emergency sessions, the last possible meeting began with various amendments still to be discussed. At this point, however, as if by magic, the Faculty seemed to realize that further delay courted disaster. In contrast to the pace of earlier meetings, the remaining amendments were quickly disposed of. After a few members rose to express doubts and reservations, the new curriculum passed by a vote of 164 to 14 with 11 abstentions.

The other reform projects went more smoothly, since they did not require faculty approval. Dean Skocpol's Task Force on Teaching and Career Development produced a detailed report with many recommendations similar to those suggested in chapter 12—more extensive preparation and mentoring for teaching fellows and new assistant professors; more detailed documentation of classroom performance and other contributions to teaching in considering appointments and promotions; funds for course development and experiments in new methods of teaching; and improved forms of student evaluation to provide more useful feedback for instructors. In addition, the report provided that all available information bearing on the quality of teaching of each graduate student and junior faculty member would be compiled in dossiers that would be made available to prospective employers. All faculty members would be required to include an account of their teaching in the annual reports they submitted to the dean. With the aid of these reports and other pertinent evidence, teaching would henceforth be given equal weight with research in setting salaries. A new Web site would be created to publicize promising experiments in pedagogy and other relevant information about teaching and learning. Finally, the Task Force offered various suggestions for encouraging more discussion and cooperation in improving the quality of courses and teaching.

The report on teaching was distributed to all members of the faculty, and ample time was set aside at a subsequent meeting to discuss its contents. Our hope was to use this occasion to air significant concerns, allay fears, and generate support for the proposals. Unfortunately, attendance at the meeting was sparse, and the discussion was rather desultory. Whether this response indicated general acceptance of the proposals or a widespread lack of interest in the entire subject was not immediately clear.

Meanwhile, Provost Hyman's Committee on Learning in Science and Engineering came quickly to a set of sensible conclusions similar to those expressed in earlier reports from the National Academy of Sciences. The Committee warmly endorsed a process already underway to create a series of ambitious new entry-level, or "portal," courses in the life sciences and physical sciences. One such interdisciplinary course had just been introduced in the life sciences and attracted a large and enthusiastic student audience. In fact, while walking back to my office one day, I encountered the organizer of our largest union, who rushed up, kissed me on the cheek, and announced that she was auditing the new life science course and found it the most interesting experience she had had at Harvard. Apparently, many students agreed.

As a result, twice as many undergraduates as in earlier years went on to take advanced life science courses, and many more freshmen decided to major in science.

The rest of the Committee's recommendations were likewise uncontroversial. The final report called for a large-scale conversion of student laboratories so that undergraduates could spend much more of their class time doing "hands-on science" instead of listening to lectures. In addition, the report urged that greater efforts be made to expand opportunities for undergraduates to assist faculty scientists with their projects in order to gain still more direct experience in the process of scientific research. With some 10,000 faculty investigators at work in the Medical School and its affiliated hospitals, the prospects for multiplying these apprenticeships seemed promising indeed.

The evaluations of student progress in writing and critical thinking also proceeded as planned, although heroic efforts were required to enlist the several hundred student volunteers needed for an adequate sample. The results of these assessments were still being tabulated as this afterword was written. We did complete one other evaluation, however, which sought to ascertain what fraction of the exam questions given to undergraduates tested higher-order thinking skills as opposed to mere recall or comprehension of written material. Readers may remember from chapter 4 that earlier studies of selective colleges and universities had concluded that only 15 to 18 percent of examination questions asked students to use critical thinking skills even though more than 90 percent of all college professors considered the development of these skills to be the most important aim of undergraduate education. Because of complications encountered in carrying out the study, our review was limited to the exams in only two large departments—economics and political science. Fortunately, in contrast to the earlier published studies, the results showed that between two-thirds and three-quarters of the exam questions in these departments called for the exercise of critical thinking.

All in all, much was accomplished through the series of measures just described. In addition to the reports on general education, teaching, and science instruction, College officials made strenuous efforts to implement the plan to overhaul our advising system that the Faculty had approved the previous year. As a result, undergraduate advising gained much higher marks from students than it had in the past. Taken together, therefore, thanks to the efforts of many people, the changes approved or put in place over the course of the year amounted to the most comprehensive reform of the undergraduate program in Harvard's history.

At the same time, these accomplishments, important as they are, have merely established a framework for improvement. Their ultimate significance will turn on the commitment of the faculty and the efforts of the new administration to implement the programs. Decades earlier, when the Core Curriculum was passed, it was followed by more than 100 new or heavily revised courses of which more than 75 percent were taught by tenured faculty. But that curriculum was three years in the making and was preceded by innumerable meetings and informal discussions reaching into every corner of the College. Although the process consumed a great deal of time, when the final votes at last took place, many professors felt a genuine sense of ownership of the new curriculum and a keen desire to implement their handiwork successfully. In contrast, though members of the General Education Task Force spent much time meeting informally with faculty groups, the program was developed in a single year, as were most of the other reforms discussed in this afterword. How much faculty ownership and commitment were generated during this brief period remains to be seen. Although the program passed overwhelmingly, fewer than one-third of all the members of the faculty actually attended the meetings leading up to the decisive vote. What the other two-thirds think about the new curriculum is still unknown. Much of what happens next will depend on their attitude.

What did I learn from this chance to test my ideas about undergraduate education? Certainly, I discovered more faculty interest in teaching and learning than I had encountered as president many years before. The new "portal" courses in the sciences were attracting outstanding scientists to create and teach the new offerings even though the assignment demanded a great deal of time and effort. Moreover, instead of concentrating exclusively on what kinds of courses should be required, the recent review included a committee on pedagogy from the very start. Thereafter, when Dean Skocpol formed her task force on teaching and looked for highly respected senior faculty to serve, each professor she asked accepted immediately. The formation of committees on general education and teaching science met with a similar response. In each case, everyone who served worked hard and produced excellent reports.

At the same time, our attempts at reform revealed some of the difficulties of trying to carry out a successful effort to improve the quality of general education. Time-consuming as it was, the process of developing a new curriculum did not provide opportunities for dealing adequately with all the important issues. In particular, the standard procedure of appointing a committee to draft a report and then debating it in a full faculty meeting left little room for thinking through problems as difficult as figuring out how to achieve the goals of general education within the handful of courses allotted to the task. How could a single course prepare students properly for citizenship? What could one or two courses convey that would equip undergraduates to function more easily and knowledgeably in a world where other countries and cultures would impinge in so many ways on their future lives? What exactly was a course on history supposed to impart that would have lasting value for students majoring in physics or French literature? Such questions are too complicated to be pursued successfully in a large faculty meeting. Even the committees that propose a new curriculum seem unequal to the task, composed as they usually are of a handful of professors drawn from widely different disciplines and forced to resolve a formidable array of issues in a limited amount of time. If none of the existing forums are equipped to resolve these issues, however, they will be left for individual professors to decide as they prepare their separate courses. And that means that the questions will never have the benefit of the sustained discussion they deserve.

I also learned how difficult it is to institute a continuous process of improving education in which weaknesses are regularly identified, followed by experimentation, evaluation, and gradual progress by informed trial and error. No one openly criticizes such an effort, but few members of the faculty embrace it. They may fear that they will be victimized by crude methods of measuring student learning that ignore the subtler values they are trying to convey, or that attempts to evaluate teaching will expose problems in their pedagogy they are unable to correct, or that efforts to improve education in this way will demand more time than they can easily spare. Whatever the cause, our attempts to launch such a process did not provoke much interest. The nearest approximation to a process of continuous improvement was the recommendation of Dean Skocpol's Task Force that funds be set aside to experiment with new methods of teaching, evaluate their success, and publicize the results. What will come of that proposal, however, and how many innovations it will produce remain open questions. For the time being, Harvard—along with a great many other universities—still has far to go to become a "learning organization" as that term has come to be used in most other well-run organizations.

Nevertheless, I remain resolutely optimistic about the prospects at Harvard and elsewhere for substantial reform in teaching and learning. For one thing, pressure is building in the outside world to make universities more accountable and more effective in their teaching. From the secretary of education to state legislatures and accreditation bodies, officials are demanding data to show what students are learning to justify the amounts of taxpayers' money invested in their education. Although most of these efforts are flawed, they will at least force universities to offer *some* positive response.

In addition, as Thomas Friedman has explained in detail in his recent book, *The World Is Flat,* American students are no longer competing for suitable jobs only with themselves. Thanks to the Internet, companies now find it possible to employ educated young people overseas to complete American tax returns, read CAT scans and X rays, work in corporate research laboratories, and fill other jobs traditionally reserved for American university graduates. As foreign students compete for a place in the world's leading economy and as governments from Europe to China seek to upgrade their universities, faculties in the United States will come under increasing pressure to improve their educational programs.

Meanwhile, throughout American higher education, as at Harvard, professors are expressing more interest in teaching and learning and devoting more time and effort to these subjects. As the Carnegie Foundation's periodic surveys make clear, faculty members over the past twenty-five years have been steadily giving a higher priority to instruction relative to research. This trend is evident in all types of institutions, from liberal arts colleges to research universities.

My chief reason for anticipating reform, however, arises from a different source. At present, faculty behavior with respect to teaching and learning is in conflict with some of the most fundamental and widely shared values in American higher education. Almost all professors would agree that a fundamental aim of college is to help students grow to fulfill their potential. In practice, however, too few faculties make serious efforts to ascertain how much their students are actually learning during their four undergraduate years or which students are falling short of their apparent potential in mastering the learning objectives they are supposed to achieve. Moreover, in reviewing their undergraduate program and discussing educational issues, most faculties continue to rely on impressions gained from personal experience. They do not examine the available evidence carefully, or take account of relevant research, or conduct experiments to find out more about student learning as they do as a matter of course when engaged in their regular scholarly work.

This tension between the behavior of faculty and their underlying values reflects an inherently unstable condition. Once faculties receive persuasive evidence that large numbers of their students are not living up to their potential in achieving important educational goals or that different teaching methods could do a better job than those commonly used in promoting student learning, they will find it difficult to continue the status quo.

Increasingly, with encouragement from accrediting agencies and enterprising deans and department chairs, efforts are bound to be made to conduct the kind of evaluation and research that will make clear the conflict between academic ideals and educational realities. Granted, not everything that matters in education can be measured or demonstrated empirically—far from it. But enough can be done to reveal the underlying problems with sufficient clarity to evoke a creative response from the faculty.

It is this prospect that leaves me hopeful about the outlook for significant educational reform. I doubt that it will be demands from the federal government or prodding from corporations or even pressure from students that will ultimately bring about more determined efforts to examine and improve the process of teaching and learning. Rather, it will be the growing realization on the part of faculties themselves that they are not now acting in full accordance with the ideals that underlie their profession and help to give it meaning. If resourceful academic leaders can hasten that realization and encourage a creative response, the next twenty-five years could turn out to be among the most creative and most productive periods in the long history of higher education.

NOTES

INTRODUCTION

1. National Commission on Excellence in Education, *A Nation at Risk: The Imperative of Education Reform* (1983).

2. William J. Bennett, *To Reclaim a Legacy: A Report on the Humanities in Higher Education* (1984); Lynne Cheney, *Tyrannical Machines: A Report on Educational Practices Gone Wrong and Our Best Hopes of Setting Them Right* (1990). Both reports were issued while the authors were serving as head of the National Endowment for the Humanities.

3. Dinesh D'Souza, *Illiberal Education: The Politics of Race and Sex on Campus* (1991); Charles Sykes, *Profscam* (1988).

4. The subtitles of many of the books reveal even more clearly the prevailing tone of the authors: Allan Bloom, *The Closing of the American Mind: How Higher Education Has Failed Democracy and Impoverished the Souls of Today's Students* (1987); Bill Readings, *The University in Ruins* (1996); Bruce Wilshire, *The Moral Collapse of the University: Professionalism, Purity, and Alienation* (1990); Roger Kimball, *Tenured Radicals: How Politics Has Corrupted Higher Education* (1990); Peter Shaw, *The War against the Intellect: Episodes in the Decline of Discourse* (1989); Martin Anderson, *Impostors in the Temple: American Intellectuals Are Destroying Our Universities and Cheating Our Students of Their Future* (1992); Page Smith, *Killing the Spirit: Higher Education in America* (1990).

5. Allan Bloom, *The Closing of the American Mind*, p. 337. See also Jerry G. Gaff, *General Education Today: A Critical Analysis of Controversies, Practices, and Reforms* (1983), p. 187; Stanley N. Katz, "Liberal Education on the Ropes," 51 *Chronicle of Higher Education* (April 1, 2005), p. B6.

6. Bill Readings, *The University in Ruins* (1996), p. 10.

7. The quoted words appear at p. xxiv of Wilshire's book. See also Allan Bloom, *The Closing of the American Mind*; Thomas E. Boudreau, *Universities: The Social Restructuring of American Undergraduate Education* (1998).

8. See, for example, Allan Bloom, *The Closing of the American Mind*; Peter Shaw, *The War against the Intellect*; Jacques Barzun, *The Culture We Deserve: A Critique of Disenlightenment* (1989).

9. See, for example, Roger Kimball, *Tenured Radicals*.

10. Quoted by Richard H. Hersh, "The Liberal Arts College: The Most Practical and Professional Education for the Twenty-First Century," *Liberal Education* (Summer 1997), pp. 27, 28.

11. Eric Gould, *The University in a Corporate Culture* (2003), p. 197.

12. For a slightly less harsh elaboration of the same points covered by Sykes in *Profscam*, see Page Smith, *Killing the Spirit*.

13. See Thomas L. Friedman, "It's a Flat World after All," *New York Times Magazine* (April 3, 2005), p. 32.

14. This phenomenon is not unprecedented. In 1905, Calvin Thomas noted that, "Notwithstanding all the attacks that are made upon college, notwithstanding all the satiric questionings of its utility, its popularity steadily increases. Men decry it, crack jokes about it, and—send their sons to college." "The New Program of Studies at Columbia College," 29 *Educational Review* (1905), p. 335.

15. See Alexander W. Astin, *What Matters in College? Four Critical Years Revisited* (1993), p. 276; Philip G. Altbach, Patricia J. Gumport, and D. Bruce Johnstone, *In Defense of Higher Education* (2001), p. 282. Astin's study, which will be cited often in the chapters that follow, is a massive survey of more than 24,000 students at a wide variety of colleges from their entry as freshmen in 1985 until they graduated in or before 1991. The author based his work on students' impressions about their college careers as well as the results of objective tests taken before the students arrived on campus (e.g., SATs and ACTs) and when they were seniors (e.g., Graduate Record Exams, Law School Admissions Tests). In conducting his study, Astin utilized 131 characteristics of entering freshmen, 192 environmental variables (relating to, e.g., nature and size of institution, student body, and faculty), and 82 outcome measures ranging from cognitive factors to attitudes, values, and beliefs.

16. Alexander W. Astin, *What Matters in College?*, p. 275, reporting that 77.3 percent of seniors were satisfied or very satisfied with "opportunities to discuss course work and assignments out of class with professors," while 62.7 percent were satisfied or very satisfied with the amount of contact with faculty and administrators.

17. Idem, p. 310.

18. Idem, p. 277.

19. See William G. Bowen and Derek Bok, *The Shape of the River: Long-Term Consequences of Considering Race in College and University Admissions* (1998), pp. 194–208.

20. For a detailed account of the multitude of studies that document these conclusions, see Ernest T. Pascarella and Patrick T. Terenzini, *How College Affects Students: Findings and Insights from Twenty Years of Research* (1991) and, by the same authors, *How College Affects Students*, Vol. 2: *A Third Decade of Research* (2005). In these works, the authors have reviewed several thousand studies conducted from 1969 to 2005. In drawing conclusions from this body of research, the authors take careful account of the strengths and weaknesses of the methods used by the investigators. Their books summarize the results of research for a wide variety of outcomes, including cognitive skills, verbal and quantitative competence, and psychosocial changes in attitudes and values. Pascarella and Terenzini have compiled the most current comprehensive analysis of existing research on the impact of college, and their books will be cited repeatedly in the chapters that follow.

CHAPTER ONE   THE EVOLUTION OF
AMERICAN COLLEGES

1. The classic study of the evolution of college curricula in America is Frederick Rudolph, *Curriculum: A History of the American Course of Study since 1636* (1977); the most complete study of American universities from the nineteenth century to the 1920s is Laurence Veysey, *The Emergence of the American University* (1965; First Phoenix Edition, 1970); another, more concise, his-

tory is Christopher J. Lucas, *American Higher Education: A History* (1994); still another historical account is Arthur M. Cohen, *The Shaping of American Higher Education: Emergence and Growth of the Contemporary System* (1998).

2. Laurence Veysey, *The Emergence of the American University*, pp. 33–34.

3. Frederick Rudolph, *Curriculum*, points out at p. 95 that "the central institution of extracurricular life [in the early nineteenth century] was the literary society; the debater, the orator, the essayist were the heroes of the extracurriculum."

4. "Original Papers in Relation to a Course of Liberal Education," 15 *American Journal of Science and Arts* (1829).

5. Calvin B. Hulbert, *The Distinctive Idea in Education* (1890), p. 11. (Hulbert served as president of Middlebury College.)

6. Quoted in Frederick Rudolph, *Curriculum*, p. 107.

7. Laurence Veysey, *The Emergence of the American University*, p. 113.

8. Quoted in Frederick Rudolph, *Curriculum*, p. 120.

9. Quoted in W. B. Carnochan, *The Battleground of the Curriculum: Liberal Education and the American Experience* (1993), p. 20.

10. Frederick Rudolph, *Curriculum*, p. 196.

11. Idem, p. 227. As Rudolph points out at p. 209, "Electives drew to the course of study young men and women for whom the classical tradition held no attraction, but they also made possible a growing number of marginally motivated students who majored in the extracurriculum while attending or not attending, as it might be, courses sufficiently undemanding not to interfere with their priorities."

12. Idem, p. 12.

13. LeBaron Briggs, *Routine and Ideals* (1904), p. 202.

14. Quoted in Page Smith, *Killing the Spirit: Higher Education in America* (1990), p. 73.

15. Quoted in ibid., p. 43.

16. Quoted in Kai Bird, *The Color of Truth: McGeorge Bundy and William Bundy: Brothers in Arms* (1998), p. 58. William Prox-

mire, reflecting on pre-war Yale, reported that "most of my class-mates were wholly preoccupied with sports and girls, and grades, and bull sessions about sports and girls and grades—in that order." Diana Dubois (ed.), *My Harvard, My Yale* (1982), p. 187.

17. Interview with Geoffrey Kabaservice, June 22, 1997, noted in Kabaservice, *The Guardians: Kingman Brewster, His Circle, and the Rise of the Liberal Establishment* (2004), pp. 62–63.

18. Nevitt Sanford (ed.), *The American College: A Psychological and Social Interpretation of the Higher Learning* (1962), p. 13. See also Philip E. Jacob, *Changing Values in College* (1957).

19. Philip E. Jacob, *Changing Values in College*, p. 4.

20. Quoted by Laurence Veysey, *The Emergence of the American University*, p. 107.

21. Abraham Flexner, *The American College: A Criticism* (1908), p. 7.

22. Quoted in Bruce A. Kimball, *Orators and Philosophers: A History of the Idea of Liberal Education* (1986), p. 196.

23. Robert M. Hutchins, *The Higher Learning in America* (1936; Transaction Press Edition, 1995), p. 60.

24. Frederick Rudolph, *Curriculum*, p. 288.

25. Laurence Veysey, "Stability and Experience in the American Undergraduate Curriculum," in Carl Kaysen (ed.), *Content and Context: Essays on College Education* (1973), pp. 1, 58–59. According to Veysey, the principal animating themes have been utility (vocationalism and other practical pursuits), culture (emphasizing the humanities and British traditions of educating "gentlemen"), and scholarship (borrowing from German traditions of research and scholarly investigation).

26. "The Ph.D. Octopus" (1903), *Memories and Studies* (1911), p. 329.

27. Julie A. Reuben, *The Making of the Modern University: Intellectual Transformation and the Marginalization of Morality* (1996), pp. 176–78.

28. Rexford G. Tugwell, "Experimental Economics," in Tugwell (ed.), *The Trend of Economics* (1924), p. 394.

29. Steven Brint, Mark Riddle, Lori Turk-Bicalei, and Charles S. Levy, "From the Liberal Arts to the Practical Arts in American Colleges and Universities," 76 *The Journal of Higher Education* (2005), p. 151.

30. Frederick Rudolph, *Curriculum*, p. 117.

31. Idem, pp. 186–88.

32. Christopher Jencks and David Riesman, *The Academic Revolution* (1968), p. 199.

33. The trends for most of this period are contained in Alexander W. Astin, Leticia Oseguera, Linda J. Sax, and William S. Korn, *The American Freshman: Thirty-Five Year Trends, 1966–2001* (2002), p. 16. The current figures for being very well off financially are for 2004, *51 Chronicle of Higher Education* (February 4, 2005), p. A-33. The current figure cited for developing a meaningful philosophy of life is for 2003, Linda J. Sax, Alexander W. Astin, Jennifer A. Lindholm, William S. Korn, Victor B. Saenz, and Kathryn M. Mahoney, *The American Freshman: National Norms for Fall 2003* (2004), p. 27.

34. John Henry Cardinal Newman, *The Idea of a University* (1852). Even in 1852, when Newman's famous book appeared, British universities had long been preparing students for professions such as the ministry, law, and medicine.

35. For an example of the tendency to write as if vocational courses had largely replaced courses in the humanities and other liberal arts subjects, see James Engell and Anthony Dangerfield, "The Market-Model University: Humanities in the Age of Money," *Harvard Magazine* (May–June 1998), p. 48.

36. Charles Sykes, *Profscam* (1988), p. 53.

37. Quoted in Hugh Hawkins, *Between Harvard and America* (1972), p. 274.

38. Robert C. Angell, *The Campus: A Study of Contemporary Undergraduate Life in the American University* (1928), p. 36.

39. Much the same is true of Sykes's claim about the faculty's lack of contact with undergraduates. As Laurence Veysey observes, "Between undergraduates and their professors at the end of the

nineteenth century, a gulf yawned so deep that it could appropriately be called 'the awful chasm'"; *The Emergence of the American University*, p. 294.

40. Interestingly, one of the critics, Page Smith, a historian, does not make such a claim. He shows, on the contrary, that most problems of contemporary undergraduate education have deep roots; *The Killing of the Spirit: Higher Education in America* (1990).

CHAPTER TWO FACULTY ATTITUDES TOWARD UNDERGRADUATE EDUCATION

1. Carolyn J. Mooney, "New U.S. Survey Assembles Statistical Portrait of the American Professoriate," 36 *Chronicle of Higher Education* (February 7, 1990), pp. A-15, A-18.

2. Ernest L. Boyer, *Scholarship Reconsidered: Priorities of the Professoriate* (1990), Table A-26; see generally Lionel S. Lewis, *Marginal Worth: Teaching and the Academic Labor Market* (1996), pp. 27–33, 147–57.

3. U.S. Department of Education, National Center for Educational Statistics, *Background Characteristics, Work Activities, and Compensation of Faculty and Instructional Staff in Postsecondary Institutions: Fall, 1998* (April 2001), pp. 46 et seq.

4. Linda J. Sax, Alexander W. Astin, William S. Korn, and Shannon K. Gilmartin, *The American College Teacher: National Norms for the 1989–1999 HERI Faculty Survey* (1999), p. 17.

5. Alexander W. Astin, *What Matters in College: Four Critical Years Revisited* (1993), p. 275.

6. Joan S. Stark and Lisa R. Latucca, *Shaping the College Curriculum: Academic Plans in Action* (1999), p. 215.

7. G. Jeffrey McDonald, "Search for Meaning on Campus," *Boston Globe* (June 12, 2005), p. A29.

8. See pp. 59–61.

9. George D. O'Brien, *All the Essential Half-Truths about Higher Education* (1998), p. 80.

10. Association of American Colleges, *Liberal Learning and the Arts and Sciences Major*, Vol. 2: *Reports from the Field* (1991), p. 13. In 1995, the Association of American Colleges was renamed the Association of American Colleges and Universities.

11. Association of American Colleges, *Integrity in the College Curriculum: A Report to the Academic Community* (1985), p. 2.

12. See, for example, John McLeish, *The Lecture Method* (1968); Lion Gardiner, *Redesigning Higher Education: Producing Dramatic Gains in Student Learning* (1994), p. 46.

13. See, for example, L. Meiskey, A. Healy, and L. Bourne, "Memory for Classroom Algebra," 2 *On Teaching and Learning* (1990), p. 57; Martin A. Conway, Gillian Cohen, and Nicola Stanhope, "On the Very Long-Term Retention of Knowledge Acquired through Formal Education: Twelve Years of Cognitive Psychology," 120 *Journal of Experimental Psychology: General* (1991), p. 395.

14. See, for example, Lion Gardiner, *Redesigning Higher Education*.

15. Joan S. Stark, Malcolm A. Lowther, Michael P. Ryan, and Michele Genthon, "Faculty Reflect on Course Planning," 29 *Research in Higher Education* (1988), p. 219. In a later work, Professor Stark observed: "Generally, faculty members did not include knowledge of learning theory or pedagogical training among the types of scholarly preparation that strongly influenced their course planning. Only 30% of the college instructors we talked with had any exposure to various educational and psychological theories through formal courses or workshops that might have created awareness of alternative planning strategies." Joan S. Stark and Lisa R. Latucca, *Shaping the College Curriculum*, p. 117.

16. See, for example, Michael Moffatt, *Coming of Age in New Jersey: College and American Culture* (1988). More generally, see George D. Kuh, "The Other Curriculum: Out-of-Class Experiences Associated with Student Learning and Personal Development," 66 *The Journal of Higher Education* (1995), p. 123.

17. Richard J. Light, *Making the Most of College: Students Speak Their Minds* (2001), p. 8. Unlike regular classes, more-

over, these extracurricular experiences and chance encounters cannot be programmed through television or the Internet. Ironically, therefore, although they are neglected by the faculty, they offer the strongest reason why pundits are wrong when they claim that modern technology has made the traditional residential college a costly relic that will eventually go the way of the dinosaur.

18. According to Ernest T. Pascarella and Patrick T. Terenzini, "the research published since 1990 indicates that students' in- and out-of-class experiences are interconnected components of a complex process shaping student change and development in ways we are only beginning to understand." *How College Affects Students,* Vol. 2: *A Third Decade of Research* (2005), p. 629.

19. Allan Bloom, *The Closing of the American Mind: How Higher Education Has Failed Democracy and Impoverished the Souls of Today's Students* (1987), p. 338; William J. Bennett, *To Reclaim a Legacy: A Report on the Humanities in Higher Education* (1984); Lynne V. Cheney, *50 Hours: A Core Curriculum for College Students* (1989).

CHAPTER THREE PURPOSES

1. W. B. Carnochan, *The Battleground of the Curriculum: Liberal Education and American Experience* (1993), p. 126.

2. Bruce Wilshire, *The Moral Collapse of the University: Professionalism, Purity, and Alienation* (1990), p. xxiv.

3. Charles Anderson, *Prescribing the Life of the Mind: An Essay on the Aims of Liberal Education, the Competence of Citizens, and the Cultivation of Practical Reason* (1993), p. 4.

4. Bill Readings, *The University in Ruins* (1996), p. 6.

5. Stanley Fish, "Aim Low," 49 *Chronicle of Higher Education* (May 16, 2003), p. C5.

6. Ibid.

7. Ibid. Fish also suggests that efforts to make students more moral or better citizens might violate the university's neutrality

on political issues and hence provoke retaliation from external sources. It strains belief, however, to suppose that society would try to retaliate against a college for encouraging students to vote, or participate in their communities, or keep their word, tell the truth, and refrain from unjustified acts of violence.

8. Ibid.

9. Norman Nie, Jane Junn, and Kenneth Stehlik-Barry, *Education and Democratic Citizenship in America* (1996). In the same vein, Robert Putnam has concluded: "Education is by far the strongest correlate that I have discovered of civic engagement in all its forms." "The Strange Disappearance of Civic America," *The American Prospect* (Winter 1996), pp. 36–37.

10. See, for example, Alexander W. Astin and Linda J. Sax, "How Undergraduates Are Affected by Service Participation," 39 *Journal of College Student Development* (1998), p. 259.

11. See, for example, Patricia Gurin, Eric L. Dey, Sylvia Hurtado, and Gerald Gurin, "Diversity and Higher Education," 72 *Harvard Educational Review* (2002), p. 330.

12. Frank Lentricchia, *Criticism and Social Change* (1983), p. 2.

13. Frederic Jameson, "Marxism and Teaching," 2/3 *New Political Science* (1979/1980), pp. 31, 32.

14. In Darryl J. Glass and Barbara H. Smith (eds.), *The Politics of Liberal Education* (1992), pp. 128, 135.

15. Introduction to Henry A. Giroux and Kostas Myrsiades (eds.), *Beyond the Corporate University* (2001), p. 40.

16. Idem, p. 5.

17. Idem, p. 8.

18. See, for example, James A. Berlin, *Rhetoric, Poetics, and Cultures: Refiguring College English Studies* (1996).

19. See Sharon Crowley, *Composition in the University: Historical and Polemical Essays* (1998), pp. 64–72; Mary Trachsel, *Institutionalizing Literacy* (1992).

20. See Lion F. Gardiner, *Redesigning Higher Education: Pro-*

ucing Dramatic Gains in Student Learning (1994), p. 2; a later study from 1998–99 found that 99.5 percent of faculty in four-year colleges consider an "ability to think clearly" to be "essential" or "very important." Linda J. Sax, Alexander W. Astin, William S. Korn, and Shannon K. Gilmartin, *The American College Teacher: National Norms for the 1989–1999 HERI Faculty Survey* (1999), p. 36.

21. John E. McPeck, *Critical Thinking and Education* (1981); see also Edward Thorndike, *Principles of Teaching* (1906), especially p. 246.

22. For example, Gavriel Salomon and David N. Perkins, "Rocky Roads to Transfer: Rethinking Mechanisms of a Neglected Phenomenon," 24 *Educational Psychologist* (1989), p. 113; Darrin R. Lehman and Richard E. Nisbett, "A Longitudinal Study of the Effects of Undergraduate Training on Reasoning," 26 *Developmental Psychology* (1990), p. 952.

23. For example, Wilbert J. McKeachie, Paul Patrick, Y. Guang Lin, and David A. F. Smith, *Teaching and Learning in the College Classroom: A Review of the Research Literature* (1986), p. 35; Richard E. Nisbett, Geoffrey T. Fong, Darrin R. Lehman, and Patricia W. Cheng, "Teaching Reasoning," 238 *Science* (1987), p. 625.

24. For example, William A. Galston, "Political Knowledge, Political Engagement, and Civic Education," 4 *Annual Review of Political Science* (2001), pp. 217–19; see generally Warren E. Miller and J. Merrill Shanks, *The New American Voter* (1996).

25. Martin Luther King Jr., *Where Do We Go from Here: Chaos or Community?* (1968), p. 167.

26. "Curricula that emphasize breadth of knowledge may prevent organization of knowledge because there is not enough time to learn anything in depth." John D. Bransford, Ann L. Brown, and Rodney R. Cocking (eds.), *How People Learn: Brain, Mind, Experience, and School* (1999), p. 5.

27. Aristotle, *Politics* (Jowett translation, Book 8, Section 2) (1905), p. 301.

28. William D. Schaefer, *Education without Compromise: From Chaos to Coherence in Higher Education* (1990), p. 126.

29. Robert Paul Wolff, *The Ideal of the University* (1969), p. 20.

CHAPTER FOUR   LEARNING TO COMMUNICATE

1. Richard J. Light, *Making the Most of College: Students Speak Their Minds* (2001), p. 54.

2. Charles F. Adams, Edwin L. Godkin, and Josiah Quincy, "Report of the Committee on Composition and Rhetoric," in *Reports of Visiting Committees of the Board of Overseers* (1897), pp. 401, 410.

3. "Statement of Principles and Standards for Post-Secondary Teaching and Writing," 40 *College Composition and Communication* (1989), p. 329.

4. Sheryl I. Fontaine and Susan Hunter, *Writing Ourselves into the Story: Unheard Voices from Composition Studies* (1993), p. 281.

5. Ibid., p. 44.

6. See Gary A. Olson and Joseph M. Moxley, "Directing Freshman Composition: The Limits of Authority," 40 *College Composition and Communication* (1989), p. 51.

7. Joseph Harris, "Meet the New Boss, Same as the Old Boss: Class Consciousness in Composition," 52 *College Composition and Communication* (2000), pp. 43, 57.

8. Alexander W. Astin, *What Matters in College: Four Critical Years Revisited* (1993), p. 130.

9. For an account of the development of writing across the curriculum, see David R. Russell, *Writing in the Academic Disciplines, 1870–1990* (1991).

10. Edward M. White, *Developing Successful College Writing Programs* (1989), p. 33.

11. Ernest T. Pascarella and Patrick T. Terenzini, *How College Affects Students*, Vol. 2: *A Third Decade of Research* (2005), pp. 156, 573.

12. Joe M. Steele, "Assessing Reasoning and Communication Skills of Postsecondary Students," paper presented at the meeting of the American Education Research Association, San Francisco (1986).

13. Dean Whitla, *Value Added: Measuring the Impact of Undergraduate Education*, study completed for the Office of Instructional Research and Evaluation, Harvard University (1978). In addition to the studies cited in the text, George Hillocks Jr. has produced a book comparing the effects of different methods of teaching composition: *Research on Written Composition* (1986).

14. From the unpublished summary of a Harvard study conducted by Nancy Sommers with support from the Andrew W. Mellon Foundation.

15. William G. Bowen and Derek Bok, *The Shape of the River: Long-Term Consequences of Considering Race in College and University Admissions* (1998), p. 212.

16. Alexander W. Astin, *What Matters in College*, p. 223.

17. See Ann R. Gere, "Empirical Research in Composition," in Ben W. McClelland and Timothy R. Donovan (eds.), *Perspectives on Research and Scholarship in Composition* (1985), p. 110.

18. These developments are described at length in James A. Berlin, *Rhetoric and Reality: Writing Instruction in American Colleges, 1900–1985* (1987).

19. George Hillocks Jr., *Research on Written Composition*, p. 225.

20. Marilyn Sternglass, *Time to Know Them: A Longitudinal Study of Writing and Learning at the College Level* (1997), p. 295.

21. Mina Shaughnessy, *Errors and Expectations: A Guide for the Teaching of Basic Writing* (1977), pp. 284, 292.

22. Donald M. Murray, "Teach Writing as a Process, Not Product," *The Leaflet* (November 1972), p. 11. This essay is reprinted in Richard L. Graves (ed.), *Rhetoric and Composition: A Sourcebook for Teachers* (1976), p. 79.

23. "Process theory constructs students as unique individuals who should be encouraged to develop their personal voices.

Process-oriented teachers view students as naturally capable writers whose abilities have for some reason lain dormant prior to their encounter with the process-oriented classroom." Sharon Crowley, *Composition in the University: Historical and Polemical Essays* (1998), p. 220.

24. See W. Ross Winterowd, *A Teacher's Introduction to Composition in the Rhetorical Tradition* (1994), p. 100.

25. Alan W. France, *Composition as a Cultural Practice* (1994), p. 2.

26. Ray Wallace and Susan L. Wallace, "Readerless Writers: College Composition's Misreading and Misteaching of Entering Students," in Ray Wallace, Alan Jackson, and Susan L. Wallace, *Reforming College Composition: Writing the Wrongs* (2000), pp. 92, 93.

27. Barbara Leigh Smith, "Writing across the Curriculum: What's at Stake," 3 *Current Issues in Higher Education, 1983–84* (1984), p. 1.

28. Alan Jackson, "Cognition and Culture," in Ray Wallace, Alan Jackson, and Susan L. Wallace, *Reforming College Composition*, p. 249.

29. Edward M. White, *Developing Successful College Writing Programs*, p. 164.

30. Niccolo Machiavelli, *The Prince* (1515), translation by Peter Bondanella (2005).

31. Thomas Sheridan, *A Case for Lectures in Elocution: Together with Two Dissertations on Language; and Some Other Treats Relative to Those Subjects* (1762), pp. ii, 1.

32. Brian H. Spitzberg and William R. Cupach, *Interpersonal Communication Competence* (1984), p. 187.

33. June H. Smith and Patricia H. Turner, "A Survey of Communication Department Curriculum in Four-Year Colleges and Universities," 1 *JACA* (1993), pp. 34, 40.

34. Ellen L. Vinson, "General Education and Enrollment Trends at Private Baccalaureate Colleges, 1975–2000" (Ph.D. dissertation, College of William and Mary, March 2002), p. 97.

35. *Criteria for Accreditation: Commission on Colleges of the Southern Association of Colleges and Schools* (11th Ed., 1997), p. 27.

36. Sherwyn P. Morreale and Philip M. Backlund, "Communication Curricula: History, Recommendations, Resources," 51 *Communication Education* (2002), p. 2.

37. For example, John T. Morello, "Comparing Speaking across the Curriculum and Writing across the Curriculum Programs," 49 *Communication Education* (2000), pp. 99, 101–2.

38. Gustav W. Friedrich, "Speech Communication Education in American Colleges and Universities," in Thomas W. Benson (ed.), *Speech Communication in the 20th Century* (1985), pp. 235, 248.

39. Joe M. Steele, "Assessing Reasoning and Communication Skills of Postsecondary Students." More generally, see Ronald E. Bassett and Mary E. Boone, "Improving Speech Communication Skills: An Overview of the Literature," in Rebecca B. Rubin (ed.), *Improving Speaking and Listening Skills* (1983), p. 83.

40. Alexander W. Astin, *What Matters in College*, p. 223; Alexander W. Astin, Jennifer R. Kemp, and Jennifer A. Lindholm, "A Decade of Change in Undergraduate Education: A National Study of System 'Transformation,'" 25 *The Review of Higher Education* (2002), pp. 141, 152.

41. *Wall Street Journal*, "Work Week" (December 29, 1998), p. A-1. See also Stephen C. Harper, "Business Education: A View from the Top," 12 *Business Forum* (1987), p. 24.

42. Bruskin Associates, "What Are Americans Afraid Of?" *The Bruskin Report* (1973), No. 53.

43. On the effectiveness of speech and listening training, see Joe M. Steele, "Assessing Reasoning and Communication Skills of Postsecondary Students"; Ronald E. Bassett and Mary E. Boone, "Improving Speech Communication Skills."

44. See, for example, Alison Schneider, "Taking Aim at Student Incoherence," 45 *Chronicle of Higher Education* (March 26, 1999), p. A-16.

CHAPTER FIVE LEARNING TO THINK

1. Ernest T. Pascarella and Patrick T. Terenzini, *How College Affects Students: Findings and Insights from Twenty Years of Research* (1991), p. 155.

2. Ernest T. Pascarella and Patrick T. Terenzini, *How College Affects Students*, Vol. 2: *A Third Decade of Research* (2005), p. 205. Interestingly, the same authors had concluded some years earlier that the gains in critical thinking were approximately twice as large; *How College Affects Students*, p. 158. The more recent estimate reflects the results of work done in the 1990s.

3. Alexander W. Astin, *What Matters in College: Four Critical Years Revisited* (1993), p. 223.

4. William G. Bowen and Derek Bok, *The Shape of the River: Long-Term Consequences of Considering Race in College and University Admissions* (1998), p. 212.

5. See, for example, Chau-kiu Cheung, Elisabeth Rudowicz, Anna S. Kwan, and Xiau Dong Yue, "Assessing University Students' General and Specific Critical Thinking," 36 *College Student Journal* (2002), p. 504.

6. This commonplace observation has been confirmed by a variety of empirical studies. Summarizing this work, Ernest Pascarella and Patrick Terenzini conclude that the level of effort and involvement in academic work has important effects on the growth of critical thinking; *How College Affects Students*, Vol. 2, p. 208.

7. George D. Kuh, "What We're Learning about Student Engagement from NSSE: Benchmarks for Effective Educational Practices," *Change* (March–April 2003), pp. 24, 27.

8. George D. Kuh, Shouping Hu, and Nick Vesper, "They Shall Be Known by What They Do: An Activities-Based Typology of College Students," 41 *Journal of College Student Development* (2000), pp. 228, 241.

9. Alexander W. Astin, Jennifer Kemp, and Jennifer A. Lindholm, "A Decade of Change in Undergraduate Education: A Na-

tional Study of System 'Transformation,'" 25 *The Review of Higher Education* (2002), p. 141.

10. Arthur Levine and Jeannette S. Cureton, "What We Know about Today's College Students," *About Campus* (March–April 1998), pp. 4, 7.

11. Patricia M. King and Karen S. Kitchener, *Developing Reflective Judgment: Understanding and Promoting Intellectual Growth and Critical Thinking in Adolescents and Adults* (1994).

12. See, for example, Robert A. Mines, Patricia M. King, Albert B. Hood, and Phillip K. Wood, "Stages of Intellectual Development and Associated Critical Thinking Skills in College Students," 31 *Journal of College Student Development* (1990), p. 538.

13. Kitchener and King, *Developing Reflective Judgment*, pp. 165–69.

14. Idem, pp. 224–26. Oddly, students appear to make greater progress in addressing unstructured problems than they do in mastering critical thinking about more structured problems; Ernest T. Pascarella and Patrick T. Terenzini, *How College Affects Students*, Vol. 2 (2005), p. 574. The quoted words are from Barry M. Kroll, *Teaching Hearts and Minds: College Students Reflect on the Vietnam War in Literature* (1992).

15. See, for example, Lion F. Gardiner, *Redesigning Undergraduate Education: Producing Dramatic Gains in Student Learning* (1994), p. 10.

16. Ibrahim A. Halloun and David Hestenes, "The Initial Knowledge State of College Physics Students," and "Common Sense Concepts about Motion," both published in 53 *American Journal of Physics* (1985), pp. 1043 and 1056.

17. Ernest T. Pascarella and Patrick T. Terenzini, *How College Affects Students*, Vol. 2, p. 205.

18. For example, Wilbert J. McKeachie, Paul Patrick, Y. Guang Lin, and David A. Smith, *Teaching and Learning in the College Classroom: A Review of the Research Literature* (1986), p. 69.

19. Robert E. Slavin, *Cooperative Learning: Theory, Research, and Practice* (1990) (49 of 60 studies showed an advantage for team

learning over individual learning); David W. Johnson, Roger T. Johnson, and Karl A. Smith, *Cooperative Learning: Increasing College Faculty Instructional Productivity* (1991), p. 38 (summarizing the results of some 375 studies over the preceding 90 years).

20. David W. Johnson, Roger T. Johnson, and Karl A. Smith, *Cooperative Learning*, pp. 6–8.

21. Ernest T. Pascarella and Patrick T. Terenzini, *How College Affects Students*, Vol. 2, p. 104.

22. Mary E. Huba and Jann E. Freed, *Learner-Centered Assessment on College Campuses: Shifting the Focus from Teaching to Learning* (2000), p. 219.

23. For example, John D. Bransford, Ann L. Brown, and Rodney Cocking (eds.), *How People Learn: Brain, Mind, Experience, and School* (1999), p. 55.

24. See, for example, Paul J. Black and Dylan Williams, "Assessment and Classroom Learning," 5 *Assessment and Education* (1998), p. 7. Researchers established long ago that proper feedback improves learning; for example, Ellis B. Page, "Teacher Comments and Student Performance: A Seventy-Four Classroom Experiment in School Motivation," 49 *Journal of Educational Psychology* (1958), p. 173.

25. Robert T. Blackburn, Glen R. Pollino, Alice Boberg, and Colman O'Connell, "Are Instructional Improvement Programs off Target?" 2 *Current Issues in Higher Education* (1980), p. 32. Arthur Chickering and Zelda F. Gamson also estimate that teachers in the average college classroom lecture 80 percent of the time; *Applying the Seven Principles for Good Practice in Undergraduate Education* (1991), p. 1.

26. Karron G. Lewis and Paul Woodward, "What Really Happens in Large University Classes?" paper given at the American Educational Research Association annual conference, New Orleans, 1984. See also Carolyn L. Ellner and Carol P. Barnes (eds.), *Studies of College Teaching: Experimental Results, Theoretical Interpretations, and New Perspectives* (1983), reporting that videotaping classes in 40 undergraduate institutions revealed that only 4 percent

of class time was devoted to questions and answers, and that most of the questions called only for recall, not higher-order thinking skills.

27. See, for example, Richard Panek, "101 Redefined: Colleges Rethink the Large Lecture Course," *New York Times, Education Life* (January 16, 2005), p. 32.

28. Ernest T. Pascarella and Patrick T. Terenzini, *How College Affects Students*, Vol. 2, p. 101.

29. See, for example, Norman Frederiksen, "The Real Test Bias: Influences of Testing on Teaching and Learning," 39 *American Psychologist* (1984), p. 193.

30. For an extended treatment of the methods of assessing students, see Grant Wiggins, *Educative Assessment: Designing Assessment to Inform and Improve Student Performance* (1998).

31. John M. Braxton, "Selectivity and Rigor in Research Universities," 64 *The Journal of Higher Education* (1993), p. 657. In a study of 52 liberal arts colleges conducted eight years earlier, Braxton and Robert C. Nordvall found that more selective schools asked for critical thinking in 32 percent of their exam questions, while less-selective schools tested critical thinking in only 16 percent of their questions; "Selective Liberal Arts Colleges: Higher Quality as Well as Higher Prestige?" 56 *The Journal of Higher Education* (1985), p. 538.

32. Ohmer Milton, *Will That Be on the Final?* (1982).

33. Linda J. Sax, Alexander W. Astin, William S. Korn, and Shannon K. Gilmartin, *The American College Teacher: National Norms for the 1989–1999 HERI Faculty Survey* (1999), p. 36.

34. Karl Jaspers, *The Idea of the University* (1959), p. 57.

35. *A Turning Point in Higher Education: The Inaugural Address of Charles William Elliot as President of Harvard College, October 19, 1869* (1969), p. 11.

36. John McLeish, *The Lecture Method* (1968), p. 10; see also Lion F. Gardiner, *Redesigning Higher Education* (1994), pp. 46–50.

37. See, for example, Alice F. Healy, David W. Fendrich, Robert J. Crutcher, William T. Wittman, Antoinette T. Gesi,

K. Anders Ericsson, and Lyle E. Bourne Jr., "The Long-Term Retention of Skills," in Alice F. Healy, Stephen M. Kosslyn, and Richard M. Shiffrin, *From Learning Processes to Cognitive Processes: Essays in Honor of William K. Estes*, Vol. 2 (1992), p. 87. The initial study on this point is Norman J. Slemecka and Peter Graf, "The Generation Effect: Delineation of a Phenomenon," 4 *Journal of Experimental Psychology: Human Learning and Memory* (1978), p. 592.

38. "It may tentatively be suggested that learning exercises that require the practical application of knowledge (i.e., active learning) lead to levels of retention that do not show a rapid decline with time"; Martin A. Conway, Gillian Cohen, and Nicola Stanhope, "On the Very Long-Term Retention of Knowledge Acquired through Formal Education: Twelve Years of Cognitive Psychology," 120 *Journal of Experimental Psychology: General* (1991), pp. 395, 407.

39. See, for example, Deborah Stipek, *Motivation to Learn: From Theory to Practice* (3d Ed., 1998), p. 165.

40. See, for example, David A. Garvin, *How Professional Schools Teach Professional Skills: The Case Method in Action* (2003).

41. See Howard Hughes Medical Institute, *Bye-Bye Bio 101: Teach Science the Way You Do Science* (April 22, 2004), http://www.eurekalert.org/pub_releases/2004-04/hhmi-bb1041904.php.

42. Michael M. Lewis, *Moneyball: The Art of Winning an Unfair Game* (2003).

43. Lynn A. Steen (ed.), *Mathematics and Democracy: The Case for Quantitative Literacy* (2001), pp. 16–17.

44. See, for example, Deborah Hughes-Hallett, "The Role of Mathematics Courses in the Development of Quantitative Literacy," in Bernard L. Madison and Lynn A. Steen (eds.), *Quantitative Literacy: Why Numeracy Matters for Schools and Colleges* (2003), p. 91.

45. William H. Schmidt, Curtis C. McKnight, Leland S. Logan, Pamela M. Jakwerth, and Richard T. Houang, *Facing the Consequences: Using TIMSS for a Clear Look at U.S. Mathematics and Science Education* (1999), p. 226; Pascal D. Forgione,

U.S. Commissioner of Education Statistics, *Questions and An-swers: 12th Grade TIMMS Results* (1995), http://www.col_ed.org/smenws/tim55/12th.html.

46. Ernest T. Pascarella and Patrick T. Terenzini, *How College Affects Students* (1993), pp. 70, 569. For all undergraduates, quantitative skills are thought to rise by approximately one-half of a standard deviation (or about 19 percentile points), a gain roughly equal to the estimated gain in critical thinking and one-half of the estimated gain in reflective judgment (i.e., reasoning about ill-structured problems); Pascarella and Terenzini, *How College Affects Students,* Vol. 2, p. 574.

47. Bernard L. Madison, "Articulation and Quantitative Literacy," in Bernard L. Madison and Lynn A. Steen, *Quantitative Literacy: Why Numeracy Matters* (2003), pp. 153, 162.

48. Uri Treisman, "Studying Students Studying Calculus: A Look at the Lives of Minority Mathematics Students in College," *The College Mathematics Journal* (1992), p. 362.

49. Mazur's teaching is described in Sheila Tobias, *Revitalizing Undergraduate Science: Why Some Things Work and Most Don't* (1992), p. 114; see also Eric Mazur, *Peer Instruction: A User's Manual* (1997).

50. Catherine H. Crouch and Eric Mazur, "Peer Instruction: Ten Years of Experience and Results," 69 *American Journal of Physics* (2001), p. 970.

51. See Association of American Colleges, *Integrity in the College Curriculum: A Report to the Academic Community* (1985), p. 29.

52. Compare the discussions of different disciplines in Association of American Colleges, *Liberal Learning and the Arts and Sciences Major,* Vol. 2: *Reports from the Fields* (1991).

53. Karen Schilling, *Assessing Models of Liberal Education: An Empirical Comparison* (ERIC Document Reproduction Service No. ED 359 864) (1991); Sheila Wright, "Fostering Intellectual Development of Students in Professional Schools through Interdisciplinary Coursework," 16 *Innovative Higher Education* (1992), p. 251.

54. Association of American Colleges, *Reports from the Fields: Project on Liberal Learning, Study-in-Depth, and the Arts and Sciences Major* (1991), p. 28.

55. Ernest T. Pascarella and Patrick T. Terenzini, *How College Affects Students*, pp. 65–66, 614.

56. Idem, pp. 118–20. See also Lamont Flowers, Steven J. Osterlind, Ernest T. Pascarella, and Christopher T. Pierson, "How Much Do Students Learn in College?: Cross-Sectional Estimates Using the College BASE," 72 *The Journal of College Education* (2001), pp. 566, 574. "A second major trend supported in the data is that the vast majority of college impact on C BASE scores appears to take place in the first two years of college." The C BASE tests attempt to measure reasoning in English, mathematics, science, and social studies.

57. Idem, p. 139.

58. Alexander W. Astin, *What Matters in College*, pp. 236–41, 302–10, 370–72.

59. Idem, p. 276.

60. Idem, pp. 375–76, 383. See also Alexander W. Astin, "Involvement in Learning: Lessons We Have Learned," 37 *Journal of College Student Development* (1996), p. 123.

61. Pascarella and Terenzini, *How College Affects Students*, p. 619.

62. "While much has been made of the importance of recognizing and adapting educational programs and experiences so that they are more responsive to individual differences among students, there is little evidence to suggest that the challenge has been taken seriously on more than a handful of campuses"; idem, p. 645. This is especially regrettable since studies indicate that the greatest gains in critical thinking come from matching methods of teaching to differences in the learning styles of students; Rita Dunn, Shirley Griggs, Jeffery Olson, Mark Beasley, and Bernard Gorman, "A Meta-Analytic Validation of the Dunn and Dunn Learning Styles Model," 88 *Journal of Educational Research* (1995), p. 353.

CHAPTER SIX BUILDING CHARACTER

1. David Brooks, "'Moral Suicide,' à la Wolfe," *New York Times* (November 16, 2004), p. A27.

2. See generally Daniel Callahan and Sissela Bok (eds.), *Ethics Teaching in Higher Education* (1980), especially Douglas Sloan, "The Teaching of Ethics in the American Undergraduate Curriculum, 1976–1996," p. 1.

3. *Who's Who among American High School Students: 29th Annual Survey of High Achievers, Cheating and Succeeding: Record Numbers of Top High School Students Take Ethical Shortcuts* (1998), p. 1.

4. Josephson Institute of Ethics, *Report Card 2002: The Ethics of American Youth* (2002). Fortunately, self-reports of cheating seem to have declined somewhat in 2004, although this single annual report is not sufficient to demonstrate a trend; Josephson Institute of Ethics, *Report Card 2004: The Ethics of American Youth* (2004), available on line at http://josephsoninstitute.org/Survey2004/.

5. Josephson Institute of Ethics, *Report Card 2002*, p. 6.

6. Ibid.

7. See, for example, Donald L. McCabe and Linda K. Trevino, "Honor Codes and Other Contextual Influences," 64 *The Journal of Higher Education* (1993), p. 522; see studies cited in Margaret P. Jendrek, "Faculty Reactions to Academic Dishonesty," 30 *Journal of College Student Development* (1989), p. 401.

8. See, for example, Donald L. McCabe, Linda K. Trevino, and Kenneth D. Butterfield, "Cheating in Academic Institutions: A Decade of Research," 11 *Ethics and Behavior* (2001), pp. 219, 223; Gary Pavela, "Applying the Power of Association on Campus: A Model Code of Academic Integrity," 9 *Synthesis: Law and Policy in Higher Education* (1997), p. 637. Arthur Levine and Jeannette S. Cureton, however, argue that the number of students who acknowledge having cheated did not rise from 1976 to 1993; *When Hope and Fear Collide: A Portrait of Today's College Student* (1998), p. 126.

9. David Callahan, *The Cheating Culture: Why More Americans Are Doing Wrong to Get Ahead* (2004), especially pp. 20–24.

10. Tammy Joyner, "Corporate Crime Not Limited to Bigwigs," *Atlanta Journal-Constitution* (August 6, 2002), p. A1.

11. Alan Wolfe, *Moral Freedom: The Impossible Idea That Defines the Way We Live Now* (2001), p. 195.

12. Harvard University, *General Education in a Free Society* (1945), pp. 72–73.

13. Howard R. Bowen, *Investment in Learning: The Individual and Social Value of American Higher Education* (1977), p. 220.

14. Ernest T. Pascarella and Patrick T. Terenzini, *How College Affects Students: Findings and Insights from Twenty Years of Research* (1991), p. 366.

15. Idem, p. 366; Ernest T. Pascarella and Patrick T. Terenzini, *How College Affects Students*, Vol. 2: *A Third Decade of Research* (2005), p. 347.

16. Andre Schlaefli, James R. Rest, and Stephen J. Thoma, "Does Moral Education Improve Moral Judgment?: A Meta-Analysis of Intervention Studies Using the Defining Issues Test," 55 *Review of Educational Research* (1985), p. 319; Ernest T. Pascarella and Patrick T. Terenzini, *How College Affects Students*, Vol. 2, p. 348.

17. Ernest T. Pascarella and Patrick T. Terenzini, *How College Affects Students*, Vol. 2, p. 359.

18. Ernest T. Pascarella and Patrick T. Terenzini, *How College Affects Students*, p. 357, reporting that discussions of moral dilemmas are particularly effective in encouraging students to approach ethical questions through principled reasoning.

19. Ernest T. Pascarella and Patrick T. Terenzini, *How College Affects Students*, Vol. 2, pp. 354–55.

20. G. Blakemore Evans, *The Riverside Shakespeare* (1974), p. 256.

21. Alan L. Otten, "Politics and People," *Wall Street Journal* (April 11, 1974), p. 12.

22. For example, Wendy Fischman, Becca Solomon, Deborah

Greenspan, and Howard Gardner, *Making Good: How Young People Cope with Moral Dilemmas at Work* (2004), p. 161.

23. Ernest T. Pascarella and Patrick T. Terenzini, *How College Affects Students*, p. 363; in a subsequent volume, Pascarella and Terenzini add that, having looked at research carried out in the 1990s, "we also found extensive evidence of a positive relationship between level of principled moral reasoning and the likelihood of principled behavior in a wide range of settings"; *How College Affects Students*, Vol. 2, p. 582.

24. James R. Rest and Darcia Narváez, "Summary: What's Possible," in James R. Rest and Darcia Narváez, *Moral Development and the Professions: Psychology and Applied Ethics* (1994), p. 213.

25. *Harvard University Gazette* (October 17, 1986), pp. 1, 8.

26. See generally Martin Hoffman, *Empathy and Moral Development: Implications for Caring and Justice* (2000); for a thoughtful, more popular, treatment, see Alfie Kohn, *The Brighter Side of Human Nature: Altruism and Empathy in Everyday Life* (1990).

27. Donald L. McCabe, Linda K. Trevino, and Kenneth D. Butterfield, "Academic Integrity in Honor Code and Non–Honor Code Environments: A Qualitative Investigation," 70 *The Journal of Higher Education* (1999), p. 211.

28. Donald L. McCabe, "Faculty Responses to Academic Dishonesty: The Influence of Student Honor Codes," 34 *Research in Higher Education* (1993), p. 647.

29. Margaret P. Jendrek, "Faculty Reactions to Academic Dishonesty," 30 *Journal of College Student Development* (1989), p. 401.

30. Gary Pavela, "Donald McCabe on 'Faculty Attitudes toward Academic Integrity,'" 9 *Synthesis: Law and Policy in Higher Education* (1997), pp. 637, 642.

31. Sissela Bok, *Mayhem: Violence as Public Entertainment* (1998), p. 70.

32. Ernest T. Pascarella and Patrick T. Terenzini, *How College Affects Students*, Vol. 2, p. 369.

33. Janet Eyler and Dwight E. Giles Jr., *Where's the Learning in Service Learning?* (1999), p. 37. One study comparing the effect on moral reasoning between students in a course on ethics and students who took the same course but also engaged in community service found that the latter scored significantly higher on the Defining Issues Test of Moral Reasoning; Judith A. Boss, "The Effect of Community Service Work on the Moral Development of College Ethics Students," 23 *Journal of Moral Education* (1994), p. 183. Other studies, however, have not confirmed this result; Ernest T. Pascarella and Patrick T. Terenzini, *How College Affects Students*, Vol. 2, pp. 358–59.

34. Alexander W. Astin, "Involvement in Learning Revisited: Lessons We Have Learned," 37 *Journal of College Student Development* (1996), pp. 123, 129.

35. Janet Eyler and Dwight E. Giles Jr., *Where's the Learning in Service Learning?*, p. 36.

36. Linda J. Sax and Alexander W. Astin, "The Development of 'Civic Virtue' among College Students," in John Gardner and Gretchen Van der Veer (eds.), *The Senior Year Experience: A Beginning, Not an End* (1997), p. 191.

37. Linda J. Sax, Alexander W. Astin, William Korn, and Shannon Gilmartin, *The American College Teacher: National Norms for the 1989–1999 HERI Faculty Survey* (1999), p. 36.

CHAPTER SEVEN   PREPARATION FOR CITIZENSHIP

1. John Dewey, *School and Society* (2d Ed., 1933). Quoted in Janet Eyler and Dwight E. Giles Jr., *Where's the Learning in Service Learning?* (1999), p. 154.

2. These figures are taken from the *Statistical Abstract of the United States* for the appropriate years. Those figures are in turn derived from the Census Bureau's *Current Population Survey*, November Supplements, taken from a large sample of individuals within two weeks of each election.

3. Ibid.

4. Robert D. Putnam, *Bowling Alone: The Collapse and Revival of American Community* (2000), p. 45.

5. Peter Levine and Mark H. Lopez, "Youth Turnout Has Declined by Any Measure," The Center for Information and Research on Civic Learning and Engagement (University of Maryland, September 2002), p. 9.

6. Ibid.

7. Robert D. Putnam, *Bowling Alone*, p. 252.

8. David T. Z. Mindich, *Tuned Out: Why Americans under 40 Don't Follow the News* (2005), p. 28. Mindich also points out that this trend is not compensated for by greater use of television news or the Internet.

9. Martin P. Wattenberg, *Where Have All the Voters Gone?* (2002), p. 93.

10. William A. Galston, "Political Knowledge, Political Engagement, and Civic Education," 4 *Annual Review of Political Science* (2001), p. 217.

11. American Political Science Association, Task Force on Civic Education in the Next Century, "Expanded Articulation Statement: A Call for Reactions and Contributions," 31 *PS: Political Science and Politics* (1998), pp. 636–37. For interesting commentary on earlier efforts by the APSA to address civic education, compare Hindy L. Schecter, "Civic Education: Three Early American Political Science Association Committees and Their Relevance to Our Times," 31 *PS: Political Science and Politics* (1998), p. 631, with Stephen T. Leonard, "'Pure Futility and Waste': Academic Political Science and Civic Education," 32 *PS: Political Science and Politics* (1999), p. 749.

12. Mike Bergman, "U.S. Voter Turnout Up in 2004, Census Bureau Reports," U.S. Census Bureau News, press release (May 26, 2005).

13. David C. King, "Youth Came Through with Big Turnout," *Boston Globe* (November 4, 2004), p. A15.

14. "From the earliest empirical studies of civic involvement and electoral participation, formal educational attainment has

been identified as the strongest and most consistent positive influence on the characteristics of citizenship"; Robert D. Putnam, *Bowling Alone*, p. 31. As Ernest T. Pascarella and Patrick T. Terenzini observe, studies "almost invariably indicate changes during the college years toward . . . greater interest in social and political issues and greater interest and involvement in the political process"; *How College Affects Students: Findings and Insights from Twenty Years of Research* (1991), p. 278.

15. William A. Galston, "Political Knowledge, Political Engagement, and Civic Education," p. 232, and studies cited therein. In reviewing studies on undergraduate education, Ernest T. Pascarella and Patrick T. Terenzini observe that "education produces substantially greater understanding of the principles of democratic government, greater ability to identify incumbent local and national leaders, more knowledge of political facts"; *How College Affects Students*, Vol. 2: *A Third Decade of Research* (2005), p. 329.

16. Sam L. Popkin and Michael A. Dimock, *Political Knowledge and Citizen Competence* (1999), p. 142.

17. Michael C. Johanek and John Puckett, "The State of Civic Education: Preparing Citizens in an Age of Accountability," in Susan Fuhrman and Marvin Lazerson (eds.), *The Public Schools* (2005), p. 130.

18. Idem, pp. 130, 139.

19. Derek Bok, *The Trouble with Government* (2001), pp. 405–6.

20. Linda J. Sax, Alexander W. Astin, William S. Korn, and Kathryn Mahoney, *The American Freshman: National Norms for Fall 2000* (2000).

21. Linda J. Sax, Alexander W. Astin, William S. Korn, and Kathryn Mahoney, *The American Freshman: National Norms for Fall 2003* (2003); "Survey: Fewer Students Seek Diverse Friends," 52 *Chronicle of Higher Education* (February 4, 2005), pp. A-1, A-34.

22. Anne Colby, Thomas Ehrlich, Elizabeth Beaumont, and Jason Stephens, *Educating Citizens: Preparing America's Undergraduates for Lives of Moral and Civic Responsibility* (2003), p. 45.

23. Carol G. Schneider, "Educational Missions and Civic Responsibility," in Thomas Ehrlich (ed.), *Civic Responsibility and Higher Education* (2000), pp. 98, 120.

24. Linda J. Sax, Alexander W. Astin, William S. Korn, and Shannon K. Gilmartin, *The American College Teacher: National Norms for the 1989–1999 HERI Faculty Survey* (1999), p. 36.

25. Ernest T. Pascarella and Patrick T. Terenzini, *How College Affects Students*, pp. 277–78.

26. Ernest T. Pascarella and Patrick T. Terenzini, *How College Affects Students*, Vol. 2, p. 586.

27. See Linda J. Sax and Alexander W. Astin, "Developing Civic Virtue among College Students," in John N. Gardner and Gretchen Van der Veer (eds.), *The Senior Year Experience: Facilitating Integration, Reflection, Closure and Transition* (1998), p. 133. See also Linda J. Sax, "Citizenship Development and the American College Student," in Thomas Ehrlich (ed.), *Civic Responsibility and Higher Education* (2003), p. 16: "Clearly forming a habit of volunteerism is critical to the long-run development of citizenship."

28. William E. Knox, Paul Lindsay, and Mary N. Kolb, *Does College Make a Difference? Long-Term Changes in Activities and Attitudes* (1993), pp. 91–92.

29. Dan Drew and David Weaver, "Voter Learning in the 1988 Presidential Election: Did the Debate and the Media Matter?" 68 *Journalism Quarterly* (1991), p. 27.

30. Carol G. Schneider, "Liberal Education and the Civic Engagement Gap," in Adrianna Kezar, Tony C. Chambers, and John C. Burkhardt (eds.), *Higher Education for the Public Good: Emerging Voices from a National Movement* (2005), pp. 127, 139, 140.

31. U.S. Department of Education, *The New College Course Map and Transcript Files: Changes in Course-Taking and Achievement, 1972–1993* (2d Ed., 1999), pp. 187–89.

32. Robert D. Putnam, *Bowling Alone*, p. 35.

33. Norman Nie and Sunshine Hillygus, "Education and Democratic Citizenship," in Diane Ravitch and Joseph Viteritti (eds.), *Making Good Citizens: Education and Civil Society* (2001), p. 30.

34. See David E. Campbell, *Untapped Potential: Young People and Political Mobilization*, Program in American Democracy, University of Notre Dame (2004), Campbell.91@nd.edu.

35. Robert D. Putnam, *Bowling Alone*, p. 46.

36. William E. Knox, Paul Lindsay, and Mary N. Kolb, *Does College Make a Difference?*, p. 19.

37. William A. Galston, "Political Knowledge, Political Engagement, and Civic Education," p. 218.

38. Elizabeth Beaumont, Anne Colby, Thomas Ehrlich, and Judith Torney-Purta, "Promoting Political Competence and Engagement in College Students: An Empirical Study," *Journal of Political Science Education* (in press).

39. Linda J. Sax and Alexander W. Astin, "The Development of 'Civic Virtue' among College Students," in John Gardner and Gretchen Van der Veer (eds.), *The Senior Year Experience*, p. 19. See also Miranda Yates and James Youniss, "Community Service and Political-Moral Identity in Adolescents," 6 *Journal of Research on Adolescents* (1996), p. 271; Monica Kirkpatrick, Timothy Beebe, Jeylan T. Mortimer, and Mark Snyder, "Volunteerism in Adolescence: A Process Perspective," 8 *Journal of Research on Adolescence* (1998), p. 309.

40. See generally Janet Eyler and Dwight E. Giles Jr., *Where's the Learning in Service Learning?* (1999). Ernest T. Pascarella and Patrick T. Terenzini report that community service that includes opportunities for reflection shows greater gains in civic interest and commitment than community service by itself; *How College Affects Students*, Vol. 2, p. 359.

41. Arthur Levine and Jeannette S. Cureton, *When Hope and Fear Collide: A Portrait of Today's College Student* (1998), p. 54.

42. Sidney Verba, Kay L. Schlozman, and Henry E. Brady, *Voice and Equity: Civic Voluntarism in American Politics* (1995), pp. 424–25.

43. Higher Education Act of 1998, 20 United States Code 1094(a)(23)(A), -(B), and -(C).

44. Elizabeth F. Farrell and Eric Hoover, "Many Colleges Fall

Short on Registering Student Voters," 51 *Chronicle of Higher Education* (September 17, 2004), p. A-1.

45. Quoted in Matthew Hartley and Elizabeth L. Hollander, "The Elusive Ideal: Civic Learning and Higher Education," in Susan Fuhrman and Marvin Lazerson (eds.), *The Public Schools* (2005), pp. 252, 272.

CHAPTER EIGHT   LIVING WITH DIVERSITY

1. Laurence Veysey, *The Emergence of the American University* (1965; First Phoenix Edition, 1970), p. 271.

2. Ernest T. Pascarella, Betsy Palmer, Melinda Moye, and Christopher T. Pierson, "Do Diversity Experiences Influence the Development of Critical Thinking?," 42 *Journal of College Student Development* (2001), p. 257.

3. Patricia Gurin, Jeffrey S. Lehman, and Earl Lewis, *Defending Diversity: Defending Affirmative Action at the University of Michigan* (2004), pp. 102, 130.

4. Idem, p. 102.

5. Samuel Walker, *Hate Speech* (1994), p. 127; Jack B. Harrison, "Hate Speech: Power in the Marketplace," 25 *The Journal of College and University Law* (1994), p. 478; Henry Louis Gates Jr., "Let Them Talk," *The New Republic* (September 20 and 27, 1993), p. 37.

6. Debra Humphreys, "National Survey Finds Diversity Requirements Common around the Country," http://www.diversityweb .org/Digest/FOO/survey.html.

7. See, for example, Jeffrey F. Milem and Kenji Hakuta, "The Benefits of Racial and Ethnic Diversity in Higher Education," in Deborah J. Wilds (ed.), *Minorities in Higher Education: Seventeenth Annual Status Report, American Council on Education* (2001), p. 39.

8. Stephan Thernstrom and Abigail Thernstrom, *America in Black and White: One Nation, Indivisible* (1997), pp. 387–88.

9. Arthur Levine and Jeannette S. Cureton, *When Hope and Fear Collide: A Portrait of Today's College Student* (1998), p. 91.

10. Beverly D. Tatum, *"Why Are All the Black Kids Sitting To-gether in the Cafeteria?" and Other Conversations about Race* (1997), p. 78.

11. Sharon B. Gmelch, *Gender on Campus: Issues for College Women* (1998), p. 96.

12. See, for example, Donna Henderson-King and Audrey Kaleta, "Learning about Social Diversity: The Undergraduate Experience and Intergroup Tolerance," 71 *The Journal of Higher Education* (2000), p. 142.

13. Ernest T. Pascarella and Patrick T. Terenzini, *How College Affects Students*, Vol. 2: *A Third Decade of Research* (2005), p. 581; Ernest T. Pascarella, Marcia Edison, Amaury Nora, Linda S. Hagedorn, and Patrick T. Terenzini, "Influences on Students' Openness to Diversity and Challenge in the First Year of College," 67 *The Journal of Higher Education* (1996), pp. 174, 175.

14. Idem, p. 280.

15. Alexander W. Astin, *What Matters in College: Four Critical Years Revisited* (1993), p. 146; Alexander W. Astin, Jennifer R. Kemp, and Jennifer A. Lindholm, "A Decade of Changes in Undergraduate Education: A National Study of System 'Transformation,'" 25 *The Review of Higher Education* (2002), pp. 141, 154.

16. William G. Bowen and Derek Bok, *The Shape of the River: Long-Term Consequences of Considering Race in College and University Admissions* (1998).

17. Idem, p. 194.

18. Idem, pp. 224–25, 232.

19. Idem, pp. 225–26. According to Ernest T. Pascarella and Patrick T. Terenzini, "the weight of evidence is reasonably clear and consistent in suggesting that across racial-ethnic groups, having friends of another race and being a member of an interracial friendship group has significant and positive effects on racial-ethnic attitudes and values"; *How College Affects Students*, Vol. 2, p. 311.

20. Sylvia Hurtado, "The Campus Racial Climate: Contexts of Conflict," 63 *The Journal of Higher Education* (1992), pp. 539, 552.

21. Arthur Levine and Jeannette Cureton, *When Hope and Fear Collide*, p. 71.

22. Anthony L. Antonio, "The Role of Interracial Interaction in the Development of Leadership Skills and Cultural Knowledge and Understanding," 42 *Research in Higher Education* (2001), pp. 593, 604.

23. Anthony L. Antonio, "Diversity and the Influence of Friendship Groups in College," 25 *The Review of Higher Education* (2001), pp. 63, 76, 78.

24. Arthur Levine and Jeannette S. Cureton, *When Hope and Fear Collide*, p. 72.

25. Howard J. Ehrlich, *Campus Ethnoviolence . . . and the Policy Options*, Institute Report No. 4, National Institute against Prejudice and Violence (1990), p. iii.

26. In a 1993 survey of student newspaper editors, just over half opined that race relations on their campus were "excellent" or "good," while just under half felt that they were only "fair" or "poor"; Mel Elfin with Sarah Burke, "Race on Campus," *U.S. News and World Report* (April 19, 1993), pp. 53–56.

27. Arthur Levine and Jeannette S. Cureton, *When Hope and Fear Collide*, pp. 71–91, 81.

28. Greg Tanaka, *The Intercultural Campus: Transcending Culture and Power in American Higher Education* (2003), pp. 91, 74.

29. Ernest T. Pascarella, Marcia Edison, Amaury Nora, Linda S. Hagedorn, and Patrick T. Terenzini, "Influences on Students' Openness to Diversity and Challenge in the First Year of College," pp. 174, 189; Walter G. Stephan and W. Paul Vogt (eds.), *Education Programs for Improving Intergroup Relations: Theory, Research, and Practice* (2004); Leonard Springer, Betsy Palmer, Patrick T. Terenzini, Ernest T. Pascarella, and Amaury Nora, "Attitudes toward Campus Diversity: Participation in a Racial or Cultural Awareness Workshop," 20 *The Review of Higher Education* (1996), p. 53; A. Mitchell Chang, "The Impact of an Undergraduate Diversity Course Requirement on Students' Racial Views and Attitudes," 51 *The Journal of General Education* (2002), p. 21.

For more general experimental work on altering perspectives to decrease stereotypes, see Adam Galinsky and Gordon B. Moskowitz, "Perspective-Taking: Decreasing Stereotype Expression, Stereotype Accessibility, and In-Group Favoritism," 78 *Journal of Personality and Social Psychology* (2000), p. 708.

30. Greg Tanaka, *The Intercultural Campus*, pp. 7, 152; Tommy Lee Woon, "Beyond a Leap of Faith: Addressing Second-Generation Diversity Challenges at Stanford University" (unpublished paper, February 6, 1997). For a forceful presentation of what can go wrong in racial sensitivity sessions, see Charles Alan Kors, "Bad Faith: The Politicization of the University *in Loco Parentis*," in Howard Dickman (ed.), *The Imperiled Academy* (1993), p. 153. For a more nuanced view of the pitfalls, see Marcia Baxter Magola, "Facilitating Meaningful Dialogues about Race," 2 *About Campus* (November 1997), p. 14.

31. Gordon W. Allport, *The Nature of Prejudice* (1954). Much experimental evidence confirms the contact theory; see Marilynn B. Brewer and Rupert J. Brown, "Intergroup Relations," in Daniel T. Gilbert, Susan T. Fiske, and Gardner Lindzey (eds.), *The Handbook of Social Psychology*, Vol. 2, pp. 554, 576–83.

32. Elizabeth J. Whitt, Marcia Edison, Ernest T. Pascarella, Patrick T. Terenzini, and Amaury Nora, "Influences on Students' Openness to Diversity and Challenge in the Second and Third Years of College," 72 *The Journal of Higher Education* (2001), pp. 172, 195.

33. For a discussion of the effects of intergroup dialogue and the conditions that seem to promote attitude change, see Walter G. Stephan and W. Paul Vogt (eds.), *Education Programs for Improving Intergroup Relations: Theory, Research, and Practice* (2004).

34. Sharon B. Gmelch, *Gender on Campus: Issues for College Women* (1998), p. 103. See also Beverly D. Tatum, *"Why Are All the Black Kids Sitting Together in the Cafeteria?"* p. 78.

35. Richard J. Light, *Making the Most of College: Students Speak Their Minds* (2001), pp. 180–81.

36. For a detailed survey of rising black enrollments and degrees in higher education, see Theodore Cross, "The Good News That the Thernstroms Neglected to Tell," *The Journal of Blacks in Higher Education*, No. 42 (Winter 2003/2004), p. 3.

37. Gary Orfield, *The Growth of Segregation in American Schools: Changing Patterns of Separation and Poverty Since 1968* (1993).

38. Barbara N. Solomon, *In the Company of Educated Women: A History of Women and Higher Education in America* (1985), p. 95; Helen L. Horowitz, *Campus Life: Undergraduate Cultures from the End of the Eighteenth Century to the Present* (1987).

39. Barbara N. Solomon, *In the Company of Educated Women*, p. 127.

40. *A Turning Point in Higher Education: The Inaugural Address of Charles William Eliot as President of Harvard College, October 19, 1869* (1969), p. 18.

41. Quoted in Leslie Miller-Bernal, *Separate by Degree: Women Students' Experiences in Single-Sex and Coeducational Colleges* (2000), p. 209.

42. Mabel Newcomer, *A Century of Higher Education for American Women* (1959), p. 49.

43. Barbara N. Solomon, *In the Company of Educated Women*, p. 119.

44. Mabel Newcomer, *A Century of Higher Education for American Women*, p. 203.

45. For example, Suzanne Imes, *A Look at Coeducational Living in Institutions of Higher Education* (1966); Judith Corbett and Robert Sommer, "Anatomy of a Coed Residence Hall," 13 *Journal of College Student Personnel* (May 1972), p. 215; Elizabeth A. Reid, "Effects of Coresidential Living on the Attitudes, Self-Image, and Role Expectations of Women," 131 *American Journal of Psychiatry* (1974), p. 551.

46. David A. Hoekema, *Campus Rules and Moral Community: In Place of* in Loco Parentis (1994), p. 15.

47. Norval Glenn and Elizabeth Marquardt, *Hooking Up, Hanging Out, and Hoping for Mr. Right,* Institute for American Values Report to the Independent Women's Forum (2001), p. 14

48. Dorothy C. Holland and Margaret A. Eisenhart, *Educated in Romance: Women, Achievement, and College Culture* (1990), pp. 79, 111, 149.

49. Norval Glenn and Elizabeth Marquardt, *Hooking Up, Hanging Out, and Hoping for Mr. Right,* pp. 26, 13.

50. Ernest T. Pascarella and Patrick T. Terenzini, *How College Affects Students: Findings and Insights from Twenty Years of Research* (1991), p. 326. See also studies cited on pages 293–95.

51. Norval Glenn and Elizabeth Marquardt, *Hooking Up, Hanging Out, and Hoping for Mr. Right,* pp. 61, 26.

52. See, for example, Martin D. Schwartz and Walter S. Dekesredy, *Sexual Assault on Campus: The Role of Male Peer Support* (1997), pp. 11–13; Mary P. Koss, Christine A. Gidycz, and Nadine Wisniewski, "The Scope of Rape: Incidence and Prevalence of Sexual Aggression and Victimization in a National Sample of Higher Education Students," 55 *Journal of Consulting and Clinical Psychology* (1987), p. 162. For a skeptical view of such findings, see Neil Gilbert, "The Phantom Epidemic of Sexual Assault," *Public Interest,* No. 103 (Spring 1991), p. 54.

53. One study reports that fraternity members account for 63 percent of all sexual assaults by students on campus despite making up only one-quarter of the total undergraduate population; Jennifer Scanlon, "Campus Tolerates Violence," 4 *Women in Higher Education* (April 1995), p. 19.

54. Luoluo Hong, "Toward a Transformed Approach to Prevention: Breaking the Link between Masculinity and Violence," 48 *Journal of American College Health* (2000), p. 269.

55. Alexander W. Astin, *What Matters in College,* p. 142.

56. Alan J. Berkowitz, *Man and Rape: Theory, Research and Prevention Programs in Higher Education* (1994).

CHAPTER NINE PREPARING FOR A
GLOBAL SOCIETY

1. Richard D. Lambert, "New Directions in International Education," 449 *Annals of the American Academy of Political and Social Science* (May 1980), p. 14.

2. Robert B. Woyach, *Understanding the Global Arena: A Report on the Ohio State Awareness Survey* (1989). Apparently the modest improvements from freshman to senior year were typical of the other colleges in the survey; Thomas S. Barrows, Stephen S. Klein, and John L. D. Clark, *College Students' Knowledge and Beliefs: A Survey of Global Understanding* (1981).

3. "Americans Get Low Grades in Gallup Geography Test," News Service of the National Geographic Society (July 27, 1988).

4. Martha C. Nussbaum, *Cultivating Humanity: A Classical Defense of Reform in Liberal Education* (1997), pp. 50–51.

5. Idem. The quotations appear on pp. 145, 146, 169, 68, and 145, respectively.

6. Nussbaum is not the only writer to set the bar for acquiring intercultural competence at an unrealistically high level. Marion Dobbert, for example, would demand a mastery of another language and adds that "every student and faculty member should be required to do internships in at least two target cultures and live in each for 9–12 months or more"; "The Impossibility of Internationalizing Students by Adding Materials to Courses," in Josef A. Mestenhausen and Brenda J. Ellingboe (eds.), *Reforming the Higher Education Curriculum: Internationalizing the Campus* (1998), pp. 53, 65.

7. Richard D. Lambert, *International Studies and the Undergraduate* (1989), p. 151.

8. Idem, p. 104. According to William D. Hunter, "There is currently no agreed upon definition of what it means to be globally competent or how to obtain such world-wide savvy." "Got Global Competency?" 13 *International Educator* (Spring 2004), pp. 6, 8.

9. Laura Siaya and Fred M. Hayward, *Mapping International-ization on U.S. Campuses* (2003), p. 24. More precisely, 19 percent of the slightly more than half of colleges with an international requirement required three or more courses.

10. Richard D. Lambert, *International Studies and the Under-graduate*, pp. 122–23, 114.

11. Laura Siaya and Fred M. Hayward, *Mapping Internation-alization on U.S. Campuses*, p. 7.

12. U.S. Department of Education, *The New College Course Map and Transcript Files: Changes in Course-Taking and Achieve-ment, 1972–1993* (2d Ed., 1999), pp. 187, 189.

13. Laura Siaya and Fred M. Hayward, *Mapping Internation-alization on U.S. Campuses*, p. 104.

14. Richard D. Lambert, *International Studies and the Under-graduate*, pp. 130, 133.

15. Laura Siaya and Fred M. Hayward, *Mapping Internation-alization on U.S. Campuses*, pp. 13, 21, 103.

16. See, for example, Alice C. O'Maggio, *Teaching Language in Context* (1986).

17. See generally Joel C. Walz (ed.), *Development and Super-vision of Teaching Assistants in Foreign Languages* (1992).

18. Richard D. Lambert, "Languages and International Stud-ies," in Wilga Rivers (ed.), *Teaching Languages in College: Cur-riculum and Content* (1992), p. 285.

19. Wilga Rivers (ed.), *Teaching Languages in College*, p. 381.

20. "Language teaching can affect language acquisition . . . but I must acknowledge that my conviction is based largely on intuition—and a certain educational conservatism"; Patsy Lightbowm, "Can Language Acquisition Be Altered by Instruction?," in Kenneth Hyltenstam and Manfred Pienemann (eds.), *Modeling and Assessing Second Language Acquisition* (1985), pp. 101, 106. For a somewhat dated review of the evidence, see Michael H. Long, "Does Second Language Instruction Make a Difference?," 17 *TESOL Quarterly* (1983), p. 359.

21. Alexander W. Astin, *What Matters in College: Four Critical Years Revisited* (1993), p. 223.

22. Laura Siaya and Fred M. Hayward, *Mapping Internationalization on U.S. Campuses*, p. 25. The figure of 160,000 is from Institute of International Education, *Open Doors 2003: American Students Studying Abroad*, http://opendoors.iienetwork.org/?p= 36524 (December 19, 2003).

23. See, for example, Jerry S. Carlson, Barbara B. Burn, John Useem, and David Yachimowicz, *Study Abroad: The Experience of American Undergraduates* (1990); Norman L. Kauffmann, Judith M. Martin, and Henry D. Weaver, *Students Abroad, Strangers at Home: Education for a Global Society* (1992).

24. See, for example, Norman L. Kauffmann, Judith M. Martin, and Henry D. Weaver, *Students Abroad, Strangers at Home: Education for a Global Society* (1992); K. E. Gingerich, "The Impact of Study Abroad and Didactic Cross-Cultural Coursework Experiences on the Development of White Racial Consciousness and Cultural Sensitivity," unpublished doctoral dissertation, University of Kansas (1998); D. H. Wallace, "Academic Study Abroad: The Long-Term Impact on Alumni Careers, Volunteer Activities, World and Personal Perspectives," unpublished doctoral dissertation, Claremont Graduate University (1999).

25. Jerry S. Carlson, Barbara B. Burn, John Useem, and David Yachimowicz, *Study Abroad: The Experience of American Undergraduates* (1990), p. 114.

26. Laura Siaya and Fred M. Hayward, *Mapping Internationalization on U.S. Campuses*, p. 77.

27. Richard D. Lambert, *International Studies and the Undergraduate*, pp. 31, 27.

28. Idem, p. 80.

29. Crauford D. Goodwin and Michael Nacht, *Abroad and Beyond: Patterns in American Overseas Education* (1989).

30. Katherine H. Hanson and Joel W. Meyerson, *International Challenges to American Colleges and Universities: Looking Ahead* (1995), p. 31; Patrick O'Meara, Howard D. Mehlinger, and Roxana M. Newman, *Changing Perspectives on International Education* (2001), p. 199.

31. Crauford D. Goodwin and Michael Nacht, *Missing the Boat: The Failure to Internationalize American Higher Education* (1991). On p. 112, Goodwin and Nacht observe that "the flood of foreign students lapped on the shores with hardly a notice in many places, except perhaps occasional expressions of welcome or annoyance." For a more optimistic account, see Chun-mei Zhou, George D. Kuh, and Robert M. Corini, "A Comparison of International Student and American Student Engagement in Effective Educational Practices," 76 *The Journal of Higher Education* (2005), p. 259.

32. Thomas S. Barrows, Stephen F. Klein, and John L. D. Clark, *College Student Beliefs* (1981), pp. 36, 39.

33. Alexander W. Astin, *What Matters in College*, p. 223.

34. Martha C. Nussbaum, *Cultivating Humanity*, especially pp. 113–47. Another thoughtful discussion of what intercultural competence entails is provided by Yelena Yershova, Joan DeJaeghere, and Josef Mestenhauser, "Thinking Not as Usual: Adding the Intercultural Perspective," 4 *Journal of Studies in International Education* (2000), p. 59.

35. Laura Siaya and Fred M. Hayward, *Mapping Internationalization on U.S. Campuses*, pp. 107, 109.

36. For example, Mallory Young, "It's Not Just French 101: It's an Introduction to 'Tout le Monde,'" 47 *The Chronicle Review, Chronicle of Higher Education* (May 11, 2001), p. B-12. "Two years will not give [students] true facility in a language. . . . What four semesters *will* give you is time to experience how another language works, how it differs from your own, how different cultures are affected by their different ways of speaking." See also David W. Pankenier, "College-Level Foreign-Language Requirements Do Not Work," 37 *Chronicle of Higher Education* (December 5, 1990), p. B-1.

37. Richard D. Lambert, *International Studies and the Undergraduate*, p. 72.

38. See Stephen F. Klein and John L. D. Clark, *What College Students Know and Believe about Their World* (1984), pp. 36, 38.

39. Alice C. O'Maggio, *Teaching Language in Context*, p. 357.

40. For a discussion of the problems and shortcomings, as well as the potential, of teaching culture through language courses, see Patricia R. Chaput, "Culture in Grammar," 41 *Slavic and East European Journal* (1997), p. 403.

41. Richard J. Light, *The Harvard Assessment Seminars, Second Report: Explorations with Students and Faculty about Teaching, Learning, and Student Life* (1992), pp. 75, 80.

42. Laura Siaya and Fred M. Hayward, *Mapping Internationalization on U.S. Campuses*, pp. 88–89.

43. Richard D. Lambert, *International Studies and the Undergraduate*, p. 66.

44. Patricia R. Chaput, "Language Teaching: Raising Expectations for Instructor Preparation," in Benjamin Rifkin (ed.), *Mentoring Foreign Language Teaching Assistants, Lecturers and Adjunct Faculty* (2001), p. 191.

45. Laura Siaya and Fred M. Hayward, *Mapping Internationalization on U.S. Campuses*, p. 110.

46. Exactly what such intercultural competence entails is by no means clear. For an interesting effort to develop a consensus on the question from international experts and college administrators, see Darla K. Deardorff, "The Identification and Assessment of Intercultural Competence of a Student Outcome of International Education at Institutions of Higher Education in the United States," dissertation submitted to the Graduate Faculty of North Carolina State University (2004).

47. Richard D. Lambert, *International Studies and the Undergraduate*, p. 149.

48. Laura Siaya and Fred M. Hayward, *Mapping Internationalization on U.S. Campuses*, pp. 92, 93, 99.

CHAPTER TEN   ACQUIRING BROADER INTERESTS

1. Quoted in Joseph P. Lash, *Helen and Teacher: The Story of Helen Keller and Anne Sullivan Macy* (1980), p. 315.

2. See p. 15.

3. Elizabeth A. Jones, "Is a Core Curriculum Best for Everybody?" 80 *New Directions for Higher Education* (1992), p. 37.

4. See pp. 16–17.

5. Sheila Blumstein, *A Report to the President: The Brown Curriculum Twenty Years Later: A Review of the Past and a Working Agenda for the Future* (1990), pp. 22–23.

6. Idem, p. 19. The current dean of the college, Paul Armstrong, reports that the conditions for a successful program of free choice are still in place and that Brown students continue to sample broadly from the various areas of knowledge; "Brown's Open Curriculum and General Education," essay prepared for a conference on general education in the spring of 2004 at the University of Pennsylvania.

7. Sheila Tobias, *They're Not Dumb, They're Different: Stalking the Second Tier* (1991).

8. Daniel Bell, *The Reforming of General Education: The Columbia College Experience in Its National Setting* (Anchor Edition, 1968), p. 291.

9. William J. Bennett, *To Reclaim a Legacy: A Report on the Humanities in Higher Education* (1984); Lynne V. Cheney, *50 Hours: A Core Curriculum for College Students* (1989).

10. For an interesting account of a year spent by a middle-aged journalist taking Columbia's Great Books course, see David Denby, *Great Books: My Adventures with Homer, Rousseau, Woolf, and Other Indestructible Writers of the Western World* (1996).

11. James V. Mirollo, "The Humanities in the Core Curriculum at Columbia College," in Michael Nelson and Associates, *Alive at the Core: Exemplary Approaches to General Education in the Humanities* (2000), p. 20.

12. According to Thomson and Peterson's *Competitive Colleges: Top Colleges for Top Students, 2002–03*, both campuses of St. Johns attract fewer than a thousand applicants and accept more than three-quarters of those who apply.

13. For a defense of the modes-of-inquiry approach (and much else), see Daniel Bell, *The Reforming of General Education*. For a

description of one college's deliberation leading to a modes-of-inquiry curriculum, see Phyllis Keller, *Getting at the Core: Curricular Reform at Harvard* (1982).

14. Alexander W. Astin, *What Matters in College: Four Critical Years Revisited* (1993), pp. 334, 425.

15. Ernest T. Pascarella and Patrick T. Terenzini, *How College Affects Students: Findings and Insights from Twenty Years of Research* (1991), p. 271. The same authors estimate these gains as relatively small; *How College Affects Students*, Vol. 2: A *Third Decade of Research* (2005), p. 285.

16. George D. Kuh, "How Are We Doing? Tracking the Quality of the Undergraduate Experience, 1960s to the Present," 22 *The Review of Higher Education* (1999), pp. 99, 105; Ernest T. Pascarella and Patrick T. Terenzini, *How College Affects Students*, Vol. 2, p. 285.

17. William E. Knox, Paul Lindsay, and Mary N. Kolb, *Does College Make a Difference? Long-Term Changes in Activities and Attitudes* (1993), p. 68.

18. Ernest T. Pascarella and Patrick T. Terenzini, *How College Affects Students*, pp. 320–21.

19. Ernest T. Pascarella and Patrick T. Terenzini, *How College Affects Students*, Vol. 2, p. 142. A recent survey by the National Endowment for the Arts also reveals that college graduates are more likely than adults with only a high school education to have read at least one book of literature during the preceding year (66.7 percent versus 36.7 percent). The figure for college graduates, however, has dropped from 82.1 percent in 1982; *Reading at Risk: A Survey of Literary Reading in America* (2004), p. 25.

20. Maurice P. Marchant, *Why Adults Use the Public Library: A Research Perspective* (1994); Maurice P. Marchant, "What Motivates Adult Use of Public Libraries?" 13 *Library and Information Service Research* (1991), p. 201.

21. For an intriguing example of the potential value of such inquiries, see Douglas H. Heath, "What the Enduring Effects of

Higher Education Tell Us about a Liberal Education," 47 *The Journal of Higher Education* (1976), p. 173.

CHAPTER ELEVEN PREPARING FOR A CAREER

1. Arthur Levine, "Career Education: A Prospective, a Retrospective, and a Few Guesses," in Mary Ann Rehnke (ed.), *Career Programs in a Liberal Arts Context* (1985), pp. 13, 14.

2. Ernest T. Pascarella and Patrick T. Terenzini, *How College Affects Students*, Vol. 2: *A Third Decade of Research* (2005), p. 445.

3. Joan Stark and Malcolm Lowther, *Strengthening the Ties That Bind: Integrating Undergraduate Liberal and Professional Study: Report of the Professional Preparation Network* (1988), p. 33.

4. National Center for Education Statistics, *Undergraduate Enrollments in Academic, Career, and Vocational Education* (February 2004), p. 1.

5. Ernest T. Pascarella and Patrick T. Terenzini, *How College Affects Students: Findings and Insights from Twenty Years of Research* (1991), pp. 430, 433–34, 501, 506. The authors (p. 427) find that a college education has similar effects on occupational status.

6. Alexander W. Astin, *What Matters in College: Four Critical Years Revisited* (1993), pp. 246–48.

7. William G. Bowen and Derek Bok, *The Shape of the River: Long-Term Consequences of Considering Race in College and University Admissions* (1998), pp. 103–6.

8. Good Work Project Team, "Good Work Project: An Overview" (unpublished paper, Summer 2004), p. 14; see also Wendy Fischman, Becca Solomon, Deborah Greenspan, and Howard Gardner, *Making Good: How Young People Cope with Moral Dilemmas at Work* (2004).

9. Good Work Project Team, "Good Work Project: An Overview," p. 14; see also Howard Gardner, Mihaly Csikszentmihalyi, and William Damon, *Good Work: When Excellence and Ethics Meet* (paperback edition, 2002).

10. Darrell A. Luzzo (ed.), *Career Counseling of College Students: An Empirical Guide to Strategies That Work* (2000), pp. 50–59, 81–83.

11. See generally idem.

12. Ernest T. Pascarella and Patrick T. Terenzini, *How College Affects Students*, Vol. 2, p. 446.

13. Edward A. Colozzi, "Toward the Development of Systematic Career Guidance," in Darrell A. Luzzo (ed.), *Career Counseling of College Students*, p. 297.

14. Patrick H. Hardesty, "Undergraduate Career Courses for Credit: A Review and Meta-Analysis," 34 *Journal of College Student Development* (1991), pp. 184–85; Ernest T. Pascarella and Patrick T. Terenzini, *How College Affects Students*, Vol. 2, p. 499.

15. David G. Blanchflower and Andrew J. Oswald, "Well-Being, Insecurity, and the Decline of American Job Satisfaction" (unpublished paper, National Bureau of Economic Research, July 22, 1999). As the title implies, the authors find a decline in those who report that they are very satisfied with their current job.

16. Robert E. Lane, *The Loss of Happiness in Market Democracies* (2000), pp. 168–69.

17. Mary T. Coleman and John Pencaval, "Changes in Work Hours of Male Employees, 1940–1988," 46 *Industrial and Labor Relations Review* (1993), p. 202; Robert D. Reich, *The Future of Success* (2001), p. 121, reporting that the percentage of managerial and professional personnel working an average in excess of 50 hours per week rose by more than one-third since 1985.

18. See Robert Granfield, *Making Elite Lawyers: Visions of Law at Harvard* (1992).

19. Idem, p. 46.

20. Idem, pp. 61–65.

21. Amy Delong, "Retaining Legal Talent," 29 *Capitol University Law Review* (2002), p. 893; Gregory J. Mazares, "Associate Retention of Law Firms: What Are Your Lawyers Saying about You?" 29 *Capitol University Law Review* (2002), p. 903, reporting that only two in three lawyers plan on spending their entire careers in the law.

22. Patrick Shiltz, "On Being a Happy, Healthy, and Ethical Member of an Unhappy, Unhealthy, and Unethical Profession," 52 *Vanderbilt Law Review* (1999), p. 871; Connie J. Beck, Bruce D. Saks, and G. Andrew Benjamin, "Lawyer Distress: Alcohol-Related Problems and Other Psychological Concerns among a Sample of Practicing Lawyers," 10 *Journal of Law and Health* (1990), p. 45. For a much brighter view of law as a career, see Charles Silver and Frank B. Cross, "What's Not to Like about Being a Lawyer?," 109 *Yale Law Journal* (1999), p. 1443.

23. Adam Smith, *An Inquiry Into the Nature and Causes of the Wealth of Nations* (New York: Modern Library, 1939), p. 106. On contemporary students and their unrealistic job expectations, see Mihaly Csikszentmihalyi and Barbara Schneider, *Becoming Adult: How Teenagers Prepare for the World of Work* (2000).

24. Oliver Wendell Holmes Jr., "The Profession and the Law," in *Collected Legal Papers* (1920), pp. 29–30.

25. Kenneth R. Andrews, "Liberal Education for Competence and Responsibility," in Thomas J. Donaldson and R. Edward Freeman (eds.), *Business as a Humanity* (1994), pp. 153–54.

26. Studies on the careers of liberal arts graduates versus business majors are cited and discussed in Ernest T. Pascarella and Patrick T. Terenzini, *How College Affects Students*, pp. 469–70.

27. For an overview of the research on this subject, see Michael Useem, *Liberal Education and the Corporation: The Hiring and Advancement of College Graduates* (1989), pp. 91–119.

28. Samuel C. Florman, *The Civilized Engineer* (1987), p. 202.

29. U.S. Department of Education, "Curricular Content of Bachelors' Degrees (1986)," cited in Michael Useem, *Liberal Education and the Corporation*, p. 70.

30. Alexander W. Astin, *What Matters in College*, pp. 236–41, 302–10, 371–72.

31. Norman Nie and Sunshine Hillygus, "Education and Democratic Citizenship," in Diane Ravitch and Joseph Viteritti (eds.), *Making Good Citizens: Educational and Civil Society* (2001), p. 30.

32. Quoted in Elaine Seat, J. Roger Parsons, and William A. Poppen, "Enabling Engineering Performance Skills: A Program to Teach Communication, Leadership, and Teamwork," *Journal of Engineering Education* (2001), pp. 7–8.

33. National Academy of Engineering, *The Engineer of 2020: Visions of Engineering in the New Century* (2004), p. 59.

34. Accreditation Board for Engineering and Technology, *Criteria for Accrediting Engineering Programs* (December 26, 2000).

35. See generally Rosalind Williams, "Education for the Profession Formerly Known as Engineering," 49 *Chronicle of Higher Education* (January 24, 2003), p. B12. "The convergence of technological and liberal arts education is a deep, long-term, and irreversible trend. Students need to be prepared for life in a world where technological, scientific, humanistic, and social issues are all mixed together. Such mixing will not occur if students have to decide from the outset that they are attending an 'engineering school' as opposed to a 'nonengineering school.'" Professor Williams is director of the Massachusetts Institute of Technology's Program in Science, Technology, and Society.

36. For a detailed study of teacher education, see Christopher J. Lucas, *Teacher Education in America: Reform Agenda for the Twenty-First Century* (1997); see also Robert A. Roth (ed.), *The Role of the University in the Preparation of Teachers* (1999).

37. For a harsh critique of teacher education, see, for example, Rita Kramer, *Ed School Follies: The Miseducation of America's Teachers* (1991). For a more sympathetic account of schools of education, see David F. Labaree, *The Trouble with Ed Schools* (2004).

38. Alexander W. Astin, *What Matters in College*, pp. 236–40, 370–71.

39. Jean A. King, "The Uneasy Relationship between Teacher Education and the Liberal Arts and Sciences," 38 *Journal of Teacher Education* (1987), p. 6. See also David F. Labaree, "Too Easy a Target: The Trouble with Ed Schools and the Implications for the University," 85 *Academe* (January–February 1999), p. 34.

40. Alexander W. Astin, *What Matters in College*, pp. 238–40, 370.

41. Norman Nie and Sunshine Hillygus, "Education and Democratic Citizenship," p. 30.

42. See, for example, Diana G. Oblinger and Anne-Lee Verville, *What Business Wants from Higher Education* (1998); Robert T. Jones, "Liberal Education for the Twenty-First Century: Business Expectations," 91 *Liberal Education* (Spring 2005), pp. 32, 34.

43. See Noreen R. Sharpe and Gordon D. Pritchett, "Business Curricula Should Integrate Liberal-Arts and Vocational Studies," 50 *Chronicle of Higher Education* (April 2, 2004), p. B19.

44. See, for example, Diana G. Oblinger and Anne-Lee Verville, *What Business Wants from Higher Education*; Michael Useem, *Liberal Education and the Corporation*; John W. Gardner and Gretchen Vander Veer, *The Senior Year Experience: Facilitating Integration, Reflection, Closure, and Transition* (1998).

45. George D. Kuh, "What We're Learning about Student Engagement from NSSE," 35 *Change* (March–April 2003), p. 28.

46. Michelle V. Rafter, "Liberal Arts Grads Get the Business," 83 *Workforce Management* (September 1, 2004), p. 20.

47. Michael Useem, *Liberal Education and the Corporation*, p. 69.

CHAPTER TWELVE IMPROVING THE QUALITY OF UNDERGRADUATE EDUCATION

1. *The Economist*, "Special Report: Financing Universities" (January 24, 2004), pp. 23, 24. The same study found that 8 of the 10 top-ranked universities were located in the United States; Sam Dillon, "U.S. Slips in Status as Global Hub of Higher Education," *New York Times* (December 21, 2004), pp. A1, A19. The title of Dillon's article stems from the decline in the number of foreign students attending our universities largely caused by tighter visa restrictions following the terrorist attacks of September 11, 2001.

2. "The Chronicle Survey of Public Opinion on Higher Education," 50 *The Chronicle of Higher Education* (May 7, 2004), p. A12.

3. See William G. Bowen and Derek Bok, *The Shape of the River: Long-Term Consequences of Considering Race in College and University Admissions* (1998), p. 196.

4. See generally Ernest T. Pascarella and Patrick T. Terenzini, *How College Affects Students: Findings and Insights from Twenty Years of Research* (1991).

5. William G. Bowen and Derek Bok, *The Shape of the River*, p. 212.

6. Patricia M. King and Karen S. Kitchener, *Developing Reflective Judgment: Understanding and Promoting Intellectual Growth and Critical Thinking in Adolescents and Adults* (1994), p. 167.

7. Alexander W. Astin, *What Matters in College: Four Critical Years Revisited* (1993), p. 223.

8. See Linda J. Sax, Alexander W. Astin, William S. Korn, and Shannon K. Gilmartin, *The American College Teacher: National Norms for the 1989–1999 HERI Faculty Survey* (1999), p. 35.

9. Lion F. Gardiner, *Redesigning Higher Education: Producing Dramatic Gains in Student Learning* (1994), p. 57.

10. D. Kent Johnson, James L. Ratcliff, and Jerry G. Gaff, "A Decade of Change in General Education," *New Directions for Higher Education*, No. 125 (Spring 2004), pp. 9, 17, 18. According to Joan S. Stark and Lisa Latucca, "Many colleges have devised elaborate systems for comparing students' abilities as they enter and leave college. . . . [But] little attention has been given to the connections between student outcomes and course and program plans"; *Shaping the College Curriculum: Academic Plans in Action* (1997), p. 104.

11. William G. Bowen and Derek Bok, *The Shape of the River*, pp. 72–90.

12. James L. Shulman and William G. Bowen, *The Game of Life: College Sports and Educational Values* (2001), p. 66.

13. Alexander W. Astin, *Assessment for Excellence: The Philosophy and Practice of Assessment and Evaluation in Higher Education* (1993), pp. 216–30; Peter T. Ewell, "The Role of States and Accreditors in Shaping Assessment Practice," in Lester F. Goodchild (ed.), *Public Policy and Higher Education* (1997), p. 305.

14. *National Survey of Student Engagement, 2001, NSSE Viewpoint* (2001), p. 8.

15. See *Converting Data into Action, National Survey of Student Engagement: The College Student Report* (2003).

16. Ernest T. Pascarella and Patrick Terenzini, *How College Affects Students*, p. 592.

17. Quoted by Pat Hutchins and Lee S. Shulman, "The Scholarship of Teaching: New Elaborations, New Developments," 31 *Change* (September–October 1999), pp. 10, 13. Interestingly research shows that faculty members, even in research universities, rate their own interest in teaching much higher than that of their colleagues; Mary Wright, "Always at Odds? Congruence in Faculty Beliefs about Teaching at a Research University," 76 *The Journal of Higher Education* (2005), p. 331.

INDEX

Page numbers for entries occurring in unnumbered footnotes are followed by an *n*.